SHAKESPEARE'S SOUTHAMPTON

HENRY WRIOTHESLEY, 3RD EARL OF SOUTHAMPTON
BORN 1573. MARRIED ELIZABETH VERNON
= DAUGHTER OF JOHN VERNON. HE WAS ATTAINTED =
IN THE REIGN OF ELIZABETH, BUT RESTORED IN
1603 BY JAMES 1ST. HE DIED 1624.

SOUTHAMPTON IN MIDDLE LIFE
From Palace House, Beaulieu

Shakespeare's

SOUTHAMPTON

Patron of Virginia

BY

A. L. ROWSE

. . .

HARPER & ROW, PUBLISHERS, NEW YORK

TO
ALLAN NEVINS
EMINENT HISTORIAN
GREAT AMERICAN
MOST GENEROUS OF MEN

CONTENTS

WRIOTHESLEY PEDIGREE

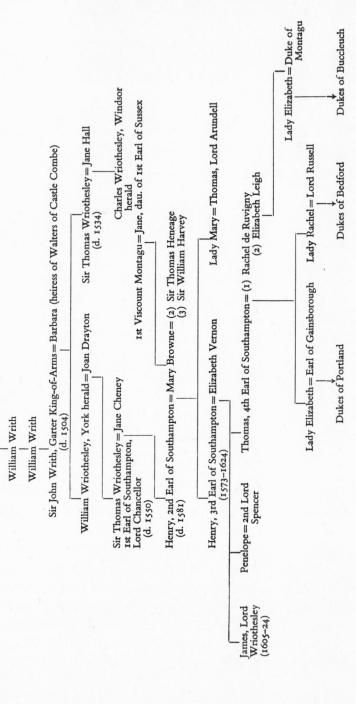

Robert Writh
|
Walter Writh
|
William Writh
|
William Writh
|
Sir John Writh, Garter King-of-Arms = Barbara (heiress of Walters of Castle Combe)
(d. 1504)

William Wriothesley, York herald = Joan Drayton   Sir Thomas Wriothesley = Jane Hall
                                                                (d. 1534)
                                                                        |
                                                           Charles Wriothesley, Windsor
                                                                    herald

Sir Thomas Wriothesley = Jane Cheney
1st Earl of Southampton,
Lord Chancellor
(d. 1550)

1st Viscount Montagu = Jane, dau. of 1st Earl of Sussex

Henry, 2nd Earl of Southampton = Mary Browne = (2) Sir Thomas Heneage
(d. 1581)   (3) Sir William Harvey

Lady Mary = Thomas, Lord Arundell

Henry, 3rd Earl of Southampton = Elizabeth Vernon
(1573–1624)

Thomas, 4th Earl of Southampton = (1) Rachel de Ruvigny
                                  (2) Elizabeth Leigh

Penelope = 2nd Lord
           Spencer

James, Lord
Wriothesley
(1605–24)

Lady Elizabeth = Earl of Gainsborough   Lady Rachel = Lord Russell   Lady Elizabeth = Duke of
                                                                                            Montagu

Dukes of Portland   Dukes of Bedford   Dukes of Buccleuch

PREFACE

THE life of Henry Wriothesley, third Earl of Southampton, offers a double interest for us, literary as well as historical. As a young man, on his first entry into public life in the early 1590's, he was Shakespeare's acknowledged patron, to whom the poet dedicated his long poems *Venus and Adonis* and *The Rape of Lucrece*, in 1593 and 1594. It is now perfectly clear that Shakespeare's Sonnets were written to and for his patron during the same period. This has always been the dominant view among literary scholars, from Malone downwards. But now, with the problem of the dating of the Sonnets settled, there is not merely no likelihood but not the remotest possibility that they could have been written for anyone else. Not only the dating, but all the circumstances and evidences, literary and historical, biographical and personal, cohere together with absolute internal and external consistency to make it impossible for this to be impugned.

Southampton's ardent and generous discipleship of Essex led to his condemnation to death and his imprisonment in the Tower for the last eighteen months of Elizabeth I's reign. He came out of it a sadder and a wiser man; in fact — I owe the remark to a friend — his career offers a striking example of what growing up can do for the character. He emerged in James's reign to become a dignified and singularly uncorrupt servant of the state in that corrupt and undignified court. Always popular, he became a man generally respected — for the qualities Shakespeare had discerned in him as a youth, the shining candour of his nature, as well as his generosity and gallantry. He was an honest and a good man.

Most of his public life falls in James's reign : it offers thus the historical interest of the transition from the Elizabethan to the Jacobean age. A Catholic to the end of Elizabeth's reign,

Southampton conformed under Scottish James, and became a champion of a vigorously Protestant and anti-Spanish foreign policy. (He died serving in the Netherlands in pursuit of it.) This led him to become a Parliament man, once more — at the end of his career as at the beginning — in opposition. A dominant concern throughout the second half of his life was his interest in America, in supporting voyages of discovery, in the plantation of Virginia ; he was Treasurer of the Virginia Company during its last years.

In writing this book I have happily incurred many obligations : above all to All Souls College and the Huntington Library, at both of which congenial places the book was written ; to Southampton's descendants, the Duke of Portland, the Duke of Buccleuch, the Duke of Bedford, and Lord Montagu of Beaulieu, for kindly allowing me to use portraits from their collections, particularly to the last for his interest in, and encouragement of, my book. I am much obliged to the Marquis of Salisbury, generous as always to scholars, for ready access to, and frequent use of, his papers; to Mr and Mrs Donald Hyde for allowing me to quote an unpublished letter of Southampton's ; and to Miss N. McN. O'Farrell for her help, now over many years, with manuscript sources. I am indebted to the Master of St. John's College, Cambridge, and to Mr. A. G. Lee, Librarian, for showing me Southampton's portrait and books there; to Mr. T. Cottrell-Dormer of Rousham Park for allowing me to consult his manuscripts and for his scholarly aid in deciphering the letters of Southampton's mother; to the Warden of All Souls, Dr. J. M. Steadman, and Professor Madeleine Doran for help with books and references ; to the Vicar of Titchfield for permitting photographs to be taken of the Southampton monument and to Mr. Charles Woolf of Newquay, who came all the way from Cornwall to take them ; and to Mr. J. Fillingham, who guided me to Titchfield.

All Souls College,   A. L. ROWSE
  Oxford
May 1965

ILLUSTRATIONS

Southampton in middle life *Frontispiece*
>From Palace House, Beaulieu
By courtesy of Lord Montagu of Beaulieu

The following are grouped in a separate section after page 148:

Palace House, Beaulieu
By courtesy of Lord Montagu of Beaulieu

Palace House, Titchfield Abbey
By courtesy of the Ministry of Works

Sir Edwin Sandys
By courtesy of B. L. Lechmere

Southampton's grandfather: the First Earl
>From Palace House, Beaulieu
By courtesy of Lord Montagu of Beaulieu

Queen Elizabeth I
>From the portrait at Corsham Court
By courtesy of Lord Methuen

King James I
By courtesy of the National Gallery of Scotland

Southampton's wife: Elizabeth Vernon
>From Boughton House
By courtesy of the Duke of Buccleuch

Southampton in the Tower
>From Boughton House
By courtesy of the Duke of Buccleuch

The Earl of Essex
>From Woburn Abbey
By courtesy of the Duke of Bedford

Southampton as a soldier
>From Welbeck Abbey
By courtesy of the Duke of Portland

Shakespeare's Dedication to Southampton
By courtesy of the Bodleian Library

Southampton at the period of the Sonnets
From the miniature by Nicholas Hilliard
By courtesy of the Fitzwilliam Museum, Cambridge

Southampton's mother: Mary Browne
From Welbeck Abbey
By courtesy of the Duke of Portland

Southampton as a boy
From the tomb at Titchfield
Photograph by Charles Woolf

The Southampton tomb at Titchfield
Photograph by Charles Woolf

CHAPTER I

The King's Servant

THE grandeur of the Wriothesley family is almost entirely due to the Reformation. Before that happy event, it is true, they had been heard of under their original name of Writh, a Wiltshire family by origin.[1]* And indeed they were already noticeably on their way up at the end of the fifteenth century, through the curious — but in the age of bastard feudalism not uncharacteristic — profession of heraldry. However, the Reformation, in particular the Dissolution of the Monasteries, with the splendid opportunities which it gave of garnering Church lands, made the classic period in the formation and establishment of English families. It was then that their fortune was made for them in the person of Thomas Wriothesley, first Earl of Southampton. He was not precisely a *novus homo*.

His grandfather, Sir John Writh, was the third Garter King-of-Arms and held the office at the time when the College of Heralds was incorporated in 1483.[2] As such he was frequently employed on diplomatic missions by Edward IV and Henry VII. The former sent him to Scotland in 1479, and again in 1480 to proclaim war in form at Edinburgh ; two years later he was sent into France. In 1483 he played his ceremonial part at the funeral of Edward IV and at the coronation of Richard III. Henry VII, somewhat improbably, increased his salary and employed him still more frequently on missions abroad : in 1485 to Maximilian, King of the Romans, two years later to Ireland, next year to Brittany. In 1491 he was sent with the

* Superior numbers refer to Notes, page 306

I

insignia of the Garter to Maximilian, in the same year to Brittany, and next year to the Duke of Burgundy. In 1494 he carried the Order of the Garter to Charles VIII of France. He was evidently a very reliable official, not merely a herald but a man of diplomacy, to whom such missions could be entrusted.

He made three prudent marriages, the first to a Wiltshire heiress, Barbara, daughter of John (probably Walters) of Castle Combe, and this enhanced his fortune. By her he had two sons, Sir Thomas and William, who each made his mark in his profession. Their father died in 1504, and was buried under a grand marble slab, subsequently destroyed by fire, in St. Giles', Cripplegate.[3]

His elder son, Thomas, was at once and somewhat unexpectedly promoted to his father's office, under whom he had served his apprenticeship. He had much the same kind of career, court ceremonies, diplomatic missions, Heralds' Office work, though to these he added scholarship and was a noted collector of heraldic antiquities. As a young pursuivant he had been present at the investiture of Prince Arthur, and years after was cited as one of the principal witnesses of the Prince's marriage to Catherine of Aragon, when the case came before Wolsey and Campeggio in 1529. Meanwhile he attended Henry VIII to Tournai in 1513, calling in form upon the town to surrender ; next year he was present at the marriage of Louis XII to Henry's buxom sister, Mary, who danced her ageing husband off his feet and into his grave, after which she felt free to marry her lover, Charles Brandon, Duke of Suffolk. In 1520 Thomas attended Henry VIII to the Field of the Cloth of Gold — a piece of nonsense as extravagant as it was insincere. Seven years later, at a switch in policy, when Wolsey needed the French alliance, Garter King-of-Arms conveyed the Garter to Francis I. Meanwhile he had been knighted when on a similar errand to the Emperor Charles V's brother, Ferdinand, when England had been at war with France in alliance with the Emperor.

This Sir Thomas had a country residence at Cricklade. He made two marriages, of which the first was to a small heiress at Salisbury and the second to a well-off widow. By the first he had several sons, of whom Charles was also a herald, Windsor herald, and became the author of the well-known *Wriothesley's Chronicle*. This important source for the history of the later years of Henry VIII's reign, that of Edward VI and into the reign of Mary, we owe to the piety and scholarly interests of the subject of this book, Shakespeare's Southampton, the third Earl, who had a transcript of it made, and that is the only existing copy. But for him it would have been lost. Sir Thomas prospered and carried the family a stage further in the world. He built himself a fine big town residence, Garter House, outside Cripplegate, in the church of which he was buried in 1534.[4] Anstis says that he bore the same motto as his father, 'Humble and Serviceable' : this changed to something grander in Norman French as they went up in the world. However, several manuscript collections of his still remain, 'which show him to have been an officer of great industry' ; and Lord Stafford called him 'the best herald that ever was since or many years before'.

What was the point of his being so fine a herald if he could not improve on his name and pedigree ?

Evidently he did not think the simple name of Writh grand enough for his station, and with that Tudor snobbery which induced the great Lord Burghley to change the form of his name from Welsh Sytsilt to Roman Cecil, Sir Thomas Writh found a Wriothesley back in the reign of King John from whom he might claim a descent and adapted his name to that. Not stopping at that, he redubbed his old father who had been content with the name of Writh as John Wriothesley *alias* Writh — which led Anstis to a passage of Augustan disapprobation :

> Though this officer was advanced to this employment by the monosyllable surname that his father used, yet he disliked the shortness of it, either with regard to the explication of the ancient

3

proverb, *Omnis herus servo monosyllabus*, or some other whimsical humour, and therefore augmented it with the high sound of three syllables : which added nothing to the smoothness in pronunciation, and after some variations in the spelling he at last settled upon Wriothesley. Wherein his brother William, York herald, concurred and their descendants followed this precedent ; and, which is somewhat particular, in order to countenance this affectation, he contributed this new-found appellation to all his paternal ancestors in the drafts he made of his own pedigree. . . . He was so very fond of this new surname thus devised by him that, when the salary granted by Henry VII was determined by his demise, he took a new one from his successor, wherein he procured his father to be styled John Wriothesley *alias* Writh, late Garter : at which time the reflection that Judge Catilin once made upon an *alias* might probably be out of his memory.

No doubt this was to the effect that an *alias* usually betokened illegitimacy.

Thus it is that we come by some difficulty in pronouncing the name : no one seems to know how to pronounce it. In fact, it is pronounced Wrisley, and may be rhymed with grisly ; later on, we find one of the name spelling himself phonetically Risley.

Sir Thomas Wriothesley's younger brother, William, married Agnes, daughter of James Drayton of London, who also seems to have been genealogically inclined, for he left notes of his family and pedigree.[5] Thomas, the eldest son, was born on the feast of St. Thomas the Apostle, 21 December 1505. His younger brother, Edward, had a grander christening as the family moved up : Edward Stafford, Duke of Buckingham, and Henry Percy, Earl of Northumberland, as godfathers.

It was a promising background for a career at Court.

Young Wriothesley was sent to Cambridge, and studied at Trinity Hall, almost certainly under Stephen Gardiner, later Bishop of Winchester, who became his early patron and afterwards colleague, and with whom his career was at times closely, though not uniformly, connected. Years after, when Wriothesley was Principal Secretary of State, we have a portrait of him in John Leland's Latin *Encomia*, a series of tributes to the leading figures at the Court of Henry VIII which serves as a kind of parallel to Holbein's drawings of them at Windsor.[6] The tone of Leland's poem is warmer and more intimate than most : he seems to have known Wriothesley and his family from boyhood. He pays tribute not only to his gifts of mind and character, his virtue — and there was never any count against his morals in Henry's Court — but to his good looks. It seems that Wriothesley was a handsome youth and won much applause at Cambridge by his performances in the comedies of Plautus. But he left the university early for a Court career, accompanying Gardiner abroad on one of his missions :

> Hinc crevit magnis certa experientia rebus
> Et fama enituit latius inde tua.

In 1529–30 we find him servant to Sir Edmund Peckham, Cofferer of the Household, and as one of the King's Messengers riding about England on government business. Next, in 1530, he was appointed a clerk of the Signet. With the rise of Thomas Cromwell to power the promising young man was absorbed into his service — Leland tells us how much Cromwell appreciated his intelligence and dexterity — and for the next crucial ten years Wriothesley lived in the closest association with the great minister who carried through the first stages of the English Reformation.

In December 1532 Wriothesley was crossing the Channel on a mission to Brussels. In October 1533 he was at Marseilles, reporting to Cromwell that his 'apparel, and play sometimes, whereat I am unhappy, have cost me above 50 crowns'.[7] Could Cromwell forward his suit for his allowances, for the friend who had helped him at his departure was not satisfied ? Wriothesley may have gone on to Rome, though he was unable to help his friend, John Salcote, the abbot of Hyde, to

Papal Bulls for his consecration as Bishop of Bangor. Nevertheless, Salcote was consecrated — and Wriothesley got a fat, beneficial lease of property from the monastery for his services. This pointed to the royal road to the future.

It is fairly certain that Wriothesley's missions concerned the King's 'great matter' of the divorce from Catherine, for there exist drafts of important documents in the clerk of the Signet's hand, with Henry's own interlineations in regard to the marriage. It is pleasant to find among Cromwell's Remembrances a memorandum to pay Wriothesley £20 alongside of one to pay Melancthon 300 crowns — as a friend abroad of the proceedings in England and one who held tolerant views of bigamy, when it came to royal persons.[8] Meanwhile, in 1534, Wriothesley was admitted to Gray's Inn, no doubt to qualify himself — useful for a future Lord Chancellor — and in 1536 got the office of 'graver' of the Tower and the reversion to that of coroner and attorney in the King's Bench. Better things were in store.

Wriothesley's grand opportunity came with the crisis of Henry's reign, the Pilgrimage of Grace, the risings in the North in 1536, against the new course set in the South. Henry was furious at this challenge to his authority from the most backward — he himself said the 'beastliest' — parts of his realm. He remained at Windsor where he took charge of the situation himself, directing forces and operations against the rebels, and in constant communication with Cromwell in London, who had the task of raising money, equipment, munitions for the forces sent north in the emergency. The lesser monasteries were already dissolved, but the Pilgrimage itself, and the cost of suppressing it, rendered inevitable the suppression of the greater monasteries : many of them superb buildings with their accumulated treasures and traditions, libraries, shrines, sculptures, stained glass, monuments, jewels, their choirs and their music.

Wriothesley was at Windsor throughout the crisis, in attendance on the King, writing his letters, sending out his commands and messages, keeping in touch with Cromwell, from his letters to whom we derive a vivid picture of this anxious time. On 15 October 'this matter hangeth yet like a fever, one day good, another bad'.⁹ Three days later they learn that 'all Yorkshire is up', and 'his Majesty appeareth much to fear this matter, and has no great trust in Darcy'. Wriothesley was writing letter after letter with the King's commands to Cromwell to shift for money to the uttermost, raising loans where he could in the City, coining the plate in the Jewel House — the consequences of Henry's extravagance were coming home to him (his careful father had left large reserves in the Treasury).

Henry wanted to know all the details of Cromwell's measures in the City, and four days later called Wriothesley back, after he had taken his leave, with the command that 'you would taste the fat priests thereabouts' — this meant the sleek prebendaries and canons of St. Paul's. Next day 'his Grace, being very merry, said there was a servant of King Edward's, his grandfather, which made once a suit unto him for 1,000 oaks that he might only obtain twenty. He is glad you remembered my lord of Wiltshire and that you wrote for so good a sum. So he trusted your request should purchase £500, or such a matter, by reason it was so great — which, being less, would else percase have wrought nothing with him.' This was pretty pointed — especially considering that the Earl of Wiltshire was Anne Boleyn's father. Here we have direct glimpses of Henry in action, as so rarely : we see what kind of man he was.

He was not ungenerous — in fact extravagantly generous to those who served his purposes. The monastic lands were annexed to the Crown in support of its revenues for the purposes of government, and with the intention of alleviating taxation. But large gifts outright were made to the King's ministers and servants, and to those in the immediate entourage of the Court — on far too big a scale and in too indiscriminate a matter. One observes immediately in the correspondence of the time the fever of avarice that set in, the greedy gaping for Church lands, the jostling and pushing, the buying and selling, the pulling down and building up, the accumulation and dispersal of fortunes, that are features conditioning much of social life for the remainder of the century.

It was natural that Wriothesley should be rewarded for his services ; it was no less natural that, now a Hampshireman with a residence at Micheldever, he should have his eye on the neighbouring Hampshire monasteries when the manna began to fall from heaven. Indeed, he was already in line as a secular official, in receipt of a fee, of the Premonstratensian house of Titchfield near Southampton : this was the regular way. He had obtained from his friend the abbot of Hyde a 61-year-long lease of the parsonage of Micheldever, with its great tithes — this was what was so advantageous, to get a lease for so exceptionally long a period without having to pay fines for renewal.[10] Here, at the end of 1536, he was building and making a garden ; his servant, Clerk, wrote : 'my young master, your son, your daughter and all your household are in good health' — in good country air, away from the city.[11] Clerk was badgering the abbots of Titchfield and Beaulieu for a horse each for his master. 'My lord of Beaulieu sent his men to take up for you his own riding horse . . . his only fault is that he is too little for you, though the biggest in all his park. I reminded my lord of the patent for you, and he only waits to have your counsel in the finishing of it.'

Wriothesley had married Jane, the daughter and heiress of William Cheney of Chesham Bois, in Buckinghamshire. We know what she looked like, from a Holbeinesque portrait of her somewhat later : a rounded face with a surprised, rather sweet, expression, small mouth and nose, regular arched eyebrows, a demure feminine appearance under the white lace cap with long lappets falling behind.[12] Very richly dressed, with the full puffed-out sleeves of the time, she holds a flower in her ringed right hand, in her left the gold chain attached to the jewelled cross upon her waist. We know that she was an educated woman who could read and write — unlike many of the ladies at the Court of Henry VIII ; for at the Huntington

Library in California exists her copy of the 1532 edition of the works of Chaucer.[13]   In this she has inscribed four times in various places throughout the book, in a bold clear hand, 'this ys Jane Southampton boke'.   She does not achieve the subtlety of a possessive apostrophe ;   nevertheless the instinct of property, the assertion of possession, is there.   She was the first owner of this new edition of Chaucer, a chief delight of Tudor readers.   She was the half-sister of Germain Gardiner, Bishop Gardiner's nephew.   In May 1537 we find Germain complaining that he has not heard from Wriothesley for a long time, yet he learns from others what he most desires — that Wriothesley is the old man still.   He will not fall out with him for not writing, 'for when the business was in the North, and you were so occupied, yet ye wrote unto me.   Commend me to my good sister, for whose sake I forbear to chide.'   He salutes Wriothesley as his 'good loving brother'.[14]

Next year, in September 1538, Wriothesley was going on a mission into Flanders when he encountered Bishop Gardiner and all his fine train returning from one of the ostentatious embassies abroad that Henry's bold policies involved him in. The Reformation was moving a step further forward, and not much love was lost between Cromwell and the more conservative Gardiner, though both were devoted and convinced Henricians.   Wriothesley sounded out Thirlby, Gardiner's colleague, as to the Bishop's attitude to the new measures, and was able to report to Cromwell that Gardiner did not seem to mislike the doings at Canterbury and wished the like were done at Winchester, his own cathedral.   This evidently refers to the destruction of the shrine of St. Thomas and the cleansing of the cathedral of its relics.   Wriothesley pumped Thirlby for more information as to Gardiner's disposition ;   Thirlby commended his wisdom and said that Gardiner had often said that he would go as far as the King, but never farther, without knowing for certain whether the King would approve it.   This was a safe position, in which most sensible men remained. Gardiner appeared to approve the new Injunctions, especially that of learning the faith in English. The Bishop said, 'Ha! I see the King will not yet leave this auricular confession. Methink I smell the King in this point.' With ill feeling and distrust increasing between the two sides, Wriothesley had 'no more than a beck and a good morrow with Germain'.[15] The ambassadorial train passed on, and Wriothesley went on his way abroad.

Meanwhile, at home in February 1537 he had been granted most of the possessions of little Quarr Abbey, on the north coast of the Isle of Wight — the stonework of the church went more usefully to build two blockhouses at East and West Cowes to guard Southampton Water.[16] In August his agent, John Hutton, has to condole with him on the death of his little son William : 'gentle Mistress Wriothesley is so wise that she will take it according to the comfort you sent to her'.[17] For himself, 'I am bound to give you, if I were not mortal, immortal thanks for your goodness'. All Wriothesley's servants take this tone with him : he seems to have had charm, to have been generous with them, and to have had the faculty of arousing their loyalty and devotion.

With the suppression of the greater monasteries now on the way it is hardly surprising that they did what they could to look after their friends, salt away beneficial leases to relatives of their abbots and priors, strip their houses of everything they could before the new secular proprietors came in. It was time that the government decided on its course before the Crown was cheated of more than was necessary in the transition — really a major measure of nationalisation. Wriothesley was promised Titchfield and Beaulieu, in both of which he already held secular office and was naturally interested. At Titchfield, before the end, the canons stripped the church of all its valuables, except for the vestment Wriothesley had given, and granted away all they could in beneficial leases and pensions.[18] The convent was £200 in debt, and expected £135 a year from the Crown in pensions to its abbot and monks. They

owed the King 200 marks for first-fruits ; the lands were left
in ruinous condition, with not an ox left, and only a dozen
rusty platters and old hangings left in the house. The commissioners assured Wriothesley, on getting his expected grant
of the abbey and its manors, that his first entry would be
expensive. The Catholic Lord Lisle had been most anxious
to obtain a grant of Beaulieu Abbey as early as 1536.[19] In
1538 Wriothesley obtained the purchase of it for his services.

In September 1538 he was down at Winchester carrying out
the government's orders — whether altogether to Bishop Gardiner's liking or no — to pull down the shrine of St. Swithin
and clear the cathedral of its treasure along with its junk, relics,
bones, and such. He reported that the commissioners had made
an end of the shrine at three in the morning — evidently to
avoid trouble from the credulous populace. The mayor with
eight or nine of his brethren were present, the Bishop's chancellor with others assisted and praised the King therefore ; the
cathedral prior and convent were conformable : all was in
legal order. There was no gold, nor ring, nor true precious
stone in the shrine, but all great counterfeits ; nevertheless, the
silver alone would amount to 2,000 marks. They had also
received the cross of emeralds, the Jerusalem cross and another
of gold, two gold chalices and other plate. The altar would be
worth taking down, but it was such a piece of work that it
would take a couple of days. 'Which done we intend both at
Hyde and St. Mary's to sweep away all the rotten bones that
be called relics : which we may not omit lest it should be
thought we came more for the treasure than for the avoiding
of the abomination of idolatry.' [20]

All government needs an admixture of humbug in its proceedings, even when it is sincerely held by its practitioners.
There follows an inventory of the shrines and jewels, the altars
and plate, of Winchester Cathedral, which shows it to
have been a treasure-house much as Spanish cathedrals are
today.

At the same time as the process of pulling down proceeded, that of building up went forward with even more energy : a new and secular, a more efficient and energetic, society arose upon the ruins of medieval religion, now antiquated and out-moded, the needs of society having left it behind. From New Year 1538 Wriothesley's agents were moving his household for him from Micheldever to Titchfield, taking possession of house and lands, holding his courts, shortly embarking upon a rapid transformation of its buildings, pulling down most of the church, refashioning the conventual premises — from Titch-field Abbey to Place House.

The surveyor summoned all the tenants together to declare to them that the monastery had been freely surrendered to the King, who, considering Wriothesley's wisdom and daily service gave it to him and his heirs for ever under the Great Seal. Formal possession was then taken, 'whereof every man is glad, and wishes it had been done seven years before, and then all are sworn to you'.[21] Such a concourse of tenants came in to receive their new leases that the court had to be held in the parish church. 'You have now many good and hearty tenants, divers of them good archers, and some bondmen whose names shall be registered. The carpenter stays from his labour in taking down the abbey church, because we would be loth to adventure with him before the change of the moon.' The pavement of the nave had been taken up, but it was so worn that scarce the tenth tile could be saved. Parishioners from Overton were expected to view the south aisle for stone to build a bell-tower for their church. Perhaps the abbey-bells would fetch £60, then the steeple might come down. Half a dozen neighbours had been to buy marble stones and altars. 'Mistress Wriothesley nor you neither be not meticu-lous nor scrupulous to make sale of such holy things, having the example of a devout Bishop of Rome, called Alexander, whose epitaph is,

> Vendit Alexander cruces, altaria Christi,
> Vendere iure potest, emerat ille prius.

Mistress, your husband will open the sense of these two verses. Plucking down the church is a small matter, as you will build a chapel.' [22]

For some time they hesitated about taking down the steeple, but Wriothesley's agents reported 'the tower or steeple misliketh every man, if anything shall be done thereto it must be before the rearing of the north side roof'. They wanted Wriothesley to see for himself before deciding what should be done. It had, of course, to come down in the interests of symmetry. By March the work was going well, but the roof of the hall was shorter than had been proposed, in order to cover the screens. 'This is a disfiguring, but may be remedied.' [23] Caen stone was imported from across the Channel for new building, while faithful John Craford bought the laver, glass, and other things from Southwick Priory ; he wished the latter were Wriothesley's and advised him to buy the ponds that fed the fish-ponds at Titchfield. 'God keep you in health and from your enemies. Your own J. C.' [24]

As for the conventual buildings, 'pantry, buttery, cellar, and larder, no man in Hampshire hath better and more handsome couched together. The kitchen is large and old, and may with little change be made new in the same place.' These were situated on the north side of the cloister — the buttery capable of holding 60 barrels of beer or wine. 'The walls be so good, the old ashlar and freestone shows like white marble. As for timber, rag, brick, and freestone, we have God's fusion ; tiles and slate we cannot lack — beware of Dover lime, there is such plenty in the Virgin's chapel made with the chalk that comes of your vaults as no man living can be better served.' Altogether 'you may have with reasonable charge an house for the King's Grace to bate and for any baron to keep his hospitality in'.

There was the point of it all : a secular residence where the King might stop on his way to or from Southampton, a country house for one of the new nobility rising upon the ruins of the Middle Ages.

Now the place was to be stocked. There were four fish-ponds, a mile in length, 'besides two fair ponds at your door', with pike, carp, tench, and bream. The abbot of Beaulieu would furnish more ; the bailiff would provide 500 carp to stock the ponds. In April 100 of the best sheep were sent from Southwick Priory to stock Titchfield.[25] The prior there was increasing Wriothesley's fee : 'he and his brethren have been so well treated that they have much cause to pray for you'. No doubt Wriothesley had done his best to see to their pensions : one good turn deserves another.

In July 1538 Beaulieu Abbey, across Southampton Water, was purchased by him for £1350 6s. 8d.[26] Craford reported that almost all the inhabitants had taken refuge there as a sanctuary.[27] The murderers and felons should immediately depart as men without hope, but the rest were debtors and of good behaviour. Wriothesley would gain credit there, where, though unseen and unknown, he is much regarded, if he would do his best for them. Wriothesley was as good as his word and intervened to save them : we find among Cromwell's Remembrances, 'the sanctuary men at Beaulieu to continue there for life'. Meanwhile, the abbot instructed Wriothesley's messenger, 'the first bringer to me of the King's pleasure and yours, to show you what he has seen and the fashion of my lewd monks which now, I thank God, I am rid of'.

Wriothesley did not propose to make Beaulieu more than a subordinate residence. He kept only the inner gate-house as a lodge, with the outer gate-house leading to it. The fine great church and most of the other buildings were razed, though the frater was usefully converted to make a parish church.[28] Titchfield was to be the chief residence, though Wriothesley was kept so hard at work that moving in had to be left to his subordinates. Craford wrote for 'fine beds, carpets, cushions, to furnish your house'.[29] With Tudor jocosity he would provide that Wriothesley 'may keep his wife quietly at London and make no waste here' ; or, another time, 'Alack ! that your wife, that sorceress, is so nigh you'. The family in the country, 'Your mother, Mistress Elizabeth, Mistress Mary, Master Anthony, are well'. There is a feeling of loyalty, of friendly intimacy between the busy courtier, the government official, and his servants and dependents.

So the house that plays such a part in our story rose, as we see it still complete in Buck's drawing in the eighteenth century and can derive a fair idea from its ruins today. Wriothesley made its chief feature the fine gate-house leading into the cloister ; on either side of this he raised the buildings to form extensive wings ; the older buildings around the cloister-court he kept, as we have seen, buttery, kitchen, cellar. Into the centre of the court he introduced a decorative conduit. Leland describes it all for us in its newness, when he was here only a year or two later. 'Over the ferry and a two miles to Titchfield by like ground', i.e. both enclosed and heathy ground mixed with bracken, for this was New Forest country, good for hunting. 'Yet in some veins about Titchfield is very good ground', i.e. arable. 'I left a pretty lake on the left a little ere I entered into Titchfield town. Master Wriothesley hath builded a right stately house, embattled and having a goodly gate, and a conduit castled in the middle of the court of it. . . . There is also a park, the ground whereof is somewhat heathy and barren.' [30]

One sees the boundary wall that Wriothesley built still today, the moulded stones from the church tumbled in with the rest. It was quick work.

Meanwhile the master was always away, earning his reward the hard way by his incessant labours for the King and Cromwell. In this same autumn of 1538 he was sent as ambassador to Charles V's sister ruling in the Netherlands, to ask for the hand of the Duchess of Milan for Henry. This was Christina of Denmark, whom we see in Holbein's famous portrait. After the death of Jane Seymour Henry was in need of a new wife, but he needed even more to head off the *rapprochement* between Charles V and Francis I, which might mean a coalition against England. To help to achieve these objectives was Wriothesley's new assignment, with Vaughan for colleague. They had some difficulty in getting a sight of the Duchess ; but when they did they found her 'a goodly personage, of stature higher than either of us and competently fair, but very well favoured, a little brown'.³¹ The ambassadors were kept kicking their heels several months, during which Wriothesley was often ill of his 'old enemy', a quartan fever. I think this means that he was a consumptive, and he was only 45 when he died. He got through a great deal of life in his short time. Before leaving the Netherlands he managed to have a few words with the personable Duchess, describing Henry to her as 'a most gentle gentleman, his nature so benign and pleasant that I think till this day no man hath heard many angry words pass his mouth. At which she seemed much tickled.' ³² It was all to no avail : the ominous peace between France and the Empire prevailed.

In these dangerous circumstances Cromwell stepped out of his own sphere, took the lead in foreign policy himself and forced upon Henry the marriage with Anne of Cleves. It was intended to put a bridle, or at least a rein, upon the Emperor ; but for Cromwell it was fatal. For when Henry encountered his German *frau* he found he could not stomach her. Wriothesley warned Cromwell what the consequences would be, and asked him to devise some way for the relief of the King, for 'if he remained in this grief and trouble, they should all one day smart for it'.³³ The King himself was more specific. He said to Cromwell, before going to church with Anne, 'I am not well handled'.³⁴ This was ominous. Henry went on that he 'was not all men. Surely, my lord, as ye know, I liked her before not well, but now I like her much worse' ; for he had felt her belly and breasts and thought she was no maid, that he was struck to the heart and left her as good a maid as he found her. Though he had lain nightly, or every second night by her, he could not perform the act of love.

In the complex nullity proceedings that followed Wriothesley had to take a leading part to clear up the mess Cromwell had made. He was called in evidence as to the King's distaste for the marriage and its nonconsummation. He was sent with the Duke of Suffolk to obtain Anne's consent ; she had the sense to yield, and promised 'not to vary, for an I did so he would slay me'.[35] The commissioners praised her conformity and advised her to stick to it. She received the rich rewards that conformity purchased from Henry. She got the immense dower of a queen — £4,000 a year, and Henry sent her a token of 500 marks in gold, with a royal message : 'when Parliament ends we shall in passing see and speak with you, and you shall more largely see what a friend you and yours have of us. Requiring you to be quiet and merry, your loving brother and friend, H. R.'

Anne took the hint sensibly, and was always both quiet and merry : for the rest of her life she had a thoroughly good time in England. It was Cromwell who paid the price and was slain — the wickedest and most inexcusable thing that Henry ever did.

The fall of the great minister, chief architect of the Reformation measures, led to a breach in the unity of Henrician policy hitherto preserved, a return to a more conservative course, of which Gardiner was the main inspiration, and a duel between the two parties, conservative and progressive that distracted the country until the issue was settled by the accession of Elizabeth. Wriothesley had been until now a secondary figure, Cromwell's subordinate, and for some time his position and his course were in doubt, though he was too able and useful a servant for the King to lose. By 1542 he had come to terms with Gardiner upon a conservative course — it should not have been too difficult with his wife's uncle, his old patron — and made himself Henry's chief instrument in the return to alliance with the Emperor, which the King always preferred as in the best interest of the country. A reluctant tribute to Wriothesley from a fellow-Henrician says 'I knew he was an earnest follower of whatsoever he took in hand, and did very seldom miss where either wit or travail were able to bring his purposes to pass'.[36]

It is from this period that we have our best portraits of Wriothesley.[37] They show a face of marked character and idiosyncrasy — impossible to mistake him for anyone else. There is aggressive determination, a bulldog tenacity, in the forward thrust of jaw and chin, obstinacy in the lower lip. Yet this is in contrast with the beautiful eyes, large and fine, intelligent and sympathetic, understanding everything. The eyebrows are arched and querulous, the nose long and sensitive, also thrust forward, questing. A full moustache and short squarish beard cover the lower part of the face. Under the flat black velvet cap, worn a little to the side, the hair is gold — as in Leland's verses : one sees how handsome a youth he must have been. This is best seen in the miniature within a gold frame, which evidently his wife wore and which she bequeathed to her son. In a portrait of him as Lord Chancellor, at Palace House, Beaulieu — with the bag of his office, with the arms of England, which carried the Great Seal, proudly beside him — one sees the emaciation of disease upon his cheeks, the eyes alert as ever, the clever fingers of his white hands long and tapering.

For his tireless services in restoring the Imperial alliance, which led to a senseless and exhausting war with France in 1544, Wriothesley was at length rewarded with the barony of Titchfield. On Audley's death he was made Lord Chancellor, and for the last three years of Henry's reign was a leading member of the government, taking precedence of everyone except the Archbishop of Canterbury. As such he had a good deal of dirty work to do, especially in persecuting Protestants — the rigour of which policy came from Henry himself, who, for all the deviation of his conduct, remained always a Catholic at heart.

The episode that has done Wriothesley most harm in the eyes of posterity was his racking of Anne Askew, though it fell within the scope of his official duty. Anne Askew was a

Protestant gentlewoman, and her examinations reveal her as a well-learned, sensible person, able to hold her own in discussion with the Church dignitaries who persecuted her, better read than they in the Scriptures, not very fanatical though steadfast, anxious not to incriminate herself or make brash challenges. But she would not give way ; it was all very provoking, and the Lord Chancellor himself had to take her in hand. What the conservative elements in control of the Council wanted to get out of her was whether she was supported by the Protestant ladies at Court — the Duchess of Suffolk, Lady Hertford, and others. Because Anne would not incriminate them, she was racked in the Tower, and later, remaining obdurate, was burned. In fact, she was probably unaware that she was but a pawn in the struggle for power, with the highest stakes, with Henry's death approaching. It was vital for the conservatives to incriminate the progressive party and get control of government, if possible, before Henry died and thus to be in power at the accession of his son.

In September 1546 we find Wriothesley taken aback by the course of the war — Charles V left his ally in the lurch and England had to sustain the whole burden of the war with France. Wriothesley was in Council from morning to night trying to raise money and stores, and meet the immense strain of the struggle with a power four times larger and with far greater resources. Deserted by the Emperor, we 'can only trust in God and look that our plainness be not deceived by the doubleness of the world as it hath been of late days. . . . But I have cast away care and will serve the state whatsoever it bring.' [38] This gives us the clue to Wriothesley's attitude, as of all Henricians : 'God preserving the King in health, I fear not but the end shall be good'. However, God did not preserve the King much longer, and unfortunately for the reactionaries the Howards were lost by the arrogance and folly of the Duke of Norfolk's son, Surrey, while Norfolk would have lost his head if Henry had not died first. It fell to Wriothesley as Lord Chancellor to announce the King's death to Parliament 'with tears in his eyes' — as well he might, considering what Henry had done for him, and that his best days were now over.

By his will Henry tried to keep the unity of his servants in their allegiance to his young son, Edward VI. He nominated the leading members of both parties as executors and to be of the Privy Council till Edward should come of age at 18. Wriothesley was one of them, and was left £500 by Henry. But the Reformation impulse, with which Edward's uncle, Hertford, was allied by conviction, made it impossible to maintain the Henrician balance and keep things as they were. It was also impossible to carry on government without a leading figure : the King's uncle was made Protector and Duke of Somerset, and at once exercised his ascendancy. Secretary of State Paget ganged up with him, and conveniently remembered (or invented) Henry's last wishes, 'as it is well known he used to open his pleasure to me alone in many things'.[39]

Henry's wishes were taken to be that they should all be promoted, either stepped up in the peerage or recruited to it — 'considering that the nobility of this realm was greatly decayed, some by attainders, some by their own misgovernment and riotous wasting, and some by sickness and sundry other means', among which might be named, more simply, the block. So Hertford was made a duke, Essex a marquis, Wriothesley, Russell, Lisle, St. John all earls, and so on. More, they were all to be awarded large grants of Crown lands to support their new titles : the Protector, 1,000 marks' worth a year to begin with, the new earls £200 a year. This was somewhat stepped up in the doing. Wriothesley, as the new Earl of Southampton, emerged with £300 a year in lands. This scandalous share-out among themselves showed what it was to have a king who was a minor — unable to protect the interests of Crown and people. And shortly, with the heavy hand of Henry VIII removed, they began to fall apart, the struggle for power to come into the open and — after a period of relaxation from Henry's severity — to eat each other alive.

The new Southampton was the first to go. On a trumped-up charge that he had issued a commission to some others, to execute Chancery law to the prejudice of Common law, the Protector forced Southampton to surrender the Great Seal. He was confined to his London house, made to give up the custody of Henry VIII's will, and to pay an immense recognisance of £4,000 until his fine was settled. (The odious Rich, who became a vehement persecutor of Protestants under Mary, now lent himself to the Protector's purposes to become Lord Chancellor.) Southampton took the sentence against him submissively and acknowledged it 'as a good, perfect and just judgment'.[40]

To Charles V's ambassador he confided what he really thought, along with protestations of service: he was the Emperor's man. He owed his downfall, he said, to the long enmity the Protector had borne him, that there was no justice in his sentence, but that a majority of the councillors would not dare go against the Protector. For himself, 'he had preferred rather the certain condemnation of the Council than a scandalous contention before the public judges, which might have resulted in great murmuring on the part of the common people'.[41] Evidently, though Southampton's case was a good one, he had rather anything than submit it to them, and be an occasion for dispute and indiscipline among the people. He was always the consistent Henrician.

There had evidently been a long story of hostility between the two men, and we learn subsequently that Wriothesley had prevented Hertford's elevation in Henry VIII's will. But Southampton now took his adversity patiently, attended Parliament quietly, and bided his time. Under Protector Somerset's lead, the Reformation impulse went forward and early in 1549 the Book of Common Prayer — with the services, above all the Mass, in English — passed through Parliament. Over this issue, according to the Imperial ambassador, Southampton lost his constancy, gave way, and agreed to everything.[42] In return for this conformity he was restored to the

Council, though the Protector used him sparingly in government.

That summer, with the risings in Norfolk and the West Country and the consequent paralysis of government, the Protector came by his downfall. In the autumn two parties within the Council — the conservatives led by Southampton and Warwick's following — combined to oust the Protector. Southampton and the ambitious Warwick, who enjoyed greater popularity — a *faux bonhomme*, more open-handed, though not more open-hearted — took the lead, when most of the secret meetings of the opposition councillors were held at Southampton's town-house, Ely Place. In September the Protector hoped to resist and retired on Windsor, taking the King with him. But he had lost his majority in the Council, the governing class and London turned against him, and Southampton had the pleasure of leading the councillors to arrest his old enemy, the Protector, and send him to the Tower.

The agitation of these events was too much for Southampton's frail health. In November he was dangerously ill ; the Imperial ambassador wrote that 'if he were to fail us now I fear matters might never be righted, for he is still in good hopes of accomplishing this. And a good part of the Council is now well-disposed, but would go astray and follow the rest without him — there is not a man among the others of sound judgment to conduct the opposition. If Southampton should not recover and Warwick stick to his course, confusion and destruction would follow.' [43]

For a time people expected that the progress of the Reformation would be halted. But Warwick had the advantage of having no religious convictions and perceived clearly that the Reformation had the driving power with it, in the governing class, above all the gentry and middle class of the more progressive south and east, most of all London. As a practical politician he threw in his lot with this, double-crossed the conservatives, and neatly stole the Protector's clothes. For a time he proposed to treat the fallen Protector gently, thus winning Paget over to his side. Somerset's forfeited property, it was rumoured, would be divided between Arundel and Southampton ; they do not seem to have got it, but to have been discarded instead — though at some point in these complex turns and changes, Southampton made an exchange of property with Warwick by which he got what came to be called Southampton House. Warwick proceeded to create new councillors among the younger men and thus to assure himself of a majority — more and more like the Kremlin, or indeed like politics in all times and places.

Early in 1550 Southampton was still at Court, but ill, and seeing which way the wind was blowing withdrew before he was ordered to do so. Nevertheless he was confined to his house, and his less intelligent abetter, the Catholic Earl of Arundel, was deprived of office, imprisoned, and sentenced to an enormous fine. Such were the penalties of losing the game. By March Warwick had won out, four recalcitrant bishops were deprived, and he was absolute master, 'thrusting his hand in deep wherever he can'.[44] Such were always the rewards of winning the stakes. He was on his way to becoming Duke of Northumberland — and eventually following the Duke of Somerset upon Tower Hill.

In March Southampton was somewhat better, but 'he regrets it', reported the ambassador to Charles V, 'desiring, as I am told, to be under the earth rather than upon it'.[45] This is what it had all come to, the scheming, labouring, jostling, pushing, grabbing — 45 years old and a desire for nothing but the grave. The time would shortly come, as happens with politicians, when the despatches and state papers, for long so full of him, are as ignorant of his name as if he had never been.

He lingered until the summer, when he received permission to leave his town-house for Titchfield, for the benefit of his health. A dying man, he was unable to go. His cousin the chronicler tells us that 'the 30 July Sir Thomas Wriothesley, Lord Wriothesley, Earl of Southampton, Knight of the

Garter, and one of the executors of King Henry VIII, departed out of this transitory life at his place in Holborn about midnight. He had been long sick, and the 3 August he was buried in St. Andrew's church in Holborn, at the right hand of the high altar, Mr. Hooper, Bishop of Gloucester, preaching there at the burial.' [46] Machyn's Diary tells us what state was held : his standard borne at the head of the procession, then the banners with his arms, next the clerks and priests, then five heralds carrying his insignia of the Garter, helmet, sword, and crest[47]. Then came the body with more banners of arms, and coats of arms covering the coffin, followed by mourners, and a hundred poor men in gowns. There was a big dinner for all the attendance, and a great dole of money, which the estate could well afford. It was all very heraldic, as befitted his descent ; the body, so suitably escorted, was afterwards removed to Titchfield where it reposes under the sumptuous, piled monument subsequently erected there.

It has always been thought that Southampton was a Catholic; the cliché 'bigoted Catholic' has sometimes been applied to him. But the fact that the Protestant Bishop Hooper — to be martyred by Catholic Mary — preached the sermon at Southampton's funeral should have alerted historians. For his will made on 21 July, nine days before his death, shows that he died a Protestant : 'First, I yield my soul wholly to the infinite mercy of almighty God, trusting assuredly to be saved by the merits of the passion of our Lord and Saviour Jesus Christ, his only son and our only mediator, the second person in Trinity.'[48] This is the Protestant formula, and it speaks the language of conviction. The fact is that Wriothesley had always been a consistent Henrician and had moved, with the movement of his time, over to the Protestant position. Therein, in part, lies his historic interest for us.

These last days of his life were occupied with making his long will, for he had much to bequeath — apparently he had not thought till this that he would die so young. His widow survived him some fourteen years, long enough to see her infant grandson, the subject of this book. As we have seen, Wriothesley's eldest son, William, died an infant in 1537. His second son, Anthony, died in 1542. His third son and heir was born in 1545, and given the propitious name of Henry : he survived to carry on the family. He was given a very grand christening, the morrow after his father had been made a Knight of the Garter on St. George's Day 1545 — apex of Wriothesley's career. The family chronicler tells us 'he had a son christened at St. Andrew's in Holborn with great solemnity : the King's Majesty, godfather ; the Earl of Essex, deputy for the King, the Duke of Suffolk the other godfather ; my Lady Mary godmother at the christening, and the Earl of Arundel godfather at the bishoping [i.e. confirmation] : the name Henry'.[49] The wardship and marriage of the boy, which fell to the Crown, were subsequently purchased by Southampton's friend, Sir William Herbert, the first Earl of Pembroke.

Southampton bequeathed to the young King Edward, 'for a remembrance of my bounden duty towards his Highness, my collar of the Garter, my gilt basin and ewer, my six gilt candlesticks and my great gilt wreathen pots, beseeching God to send him his grace, with health of body, till he be as old a king as ever any of his noble progenitors'. Alas, the prayer was of no avail : within three years the boy-king too was dead. There followed a provision the like of which I have not come across in any other wills of the period. 'For a remembrance of my duty towards my sovereign Lord, and for the great benefits that I have received at his most noble father of famous memory, the late king Henry VIII, and also of his Highness, I will that his Majesty shall have for his portion, during the minority and nonage of my son, these manors hereafter limited.' There follows a list of no less than thirteen manors, mostly in Hampshire, but including the manor of Bloomsbury in Middlesex, with a couple of rectories in addition. These extensive lands would clearly yield a large return to the Crown till the heir came of age ; the Crown would in any case have received the value of the wardship, but it may be that he wanted to specify the lands from which the revenues should accrue. Everything shows that, though as grasping at the main chance as everybody else in that age, he was also a generous man.

His bequests present us with a roll-call of his friends and associates at Court. In addition to his bequests to the King, he left Princess Mary his best standing gilt cup for a remembrance, and Princess Elizabeth his second cup of the sort. Naturally he left nothing to his enemy Somerset, but to Warwick and Arundel he left a gilt cup each of the value of £20, to their ladies gilt cups of £10. To the Earl of Sussex a cup of £10, to Sir William Herbert 'all my Garters and Georges', and to his lady a gold ring. There were gilt cups and gold rings for remembrance for his friends Sir John Wallop and Sir Nicholas Lister and their ladies, as to Sir Richard Southwell and Lady Pope ; and large legacies of £40 each to his executors, his widow, Sir Edmund Peckham, Sir Thomas Pope, William Samford, and William Pye, chaplain, the overseer to be Secretary Sir William Petre, with a legacy of plate.

There were numerous legacies to his poor relations, for maintaining two of them as students at Winchester and Oxford, £20 for his cousin Charles Wriothesley the chronicler. His household and servants were very well looked after : 40 marks each for his steward and his controller, £10 for his surveyor, all his leases in Suffolk to Anthony Rush, to every gentleman in his household without wages 20 nobles, every gentleman retainer 100 marks, every yeoman retainer 20s., all the servants their year's wages. The great household was to be kept together at his charge for three months after his death, 'to the intent my servants may in the mean season the better provide for themselves'. The large sum of £200 was to be distributed to the poor of Titchfield, Farnham, and other parishes where his lands lay. At the end there is a touching bequest to his apothecary, 'and to every of the sucklings', i.e. children in arms, £10 apiece in addition to his former legacies.

Provision for the family was carefully laid down. The widow got the usual one-third of the estate for life, and this amounted to nearly a score of manors, mostly in Hampshire, with Southampton House in Holborn for her town-house, Titchfield and Micheldever for country residences. In addition she was to have household stuff to the value of 400 marks, all her own apparel and his plate worth 400 marks and another 400 marks in ready money : she was very lushly provided for. There were five daughters of the marriage. Elizabeth was already married to Lord Fitzwalter, heir to the Earl of Sussex : they were already provided for by marriage-covenant, but in addition they received an annuity of £40 and £100 worth of household stuff, while Fitzwalter got 'four of my best great horses, one hundred pair of Almain rivets and six demi-lances'. Anne was covenanted to marry Sir John Wallop's son and heir, and over and above her dower was to receive £200 ; Mary and Katherine, besides the sums paid 'for such heirs apparents as I have bought for them', were to receive £100 each ; Mabel, as yet uncovenanted for, £400 at the day of her marriage or at 18.

His son was, of course, provided for under the conditions of the wardship, until he came of age and would succeed to the estates. Meanwhile he was to receive all the residue of the household stuff, with plate to the value of 400 marks, and 'all my harness and furniture of mine armour not hereafter bequeathed.' In the last days of his life Southampton was worried in conscience whether he had made sufficient provision for the payment of his debts and the performance of his legacies ; on 23 July he added a codicil, on the next day another, and then a third to provide for another poor relation.

Such were the rewards of success at the Court of Henry VIII, provided one kept one's head.

CHAPTER II

The Heir

FOR all Wriothesley's early death and the frustration of his career's full effect — if he had lived out the normal span he would have been a leading figure in the kingdom again under Mary — nevertheless he had established his family in the peerage. His son, in accordance with custom, became a Crown ward ; but in 1551, the year after his father's death, the wardship of the boy was sold to Sir William Herbert for £1,000.[1] Herbert was one of the inner Edwardian circle, who became first Earl of Pembroke ; this was a profitable grant for him and it was made in consideration of his personal service to the King. The value of the young heir's lands was something over £1,300 a year — a fairly usual figure for a new peerage, nothing exorbitant such as Protector Somerset or Northumberland had grabbed for themselves. There is no evidence of Pembroke having interested himself in the boy ; he seems to have grown up in the care of his mother, and she brought him up a Catholic. This was important for the future, for under Elizabeth he became a malcontent, whose conduct deviated into treason, and in consequence spent some time in prison. It is also probable that, without a father's supervision, he was spoiled. He grew up to be an obstinate lightweight, of whom we know little good, who quarrelled bitterly with his wife, and left an extravagant and vindictive will at her expense. He seems to have inherited his father's consumption, but none of his industry or intelligence ; he ended his useless life at the age of 36.

The first thing we hear of the Dowager Countess Jane's household is something suspicious : in January 1551 the Privy Council has to apprehend the French schoolmaster to the Southampton children, 'whether at Titchfield or elsewhere', to examine what messages he has been sending abroad.[2] We know nothing more of the family till 1564, when the young Earl at 19 was of an age to appear at Court, from which his mother evidently had kept him away. For in December there is a peremptory order from the Council, in the Queen's name, for the Countess, without further delay and notwithstanding her former excuses, to arrange for her son to be at Court before Candlemas Eve next.[3] No doubt he was under suspicion as a Catholic, perhaps for hearing Mass contrary to the laws.

The next thing we hear of him is his marriage contrary to his mother's wishes. 'Tuesday, 19 February 1566, the marriage was solemnised at London in my lord Montagu's house, by his advice, without the consent of my lady his mother.'[4] We have a portrait of him from this time, perhaps taken to celebrate the marriage, for he is wearing a splendid doublet of white seed-pearled satin, with large bulging hose in the French fashion, and a black velvet cap with little plume such as one sees in portraits of Charles IX.[5] Right hand, with the long Wriothesley fingers, on hip, his chest is bedizened with chains of gold ; stiff collar and ruff up to the ears, above it the mulish face of a sickly boy. He has the obstinate set of the Wriothesley jaw, but none of the sensitive sharpness of his father ; the eyes are fine, but uncomprehending. Viscount Montagu's grand town-house had been made out of the conventual buildings of the priory of St. Mary Overy — now Southwark Cathedral — and his father, Sir Anthony Browne, had been the recipient of large grants of monastic lands in Sussex, including Battle Abbey with all its manors in the county. Nevertheless, the Brownes remained an undeviatingly Catholic family all through the reign of Elizabeth.

This much fortified the Catholic proclivities of the young Southampton, who followed his father-in-law's depressing line in politics. Otherwise the marriage would have been very suitable. The Brownes, like the Wriothesleys, had been enriched by the Reformation and recruited to Henry VIII's new nobility : as such they were intended to stand on guard in their respective counties, in place of effete monasteries, and serve the purposes of government and society more efficiently in their localities. Neither family played the game : they both moved into opposition and gave mainly trouble. The Brownes, however, were a much older family than the Wriothesleys, going back to Richard II, and Sir Anthony Browne's marriage to a Neville had brought in a great many quarterings. Perhaps this weighed for something in the young Earl's deference to his father-in-law.

The grand crisis of Elizabeth's reign arrived with the Rising of the Northern Earls, Northumberland and Westmorland, in 1569 ; followed in 1570 by the Papal Bull of Excommunication and Deposition, absolving her subjects from their allegiance, an incitement to rebellion. This was accompanied by a complicated plot to marry the imprisoned Mary Queen of Scots to Elizabeth's cousin, the Protestant Duke of Norfolk, and thus solve the vexing problem of the succession. But the Queen declared against it ; Norfolk returned to the project against her orders and his own given word, and entered into treasonable negotiations with the Papal emissary, Ridolfi. Not until Norfolk was executed in 1572 — much against Elizabeth's inclination — did she and Cecil surmount the opposition in all its forms. Throughout the prolonged crisis they had the constant support of the country in general, expressed in Parliament, and of all sensible people. Against them they had arrayed the militant remnants of the old faith, a considerable section of the nobility, and at times even a majority of the Privy Council.

It was hardly to be expected that Lord Montagu and his son-in-law would be of the number of ordinary sensible people, but they could hardly have behaved in a manner more silly. It seems that in the summer of 1569 a number of supporters of

the marriage met at Titchfield, including the Earl of Sussex,
Southampton's brother-in-law, for Cecil wrote to him to
inquire what had transpired there. When the rebellion broke
out in October Sussex was sent north to suppress it. But
Montagu and Southampton went to the Spanish ambassador,
Guerau de Spes, to ask his advice whether they should take up
arms or go over to Alba, now engaged in his merciless campaign of repression, in the Netherlands.[6] Montagu and his
son-in-law embarked for Flanders, but contrary winds drove
them back and they were forced ignominiously to land. In
Spain they were long expected to join Alba ; in fact, they had
been summoned to Court and clapped in the Tower as evident
traitors in intent.

Early next year, with the Rising of the Northern Earls
quickly suppressed and out of the way, Sussex wrote to Cecil
desiring his helping hand for the young Earl of Southampton
that 'he may be rather charitably won than severely corrected'.[7]
In June the young man was released and placed in the custody
of the Sheriff of London, with a servant to wait on him, but
to have no conference with anyone. Next month, with the
plague increasing hotly in London, the Council considerately
consigned him to the care of William More of Loseley Place
near Guildford, in healthy Surrey. Southampton wrote him :
'I assure you your guest cometh with no very goodwill, having
rather to be at my house, if it so pleased them. But since it is
their pleasure that I were out of the town, otherwise I am glad
they have placed me with so honest a gentleman and my
friend.'[8] It seems that More had had some part in bringing
up the young ward of state and that they were on friendly
terms.

The Spanish ambassador reported to Philip II that the Earl
was kept in custody only because he had been seen speaking to
the Bishop of Ross, Mary Stuart's agent in London. In September the ambassador was expecting a rising in Lancashire,
and that the moment it began Montagu, Southampton, Lum-
ley, and Arundel would take up arms. But the Lancashire

Catholics did not want Norfolk, now in prison, 'as he belongs to the Augsburg Confession' : they would have to do only with a real Catholic.9 One sees what fools these people were, incapable of pulling together in any event.

Lenient as they were with the Earl, the Council kept an eye on him and tried to bring him round to reason. In October they inquired of More whether the Earl 'do come to Common Prayer or not ; and in case he have not done so already, then we require you, as of yourself, to move and persuade him thereunto. And of that he shall do or hath done, and shall answer thereupon, we pray you to advertise us with convenient speed.'10 More duly reported Southampton's reply to his request that he should attend Common Prayer, held daily morning and evening at Loseley : 'as he was restrained of his liberty in my house, he had no disposition to come out of his chamber to pray, but rather to occupy himself there in prayer'. He added that Common Prayer was held in his own house and that he frequented the service at Court. After the Council's letter, at More's earnest solicitation, the young man came to prayers in More's parlour. We see that at this time he was a conforming Catholic : the Papal Bull had not yet had its fatal effect of a final scission.

Southampton was not out of trouble for long, before he renewed contact with the dangerous Bishop of Ross, that inveterate meddler in internal English politics. We learn from him that, at the time of the Rising in the North, Southampton had sent his servant Chamberlain, a Catholic, to report that Leonard Dacre had tried to persuade his father-in-law, Lord Montagu, to incite the Earl of Cumberland to join with the other two Northern Earls.11 Montagu had made him give over, and the Bishop had counselled Southampton to keep quiet — the Northern Earls had no chance of winning. Now in 1570 Southampton asked the Bishop to meet him in St. George's Fields. The Bishop refused, but the Earl insisted and had him conveyed to the waterside, where his servants tarried, and so they crossed over the Thames to hold their colloquy at night in Lambeth Marsh. There they were surprised by the watch ; they agreed to say that they had met by chance, and that their talk was but about Mary Stuart's health and such.

This was a simple and obvious lie,[12] for another spell in prison made the loquacious bishop tell everything. He thought that the occasion for Southampton's disturbance of mind was the departure of Lord Morley into Flanders for conscience' sake. Southampton had inquired of the sanctified bishop whether, in view of the Papal Bull, 'with his conscience he ought to obey the Queen's Majesty or no'. The political bishop answered that so long as the Queen was strong he should obey. The headstrong Earl said, 'if it were against his conscience he would rather forsake all, and follow that which he might do with his conscience'. The bishop advised him 'to be quiet now, as he had divers times counselled him to be, when he sent to him what he should do in the time of the rebellion'. He concluded, not unkindly, 'seeing him a young man, I thought it not good to deal with him in any matter of importance'.

So Southampton found himself in the Tower again in 1571. In April 1572 we find him writing to Burghley in an educated but furious headlong hand, to defend himself against complaints made of his behaviour there. If these were true, he said, 'rather I should . . . show myself lunatic than otherwise. As first, generally, for abusing the Lieutenant, for discontentation with things wherewith was no cause of mislike — in such manner that when my meat hath been brought me, I have thrown the dishes one way, the saucers and trenchers another way, that no man almost would or durst come willingly near me.'[13] There followed a long rigmarole of self-justification, ending up, 'let it be proved that ever since my coming hither I disordered dish or saucer, or used any furious words to any, I will not only never crave her Majesty's favour but wish that I might for my lunacy have Little-Ease [14] for my lodging, thereby the sooner to be restored from madness to more modesty.' This sounds convinced, if not convincing ; unfortunately such behaviour would be in keeping with what we know of him later.

On 2 June 1572 Norfolk, after long delay on the part of the Queen, received the reward of his treason on Tower Hill. At the last he protested that 'he was never a Papist, since he knew what religion meant'. Cecil received the reward of his courage, constancy, skill in holding a steady course through the long and tortuous crisis : he was made Lord Treasurer and created, modestly, a baron. The prisoners in the Tower were watched for their reaction to Norfolk's execution and Leicester's equivocal rôle throughout the business. It was reported of Southampton that he had said that Leicester was the cause of the Duke's death, and that he trusted the Earl would come to suffer in the same place where the Duke died.[15] His fellow-prisoners, however, stood by him and testified that they had never heard him speak ill of Leicester. Henry Goodere — later the respectable patron of Drayton and friend of Donne — imprisoned not thirty feet from the tower where Southampton lay, said that Southampton came to him upon the leads with a joyful countenance and the good news that Leicester had sent word that he would get him delivered.[16] Sir Henry Percy exonerated his fellow-prisoner and affirmed that the Earl had never lamented Norfolk's death. Southampton voluntarily swore his oath upon the Bible to the same effect, and that he took Leicester to be his special good Lord.

However, the young man was not released and this summer seems to have been ill. The women of the family exerted themselves to sue for mercy from the Queen. His wife wrote to Sussex in July : 'my old Lady [i.e. Southampton's mother] hath yesterday night sent unto me to go to her on Monday to the Court, to make suit to the Queen's Majesty for my lord, which I would do on my knees to do him good'.[17] She grieved to learn 'how unprepared the Queen's Majesty is as yet to receive our suit and how unwilling sundry of my lords of the Council be that I should as yet press her Majesty therein'. Shortly after she was appealing to Burghley 'for the safeguard of my lord's life, being sick, I fear, of a burning fever, as also troubled with a swelling in his stomach. He fears a dropsy if presently he seek not remedy.' The poor lady asked that she might 'have recourse to him to attend him in his sickness, if his full enlargement will not be obtained. Truly, my lord, if he be no better attended now in his sickness than commonly he is, I much fear his life will not be long.'

Nevertheless, he was not released. In February 1573 he indicted a complete submission, repenting his former courses and promising dutiful and faithful service to the Queen. This was the beginning of wisdom, and shortly the thaw began. In March his father-in-law was permitted to confer with him about family matters and legal business in the Lieutenant's presence.[18] In May Southampton was once more committed to Mr. More's custody, and allowed to ride abroad and take the air in his company.[19] The Earl was engaged in building a fine big house at Dogmersfield, in the wooded and hilly country of north Hampshire near Odiham, a residence in the splendid park of a thousand acres which his father had acquired in the share-out after Henry VIII's death.

No sooner was the Earl quit of the Tower than he began an angry altercation with the Lieutenant about the payment of his diets while within. Too tedious to go into here, it was also like him ; the Council was obliged to appoint arbitrators to settle the dispute.[20] In July he was permitted to live at Cowdray, the magnificent mansion the monastic wealth of the Catholic Brownes had enabled them to build, of which we have the grand ruins today. They were connoisseurs of sumptuous taste, and among the first people to build up a picture gallery, which in time became famous. Here Southampton and his wife made their home with her parents that summer and autumn. He continued to pay visits regularly to his building operations at Dogmersfield, though now he needed permission to remain a night away from home on account of the greater distance. This was accorded him, and by All Saints' Day he was able to report that his house was ready for the glazier : 'some of the house must be glazed before the frost, and my glass and all other things is there ready'.[21]

On Tuesday, 6 October 1573, Southampton was able to report to kindly Mr. More the birth of a son and heir. From Cowdray 'have I thought good to impart unto you such comfort as God hath sent me after all my long troubles : which is that, this present morning at three of the clock my wife was delivered of a goodly boy (God bless him!) — the which, although it was not without great peril to them both for the present, yet now, I thank God, both are in good state'.[22] Thus, against a background of trouble and only recent release from it, the subject of this book made his first appearance. No grand christening for him as there had been for his father, with Henry VIII himself as godfather and the Princess Mary for godmother. Since there is no information it is all the more likely that the child was baptized by a Catholic priest lurking in the background of that *dévot* entourage ; and as such he was brought up.

For the rest of this decade, the prosperous 1570's, when, the great internal crisis over, England forged ahead abroad as at home, Southampton was as good as his word and kept out of trouble. Such a man was not of much use to government, but he was given his proper place in the Commission of the Peace ; we find him doing his duty as such in regard to the Musters and also over Piracy matters.[23] It does not amount to much, but his leading position in the county was recognised by his being made a freeman of the borough of Southampton.

His mother, to whom he may have owed his troubles — for his canny father would never have brought him into opposition to Crown and government — died in July 1574. A rich old lady, she had a lot to leave, and her demise, with the end of her jointure and her widow's thirds out of the estate, would mean a large financial benefit to her son. In addition she left him various leases, cattle, and sheep, 'and all my household stuff in Southampton Place, Holborn ; my best cross of gold set with diamonds on one side and enamelled with green and red on the other, with a fair pearl hanging at it. A fair tablet of gold wherein is the picture of my lord his father's face, also my great flagon chain that I was wont to wear about my middle for a girdle.' [24] The old lady dripped jewels, most of them going to the women of the family, her daughters, daughter-in-law, or her little granddaughter Mary : they give a rich and sparkling impression of Renaissance taste in jewels. 'To my Lady Southampton, my son's wife, a brooch with an agate and seven little rubies, with the picture of a face upon the agate ; also a girdle of gold, with roses black and white enamelled, and wheatsheaves enamelled.' To her daughters she left books of gold, set with diamonds and rubies, with the Queen's writing therein ; girdles of gold, chains, crosses with crucifixes, brooches, jewelled rings. 'To my son's daughter, the Lady Mary, my best flower of gold set with two rubies, two emeralds and three pearls pendant, a tablet of gold with an old story in it, a pair of beads without enamel and a tablet hanging at them enamelled ; a brooch of gold with two little rubies in it. These jewels to be at her marriage. If she die, to her brother the Lord Harry.' And so we come back to the boy — in those days the name Henry was pronounced Harry, without the 'n'. The child was left certain leases directly, to go to his little sister Mary if he died. One hundred pounds' worth of plate was left to each of her daughters, and 100 marks' worth each to her grandchildren, Lord Harry and Lady Mary. She wound up with a year's wages to all her servants, and a generous legacy, 100 marks, to the poor of Titchfield and her Holborn parish. She was buried at Titchfield, to await translation to the splendid monument erected there a decade later.

Before the decade was out, in 1579, we find the Earl at loggerheads with his wife, of whom we know nothing but good, and debarring her of his board and presence. It seems that his addiction to his men-friends, with whom he surrounded himself, had something to do with this — in particular, his affection for his servant Dymoke, who became his right hand in everything. Many years later we learn that his fellow Catholic, Charles Paget — son of his father's old friend and rival, Secretary Paget — had had a hand in making this mischief between man and wife. The only direct information we have as to the breach comes from a long letter from Lady Southampton to her father. From it we derive the impression that ill-feeling had existed for some time, that Southampton had taken against his wife's family, and that the young men of his household aided and abetted him. In February 1579 his servant Edmund Pretty was sent to the Marshalsea prison for misdemeanours committed against Anthony Browne, Lord Montagu's son and heir.[25] Lady Southampton not only took her family's side in the matter but had grievances of her own against Pretty. She also had a will of her own : 'I trust your lordship and my dear friends will foresee that he be not delivered, for many great causes, which I shall hereafter open to you, till my case first take end.' [26] The Earl, refusing to see or speak to his wife, sent his favourite Dymoke with a message. This young man said to her, 'My lord, your ladyship knoweth, is resolute, yet there be means to win him.' This must have been hard to bear from a subordinate ; but if the Earl was obstinate the Countess was capable of defending herself. It seems that the Earl's precious conscience entered into the matter too — that he considered that his wife's powerful relations at Court, Burghley and Leicester, could procure protection for him. For, Dymoke told her, 'by none would he be enforced till himself listed, and that I [the Countess] would procure a protection to him for his conscience, that he might live untouched for that, with the Queen's good countenance — which by my friends be wanted.' Certainly we never hear of the Countess being out of favour at Court, or ill seen for her religion : she knew how to behave. As for Pretty, the Earl said 'he would bear him out though it cost him £500' These are the accounts of a thoroughly spoiled young man.

The Countess wanted to have her cause brought before the Council, not tried in public, and she was anxious to have the Queen herself intervene. Lady Southampton besought her father and her friends 'to take in hand my cause and to bring it to such kind of trial as shall by your wisdoms be thought best for me. My will, which long hath over-ruled your lord-ship and others in this case, I now leave to be ordered by your discretions.' In this uncomfortable situation it seems that the Countess's conduct had given ground for some suspicion. Her jealous husband charged her with seeing something too much of another of his servants at Dogmersfield. The Countess assured her father, 'by my truth, in my life did I never see him in that house, neither, I assure you, since I was by my lord for-bidden his company did I ever come in it. Desire I did to speak with him ... and I wish that the cause, with my meaning, were uttered by the party himself upon his conscience (if he have any) whereupon I coveted to speak with him ; and then I trust I shall be acquitted of greater evil than overmuch folly, for desiring or doing that which, being by my enemy mistaken, doth breed this my slander and danger. Neither had I ever done for him as I did, or used him other than as a common person of his calling, had I not seen my lord's liking so extra-ordinary for him as warranted me to friend him so far as I might without evil meaning.' This introduces us intimately, as so few evidences that remain from the age, into the familiar amenities of married life. The postscript has a more touching appeal for us : 'that your lordship shall be witness of my desire to win my lord by all such means as resteth in me, I have sent you what I sent him by my little boy. But his heart was too great to bestow upon the reading of it coming from me.'

With the increasing tension between England and Spain that led ultimately to open war, the multiplication of plots, the

Jesuit campaign initiated by Parsons and Campion in 1580 to reconcile people to Catholicism and forfeit their allegiance, Southampton might well have been in trouble again. We find his cousin Pound — later sent to Wisbech Castle as a noted Recusant in time of danger — aiding Father Campion and giving him a token to direct to Dymoke in order to gain access to Southampton.[27] The Spanish rumour was that the Earl was imprisoned again ; but there is no evidence of this, and shortly he was beyond the reach of prison or matrimonial troubles, happiness or unhappiness. On 4 October 1581, at Itchell, a smaller house of his not far from Titchfield, he died : he was 36 years old.

I think we may diagnose a consumptive strain in him inherited from his father, though when he made his will on 24 June he described himself as 'in health and perfect memory, but recalling the frailty of life'.[28] If people's wills may be regarded as in keeping with their character, Southampton's was certainly characteristic of him : it was too generous, extravagant with a touch of fantasy about it, very much concerned with the impression he would leave, with the houses he left unfinished, with leaving his favourite Dymoke well provided for. With the generosity characteristic of the Wriothesleys, 100 marks were to be distributed in alms at his funeral, £200 to be provided for the poor people on his estates to pray for his soul and the souls of his ancestors, and £3 to every almshouse in London and Hampshire for the same purpose 'as soon as possible after my decease'. He left a very large sum, £1,000, for monuments to be built and the chapel embellished in the church at Titchfield, within five years after his death, 'new side windows of stone to be made, the roof plastered with pendants being set full of my arms and all the walls plastered like my house in Dogmersfield, and the same fair paved and divided with iron grating from the church. Also two fair monuments there to be made, the one for my lord my father (whose body I would have thither to be brought and there buried) and my lady my mother ; the other for me, with portraitures of white alabaster or such like upon the monuments.'

In the end one very large and splendid monument for them all was raised, probably under the inspiration of the connoisseur Montagus, for its character much resembled that raised at about the same time in their parish church at Midhurst. That at Titchfield remains erect in all its glory. It is of three tiers, of coloured marbles and alabaster, with a tall obelisk at each corner symbolising eternity. On the topmost tier, alone in state lies the Lord Chancellor in his robes, the collar of the Garter around his neck ; below him, on the next level, lie his Countess Jane on his right, on his left his son, the second Earl, in armour. Beneath this last, on the north side of the great tomb chest are depicted his wife and his little boy — aged 8 at his father's death — kneeling on either side of a prayer-desk. Disposed about the monument are the symbols of Renaissance taste and family pride : the lions'-masks and laurel wreaths, the heraldic animals and coroneted coat of arms with all the quarterings, the panels of black touch with the story of the family in gold lettering. In the vault beneath are buried the later descendants. There in their marble effigies they have lain, the shifting lights of day coming in upon them, the enshrouding shadows of the night, grey of dawn, the colours of sunset, through the vicissitudes now of close on four centuries.

A vindictive provision in his will was that his little daughter should be taken away from the care of her mother : he willed that she be brought up by his sister, Catherine Cornwallis, or his aunt Laurence, and if both of these should refuse or die she was to be placed in some good virtuous house at the pleasure of his executors, provided always that she be not in the house with her mother. This unnatural dispensation was set aside by the Queen.

Thomas Dymoke was much in his master's mind : he and the other gentlemen of the Earl's bedchamber were to have £40 each above their wages, and Dymoke another £200 two years later. 'My will is that the said Thomas, for the good opinion and trust I have of him, should be specially one of those appointed after my decease to be attentive to, and daily about, the person of my son and heir Lord Wriothesley, to have care and charge thereof, whose duty in that behalf to be carefully and honestly performed I nothing doubt.' It is unlikely that this wish would be carried out : the widowed Countess would see to that. Dymoke was to have the keeping of the house in Whitley Park till his son came of age, with 10 marks a year for his trouble, with the right to keep so many of his cattle, with loads of hay from Titchfield meadow and as much wood as he could burn. 'And that he may remember what a good lord and master I have been to him, that he be good to my son, I leave him £10 a year for life. . . . I give my bay horse to Thomas Dymoke, who hath broken and made him.' Such were the terms they were on. To make all sure, he was made an executor, along with Charles Paget ; and if there were any dispute among the executors these two were to decide.

The wardship of the Earl's son would fall to the Queen, with one-third of the annual value of the estate, but in addition he left her a splendid ring of 200 marks' value, 'meekly beseeching her Majesty not to think of the value of the ring, but of the good will of the giver, and I beseech her to be good to my little infants, whom I hope to be good servants and subjects of her Majesty and of the state'. To his little daughter, Mary, he left the exceptionally large sum of £2,000 at 18 for her dowry. Jewels, plate, silver pots, rings, cash were left to relatives and friends, but noticeably more to his gentlemen-servants — Edmund Pretty, among others, was to have £100. Finally, Thomas Dymoke again : 'I straightly charge my heir, when he comes of age, to make to Thomas Dymoke, my man, a lease of what I have leased him'.

He must have been much under Dymoke's spell : as the Countess had complained to her father, 'this house is not for them that will not honour Dymoke as a god'.

It was in some respects an outrageous will, but out of it posterity acquired a magnificent monument.

CHAPTER III

Lord Burghley and his Ward

It was understandable that the Countess should object to the late Earl's will, but also it led to prolonged trouble in itself. For one thing the bequests he made were more than the estate could bear ; for another, the legacies were such that it made the wardship of the son an unprofitable matter and little was left to maintain him in his minority. The very next day after the Earl's death Dymoke rushed off to prove the will, 'by his own bare oath without the knowledge of any of the rest of the executors', the Countess complained ; but this put her in hope that the will might be successfully challenged, or at least some of its provisions set aside.[1]

She took up her pen to appeal to Leicester and make a fight for it. She regretted, tactfully, that the wardship had not come to Leicester : 'that my boy is past your hand I can but sorrow . . . that the whole state of this earldom he is of trust to enjoy should rest in the hands of so unworthy a person as gentle Mr. Dymoke, void of either wit, ability, or honesty to discharge the same, doth so vex me as in truth, my lord, I am not able to express'. On the other hand, her husband had not been able to interfere with her jointure, so that she had her widow's third of the estate and was independent : 'my assurance of living rested not in his hands to bare'. Her ill experience of marriage had persuaded her not to undergo the yoke again : 'well, my lord, I am now free and, be you sure, to the greatest prince that liveth will I not tie myself in the like condition, neither for my quiet nor credit'. Nor did she until a good many years had passed, and then in special circumstances that made her action a defence for the family, as we shall see.

Our only portrait of her — a fine one, by Hans Eworth — shows her as a girl of 13, not long before her marriage. (She was married young, and was several years junior to her husband.) But already she looks a grown woman, maturer than he. There is the beautiful long oval of the face with the high forehead, which she handed on to her son. The features are very regular, with fine intelligent eyes under delicately arched brows, auburn hair drawn back from the temples under fashionable French hood. She is smartly dressed in tight bodice and tight sleeves, puffed at the shoulders and slashed all over for the white material underneath to appear through the cherry-coloured silk. With a high ruff up to her ears and ruffs at her wrists, her ringed hands clasp her gloves. What stands out from the early Elizabethan finery is that this girl has character : there is an amused, alert expression in the eyes, a humorous look about the pouting lips with the upward turn at the corners. Already mistress of herself, she is a real person, capable of defending herself.

Now, at the end of October 1581, she returned to the charge with another letter to Leicester. 'The hard dealing of my lord towards me in his life was not unknown unto your lordship, and how he hath left me at his death is too apparent to all, making his servant his wife, by giving to him all and to myself nothing that he could put from me.' We observe how well she can express herself — she had been well educated — at a time when most ladies at Court could hardly write. And we learn something important about her son. 'That my little son refused to hear service is not my fault that hath not seen him almost this two years. I trust your lordship esteems me to have some more discretion than to forbid him that which his few years can not judge of. Truly, my lord, if myself had kept him, he should in this house have come to it as my lord, my father, and all his doth. I pray your lordship let her Majesty understand this much from me to put her out of doubt

I was not guilty of that folly.' She was writing from Cowdray : what this means is that the Montagu family, though Catholics, attended the Prayer Book service in their house. This the late Earl would not do, and had kept his little son away too.

There are other indications of the Earl's stubbornness in religion. In December the Recorder of London was ordered to search Southampton House and apprehend William Spencer, noted 'to be a very bad fellow and practiser against the state', with other suspects lurking there ; the house was to be thoroughly searched for books and ornaments for Massing.[2] Among others hanging round the neighbourhood were Swithin Wells at Southampton House, Robert Gage 'at a tailor's new house in Chancery Lane where divers bad persons lodge' and Vaudrey at the Mermaid in Fleet Street.[3] All Southampton's executors were, it seems, Catholics : Charles Paget, Edward Gage, Gilbert Wells, Ralph Hare and, presumably, Dymoke. To clear up the state of affairs left by the will, interest was made to get Edward Gage released from the Marshalsea, where he was imprisoned as an obstinate Recusant. The Privy Council were considerate and obliging : they let Gage out for a term for the purpose, and extended it yet again in April since now there was a lawsuit between Lord Howard of Effingham, who had the wardship, and the executors.[4]

The upshot was that Lord Admiral Howard gave up the wardship and it was taken over by the Lord Treasurer himself, the great Lord Burghley. With his immense sense of responsibility for the state, which after all he governed, he was concerned to have young noblemen brought up the way they should go, see them properly educated to perform their part in the state to which they were born. Nor was he without an eye to attaching them to his family and the régime by marriage; there might not be much profit in the wardship, but an eventual husband for one of his granddaughters might do just as well. Evidences remain of Burghley's careful, conscientious inquiries

— as his manner was — into the circumstances and conditions of the charge he had undertaken : into the tenants of the young Earl's lands, for example. We find the Catholic family of Chamberlain occupying the house at Beaulieu. The presentation to the living of St. Andrew's, Holborn — the parish church of Southampton House, and in which the family had a chapel — belonged to the Earl. Now in his minority, in 1584, the executors — with the good will of Lord Burghley — presented Bancroft to the living, who shortly became celebrated as Bishop of London and subsequently Archbishop of Canterbury.

In June 1585 the Earl's sister, Mary, was married in the family chapel at St. Andrew's to Thomas Arundell, son and heir of Sir Matthew Arundell of Wardour Castle in Wiltshire. This Thomas Arundell was the grandson of a much abler Sir Thomas, a younger son of the family of Lanherne in Cornwall, who had made his fortune at the Court of Henry VIII and lost his head as a follower of Protector Somerset. His fortune was almost all in monastic lands, which constituted the foundation of the family at Wardour. The family conformed under Elizabeth, but lapsed back to Catholicism with this Thomas — a rather fatuous man who got into trouble with the Queen for accepting the title of Count of the Holy Roman Empire without her permission.

Lord Burghley was a strong believer in education — the right kind of education for the right kind of people : those capable of profiting from it. He seems to have sent the young peers who were his wards, as well as his own sons, to the university and, himself a loyal Cambridge man, to Cambridge. All his life the great man looked upon St. John's College as his 'nurse', where as a youth he had paid the bellman to wake him at four in the morning and had made such profitable use of his studies. Now in the autumn of 1585 he arranged for his ward to enter his old college : the boy-Earl was admitted as a Fellow-commoner on 16 October and matriculated as a

member of the university on 11 December. There he remained
for the next four years as a student, and this was very important
for his future development. It gave him — what his father had
not had — the foundation of an educated man. This, with the
aesthetic tastes of his mother's family, must have considerably
formed his outlook and inclined him towards literature : he
became fond of books and writers, appreciated their company
and set much store by being regarded as a patron of literature.
That he in turn was grateful to St. John's College is witnessed
by the munificent gift of manuscripts and books which he
subsequently made, to become a chief glory of the college
library there.[5]

In the last two decades of Elizabeth's reign Cambridge was
well recovered from the devastation wrought by the religious
chops and changes of the mid-Tudor period, with their consequences in despoiled foundations and diminished numbers.[6]
The university was now flourishing, with the age, and the
fourteen colleges were the admiration of foreigners. The
Maintenance of Colleges Act had secured their economic
foundation, the increasing returns from land reinforced their
endowment and improved the position of Fellows. Rewards
were being reaped from Whitgift's policy of strengthening the
authority of the heads of houses and academic discipline, con-
taining within decent bounds the sterile excitements of theological controversy. The predominant theology was still that
of a narrow, rebarbative Calvinism, though it was just beginning to be challenged by Peter Baro and William Barrett, and
more magisterially by Richard Hooker of Oxford. Gone for
the time — until the odious Civil War brought them back —
were the days of iconoclasm when the splendid glass of the
Middle Ages and the ornaments of the church were removed
as superstitious. (Who cares now for the nonsense they
thought, either on one side or the other, compared with the
aesthetic damage they did, the things of beauty they destroyed?)

St. John's still vied with Trinity for first place among the
colleges, but it had the disadvantage of its more Puritan

inflexion. This was again strengthened just at this time by the appointment of Whitaker as Master in 1587. For the previous two years Howland, the Master, had been virtually an absentee as Bishop of Peterborough, where he hospitably entertained junior members of the college, including Southampton.[7] Whitaker brought with him the reputation of immense theological learning and some eminence as a controversialist — for what that was worth. Unfortunately he was tinged with Puritan inclinations, and the first thing he did was to expel from his Fellowship the one member of the college of genuine philosophical originality, Everard Digby, a precursor of Bacon in his classification of the sciences. Whitaker charged him with preaching voluntary poverty, 'a popish position', at St. Mary's, attacking Calvinists as schismatics, going fishing in the time of college services, and blowing a horn and hallooing in the court. Evidently Digby, besides having an original mind of his own, was a human being. Archbishop Whitgift was no doubt right in regarding his expulsion as 'contrary to the rule of charity, I might say, of honesty also . . . I am sorry Mr. Whitaker doth so far forget himself : but without doubt, it is the violence of Preciseness, which desireth a rule and government absolute without controlment, be it never so vehement and unjust'.[8] One sees something of what archbishops had to put up with at the hands of Puritans, once they got into the saddle : neither Whitgift nor Burghley could get Digby reinstated, and the college lost the most brilliant, though not the most solemn, of its Fellows.

After this it was only to be expected that the dreary Whitaker should inhibit 'all manner of plays, and that comedy which was usually played to celebrate the Queen's day'. These Puritans were unable to kill University dramatics — mercifully, for it was one of the elements that went to the making of the marvellous Elizabethan drama that redeemed the times. Most colleges had their plays to light up the dark days between Christmas and Shrove-tide. We have evidences of the comedies — in Latin, of course — and *scenici ludi* played at

Corpus, Marlowe's college, in the 1580's. (It is worth observing that Marlowe overlapped with Southampton by some two years at Cambridge : having come up in 1580, Marlowe did not go down until 1587.) One of the best examples of University drama, Thomas Legge's *Ricardus Tertius* had been performed in the hall of St. John's ; and at the turn of the century, the three Parnassus plays, with their interesting skits on contemporary dramatists and writers, were a product of Southampton's college.

How much of all this entered the mind of a precocious youth of twelve to sixteen we are unable to say, but it must have counted for something in Southampton's later addiction to drama and literature. And St. John's College had literary associations no less than theological ones. Thomas Nashe entered as a poor sizar in 1582 ; his name remained on the books for some seven years, he said : if so he would have overlapped with Southampton. Later in his writing career he paid an eloquent tribute to the college, as 'the sweetest nurse of knowledge in all the university . . . a university within itself'.⁹ Earlier, Robert Greene, dramatist, poet, journalist, had also been a sizar, but left for Clare. Arthur Hall, translator of Homer, and a connection of the Cecils was also a member of the Cecils' family college — where Burghley's clever son, Robert, had been a Fellow-commoner briefly. Among other poets were Henry Constable and Burghley's talented, but lightheaded, son-in-law, Edward de Vere, Earl of Oxford. Altogether, the literary associations of John's were considerable and encouraging.

Such was the college that the boy of 12 entered that October day of 1585. He was three or four years under the average age for admission : evidently Burghley thought him best placed there in lieu of a school. As a young peer he would have a set of rooms to himself — as Essex had had at Trinity — with a tutor to look after him : we gather that Southampton's chamber was on the south side of the first court, as one enters the great gate of St. John's with its gilded leopards and royal emblems. Usually a big bed-chamber was shared by three or four students, as we know was Marlowe's case at Corpus, sometimes with little studies leading out of it. Around one was the rudeness and barbarousness of the age, in addition to the usual rowdiness of young students mewed up in echoing court and cloister. As the golden days of October, with the falling leaves littering the still waters of the fenland town, moved into the gloom and the long nights of winter there would be fires leaping up in the great hall — would the boy be spared the rough but regular initiation ceremony of salting ? (Francis Bacon, at Trinity, wasn't.)

It is fairly certain that at so youthful an age Southampton would be kept, like a schoolboy, at his Latin. The chief undergraduate studies, logic and rhetoric — studied in Aristotle and Ramus, Cicero and Quintilian — would come later. It is certain that he did not scale the heights of theological disputation : those rational pleasures were for adults. Like a sensible man, though a Catholic, he never displayed any interest in them. His Latin essays were called for by Lord Burghley — a good deal of a don himself — to see how his ward was getting on. We have one from June 1586, written in a beautiful Italian hand on ruled lines, on the theme 'Laboriosa juventutis studia sunt, jucunda senectutis otia' — in so far as the studies of youth are laborious the leisure of age is made agreeable — a theme very much after the great man's heart, though he had as little leisure in age as in youth.[10] Next month followed another Latin essay on 'Omnes ad studium virtutis incitantur spe premii' — all men are incited to the path of virtue by the hope of reward. (Certainly no man's adherence to the path of virtue ever paid such dividends as in Lord Burghley's case.) The boy reported to his guardian duly in Latin letters : we have one from June 1587, written rather hurriedly because the messenger was waiting to take back a reply, and promising to write at greater length when he had more time — so like a schoolboy ; but the missive was at least in Latin.

Meanwhile the great man kept his eye on the boy's affairs — amid all the pressure of state affairs, for these were the years of the open war with Spain, the English intervention in the Netherlands, the execution of Mary Queen of Scots, the Spanish Armada. Out of the Earl's lands in the Queen's hands by reason of his minority, she allowed him a small exhibition to keep him at the university. It was not enough, and Burghley was allowed to receive these rents for his ward's honourable maintenance, over and above the Queen's annuity. Early in 1587, with the increasing threat of invasion, the Privy Council ordered that the armour and weapons at Titchfield should be scoured and put in a state of readiness, placed in proper custody and not allowed to fall into the hands of any ill-affected persons, 'the rather in respect of the doubtfulness of these times, of some foreign attempts that might be intended upon the sea-coast of that shire, and namely at Portsmouth'.[11]

On 29 February 1588 Southampton was admitted a member of Gray's Inn, introduced by Burghley who had also been a student there — his nephew, Francis Bacon, now a Bencher with his chambers in the Inn was on his way to becoming its most brilliant luminary.[12] Shortly after, 11 March, we find the Earl of Kildare admitted on Southampton's introduction, and a number of young men to become well known in their day, Sir Philip Sidney's brother, Robert, his friend Fulke Greville, Edward Fitton, Burghley's absurd nephew, Posthumus Hoby, and Lord Cobham's contemptible son and heir, Henry Brooke, who helped eventually to bring Ralegh down. In July, with the Armada on its way, we find Southampton's brother-in-law, Thomas Arundell, writing from Southampton House to complain to Walsingham that he has not yet been employed in any honourable service for her Majesty such as he had been promised.[13] In October — the Armada come and gone — Arundell wrote from another of Southampton's houses, Itchell, importuning Burghley for the keepership of the New Forest for Southampton : 'my love and care of this young Earl enticeth me. Beaulieu, the most ancient house

that he hath, is so near to the Forest and the Forest so convenient for it as that the very situation may be of sufficient
force to persuade. . . . Your lordship doth love him and then,
even out of the common nature of love, must needs desire to
be requited with love and thankfulness ; such as have good
wills together with great minds are not so soon won any way
as with favour, neither is any favour so thankfully taken, and
so long remembered of men, as that which they receive in
their minority.' As if the great minister needed to be told his
business by this young Polonius! Then comes the point :
'that my Lord of Pembroke (his most feared co-rival), having
neither land nor house near thereto, should, as it were by a
perpetuity, bear the Forest from him in his own sphere and
joining to his doors, were a great discourtesy, I may more
truly say, a wrong'.[14]

From that silly letter one gets a pretty good idea of Southampton's brother-in-law. Needless to say, no action was taken.

The Earl continued to keep his terms at Cambridge, until at
Commencement the following summer, 6 June 1589, he
received by special grace the degree of Master of Arts. On his
birthday, 6 October, this year Burghley noted in his Diary
that the Earl was now 16 ; he followed it with the reminder
that his other noble wards, the Earls of Bedford and Rutland,
were 15 and 13 respectively. This was with an eye to their
future marriages, which should be matters of profit both to
Lord Burghley and to the state : in his position these interests
were one and the same. Such is the contrariness of human
nature that each one of these young Earls went over to the
opposition to the Cecils, to follow Essex — one of their own
order — into conspiracy and treason, to their own danger and
loss.

In 1590 the Earl of Rutland, now fourteen, was sent up to
Corpus Christi — three years after Marlowe had gone down,
and a year before John Fletcher, the dramatist, came up to it.
In July young Rutland reported to his guardian, Lord Burghley,
that their 'great Commencement at Cambridge' was now

finished and sent his commendations to Southampton.[15] So
Southampton was with Burghley, and it was in the Lord
Treasurer's household that these young Earls grew acquainted :
that household was a school of virtue, whose inmates turned
out somewhat otherwise than intended. (We find that next
summer, in June 1591, Southampton sent word he would visit
his young friend, Rutland, at Cambridge.)[16] Old Roger
Manners had to write the Countess to admonish Rutland and
'those about him to have care of his manners that his behaviour
be civil'.[17] Burghley allowed Southampton to spend the
summer of 1590 with his mother, for in October we find her
thanking the Lord Treasurer for the long time he had entrusted
her son with her. She now returned him, hoping that Burghley would so dispose of him as his exercises should be such as
might grace persons of his quality. And, for conclusion, only
Burghley was able to work her son's future happiness.[18]

This referred to the important subject already raised, upon
which an awkward correspondence was being entertained —
that of the Earl's marriage.

Lord Burghley had a granddaughter to marry — in fact,
several : these were the children of his favourite daughter
Anne, whom he had married in 1571 to his ward, Edward de
Vere, Earl of Oxford. It seemed at the time that it was a love-
match, but after his Italian tour in 1575–6 Oxford returned
with other tastes and proceeded to treat his wife abominably.
He was a gifted, cultivated man, both musician and charming
lyric poet ; good-looking and with a charm capable of fascinating the Queen (when he was young), he was also impulsive,
wayward, fantastic, madly extravagant, utterly spoiled — as,
one gets the impression, many of these young Elizabethan
nobles were. In the end one wonders whether he was quite
right in the head, for he proceeded to run through the whole
of his patrimony, the ancient de Vere estates — he was the
seventeenth Earl, head of one of the oldest of medieval
families.

Neglecting his wife, then making unfounded charges against her — as Burghley wrote in his Diary, he 'was enticed by certain lewd persons to be a stranger to his wife' — he was a frightful headache to the great man, who bore his troubles, at the hand of his aristocratic son-in-law, with patience and submission. Anne Cecil was Burghley's eldest daughter ; she inherited something of the mental qualities of her parents, and herself wrote verse. She had an unhappy life of it, died while still young and was given a grand funeral in Westminster Abbey, 25 June 1588, in the weeks before the Armada arrived on the coast. Burghley had all along taken charge of her affairs — in addition to so many other people's, not to mention the state's — and now there were her three daughters to look after and provide for. The eldest was Lady Elizabeth Vere, now in 1590 15 years old and therefore of an age to be married. (Lord Burghley was all in favour of marrying people off young.)

Lady Elizabeth was a couple of years junior to Southampton — what more suitable than a match between them ? It was most suitable from Southampton's point of view. Himself a Catholic, and as such in need of some protection and favour in the highest quarters, he would be marrying into the great minister's family, with its influence and alliances extending ever more widely in the peerage : all doors would be open to him. Moreover, his was only a new Reformation family : he would be marrying into a family of the old medieval nobility. From Burghley's point of view the match was no less suitable : he would be providing for his dead daughter's eldest child a handsome young earl, of intelligence and promise. And it seems that the youth, brought up in Burghley's house and by his care, had given his promise to marry the girl.

Now that the time was approaching to bring matters to the point the youth held off. Lord Burghley, growing suspicious, thought that someone else must have put a spoke in the wheel and was after so good a catch. His suspicions fell upon Sir Thomas Stanhope, who knew better than to make so powerful an enemy and excused himself thus. He had indeed seen the Countess of Southampton, but only in the way of old friendship. 'Unto her ladyship I appeal if she can appeach me of such simplicity or presumption as to intrude myself, or of the meaning of so treacherous a part toward your honour, having evermore so found myself so bound unto you as I have done : I name it treachery, because I heard before then you intended a match that way to the Lady Vere, to whom you know also I am akin.' What, then, had transpired between Sir Thomas and the Countess ? 'My lord, I confess that talking thereof, she told me you had spoken to her in that behalf. I replied, she should do well to take hold of it, for I knew not where my lord, her son, should be better bestowed. Herself could tell what a stay you would be to him and his, and for perfect experience did teach her how beneficial you had been to that lady's father [i.e. Oxford], though by him little deserved. She answered, I said well, and so she thought and would in good faith do her best in the cause ; but saith she, "I do not find a disposition in my son to be tied as yet. What will be hereafter time shall try, and no want shall be found on my behalf."' Sir Thomas assured the great man that the Countess would not dissemble with him in such a matter.[19]

Still nothing happened. So that summer, when the Court was at delightful Oatlands in Surrey, Lord Burghley took the opportunity to have a talk with the youth's grandfather, Lord Montagu, who promised to take the matter up with both the Countess and her son. This he did when they were both staying with him at Cowdray. His daughter assured him on her honour that she knew of no 'alteration of her son's mind from this your grandchild. And we have laid abroad unto him both the commodities and hindrances likely to grow unto him by change.' To this they got only a general answer from the young man that 'your lordship was this last winter well pleased to yield unto him a further respite of one year, to ensure resolution in respect of his young years'. The grandfather replied that 'this year which he speaketh of is now almost up, and therefore the greater reason for your lordship in honour and in nature to see your child well placed and provided for'. They could get nothing more out of the young man, who was content that they should tell Lord Burghley what he had said. 'And this is the most as touching the matter I can now acquaint your lordship with.' Lord Montagu ended by re-commending the care of his grandson's person and circum-stances to his ruling — he was still Lord Burghley's ward ; when Montagu and his daughter came up to London at the beginning of the term they would talk the matter over with him, 'and will be sure to frame myself (God assisting me) to your lordship's liking in this matter'. [20]

But the fact was not so much that the youth did not want to marry Lord Burghley's granddaughter as that he did not want to marry at all.

His mind was set on quite other things. With the new year, 1591, Henry of Navarre, reduced to desperate straits in his struggle to secure his throne against the Catholic League, appealed to Elizabeth for help. The appeal was fervently backed by the brilliant young Earl of Essex, now at 24 in the first flush of his favour with the Queen, looked up to by most of the younger generation at Court, especially of his own order, as their natural leader. He was clamouring, all inexperienced as he was, for the Queen to give him the command of the expedition designed for the succour of Henry of Navarre. And a very romantic affair it turned out to be that summer, with the gallant Essex trailing a pike with the common soldier, losing his brother — 'the half-arch of my house' — in a skirmish before Rouen, risking his own capture in a mad gallop through hostile country to meet the famous Henry. The expedition to Normandy aroused romantic memories in England of Henry V and Agincourt and brave John Talbot ; and these were appealed to by a new dramatist — an actor turning his hand to writing plays — one William Shakespeare with a play on the theme. It appealed so well to the audience, it fitted so well the mood of the city at this juncture, that before he was through he had written the three plays of *Henry VI*, and was on the way to recognition and fame.

As for Southampton, the boy was in France before Essex was. In January 1591 he was in Southampton, for the corporation gave him the freedom of the borough, as it had his father before him. Thence he slipped over to Normandy, for we have a letter from him to Essex, 2 March, offering his service and assuring him of his devotion. He had already offered himself to Essex verbally, now he wrote to him from Dieppe as 'from one who hath no better present to make you than the offer of himself to be disposed of by your commandment'. The boy asked his brilliant peer to accept his devotion 'and ever afford me your good opinion and favour, of which I shall be exceedingly proud, endeavouring myself always with the best means to deserve it. . . . In the mean time wishing your fortune may ever prove answerable to the greatness of your own mind, I take my leave.' [21]

It was observed in his lifetime that Southampton had two ardent passions : one for military glory, martial adventure, and renown, the second for that other glory, to shine as a patron of literature. Devotion to the sedate Lord Treasurer, a quiet life as his son-in-law, would achieve neither of these. With this letter to the leader of his order and of all the ardent spirits among the young men, he had in fact made his decision. In the end — and before ten years were out — it very nearly proved fatal.

CHAPTER IV

The Patron and the Poet

THE Normandy campaign came to nothing, and the war died down for a time, except for individual actions that lit up the scene, like the last fight of the *Revenge* in 1591, or the capture of the *Madre de Dios* in 1592. No glory came Southampton's way, but at least there were the delights of literature and the pride of being made up to by the poets. It is understandable that the promising new dramatist of the Normandy scenes of *Henry VI* should appeal to Southampton, though we know nothing whatever of the player-playwright's introduction to the notice of the young Earl.

From the fact that 'A Lover's Complaint' turned up with the *cache* of the Sonnets and was published ultimately along with it, and from its nature, we may conjecture that it bore something of the character of a diploma-piece, and served as such in the introduction of the poet to the youth who accepted his service and became his patron. It is, of course, a *jeu d'esprit*, written in inverted commas ; yet, though in the pastoral form, it has the naturalness and spontaneity, the lack of artificiality, the realism along with the charm, that bespeak Shakespeare. Malone, the best student of Shakespeare that ever was, had no doubt of it : 'in this beautiful poem, in every part of which the hand of Shakespeare is visible, he perhaps meant to break a lance with Spenser'.[1] This may be going a little far, but there are Spenserian touches in it ; the actor, ambitious to shine as a poet, had been reading Spenser to some point.

It seems no less clear that there are strokes drawn from the recognisable personality of Southampton ; the young man who is so irresistible to the maid of the story is described thus:

> Small show of man was yet upon his chin ;
> His phoenix down began but to appear . . .
>
> His qualities were beauteous as his form,
> For maiden-tongued was he, and thereof free . . .
>
> Well could he ride, and often men would say
> 'That horse his mettle from his rider takes :
> Proud of subjection, noble by the sway,
> What rounds, what bounds, what course, what
>   stop he makes !' . . .
>
> That he did in the general bosom reign
> Of young, of old, and sexes both enchanted . . .

In the story this appealing youth, with all these charms, submits them thus to the girl :

> 'Lo, all these trophies of affections hot,
> Of pensived and subdued desires the tender,
> Nature hath charged me that I hoard them not,
> But yield them up where I myself must render —
>
> That is, to you, my origin and ender ;
> For these, of force, must your oblations be,
> Since I their altar, you enpatron me.'

Whether this was a hint on the poet's part or no, the maiden could resist no longer but yielded up her virginity.

It is, in fact, a transposition of the Southampton theme we come to know so well — that of the beautiful young man visibly made for love but who will not give himself to the love of women.

This, as we have seen, was the actual situation of the adolescent Earl in these years 1590–2, and this is the situation from which Shakespeare's Sonnets take their departure. It would be only conjecture to say that the poet may have been encouraged by the family to take a hand in the family campaign to get the youth to do his duty, marry, shore up his noble house — he was its head, its last male representative — and carry on the line. Certainly no member of the family could but approve of the urgent persuasions, expressed in fluent, flattering verse, of the duty to marry and the rewards of the married state.

The very first sonnet tells us that the young man is just coming out before the notice of the world :

> Thou that art now the world's fresh ornament.

The third has a graceful compliment to his mother :

> Thou art thy mother's glass, and she in thee
> Calls back the lovely April of her prime.

Sonnet 13 refers to his dead father :

> Dear my love, you know
> You had a father : let your son say so.

Sonnet 10 urges him to uphold his house and carry on the line, instead of

> Seeking that beauteous roof to ruinate
> Which to repair should be thy chief desire.

The whole argument of the first twenty-six of the Sonnets advances this theme and urges this argument with many ingenious variations upon it :

> Look in the glass, and tell the face thou viewest
> Now is the time that face should form another.

We have a Hilliard miniature of Southampton just at this time, from which we can see the kind of young man he was. It is a very refined, aristocratic face, with the long oval he got from his mother ; rather a feminine face, with its regularity of feature, the sensitive curve of lip and nostril, the fine arched eyebrows. Above all there are the long curling tresses brought forward over his left shoulder, by which one can recognise him in all his portraits — for he was the most frequently painted man of his age — for years ahead, well beyond his marriage and into the Tower. All the same, there is a certain masculinity in the youth's feminine appearance : a cock-sure stare of the eye, an obstinacy of expression — for the expression is not feminine. It is a portrait of an ambivalent type, as Southampton continued to be, even beyond his reluctant marriage later.

And so Shakespeare describes him in Sonnet 20 :

> A woman's face, with Nature's own hand painted,
> Hast thou, the master-mistress of my passion ;
> A woman's gentle heart, but not acquainted
> With shifting change, as is false woman's fashion . . .

Indeed, he is

> A man in hue, all hues in his controlling,
> Which steals men's eyes and women's souls amazeth.
> And for a woman wert thou first created,
> Till Nature, as she wrought thee, fell a-doting,
> And by addition me of thee defeated
> By adding one thing to my purpose nothing.

So Shakespeare was not interested in him sexually — in any case, he was not in the least homosexual, unlike Marlowe who was completely so. Thus the women can have their young man :

> But since she pricked thee out for women's pleasure,
> Mine be thy love, and thy love's use their treasure.

That places the matter upon the right foundation, that which prevails throughout the whole relationship between the poet and his youthful patron.

Nor was Shakespeare, though only now beginning to be known and successful, any longer young : in 1592 he was already 28, more than half his life was over. He had had a long struggle, a harsh apprenticeship, and had come up the hard way. When he was 13 his father's affairs had begun to

go downhill, so that there was no going to the university for
him, no scholarship to an Oxford or Cambridge college such
as Marlowe fortunately gained from the King's school at
Canterbury. At 18 he had started a family, by 21 he had a
wife and three children to maintain. It was not easy to do this
as a vagrant actor — his intimate experience of the profession
is already expressed in one of the first sonnets :

> As an unperfect actor on the stage
> Who with his fear is put beside his part,
> Or some fierce thing replete with too much rage,
> Whose strength's abundance weakens his own heart . . .

When he turned to his pen and began to be successful with his
Henry VI plays, he was spitefully attacked by the envious
Robert Greene, one of the writing tribe in London — how
one recognises the type ! — with all the more venom because
the newcomer was an outsider, no university man, a mere
player, 'an upstart crow, . . . that, with his

> Tiger's heart wrapped in a player's hide,

supposes he is as well able to bombast out a blank verse as the
best of you, and, being an absolute Johannes Factotum, is in
his own conceit the only Shake-scene in a country'.[2]

The accents of personal malice do not vary much from age
to age — the personality of Shakespeare is easily recognisable
with the parody of his line from 3 *Henry VI*. And he *was* an
absolute Johannes Factotum, able to turn his hand to anything
— maddening for the mediocre, with pretentions of their own
but unable to make anything much of them. Shakespeare
resented this personal attack on him from a curmudgeonly
muckraker, and exacted a handsome apology from the publisher of it. The latter was given an opportunity of meeting
the actor and was now able to report — 'myself have seen his
demeanour no less civil than he excellent in the quality he
professes. Besides, divers of worship have reported his uprightness of dealing, which argues his honesty, and his facetious
grace in writing that approves his art.'[3]

Everything we know about Shakespeare shows that he set store by being a gentleman, behaving like one and being treated as one. It is not surprising that we do not hear of him living the life of the literary riff-raff of London : it is evident that he did not live it, and, as Aubrey corroborates later, preferred to keep to himself. The entry to a cultivated, aristocratic circle like that around Southampton was a different matter : there was a world of culture and aesthetic refinement of which he had been starved and to which anyone of sensibility would respond. We observe that it was 'divers of worship', i.e. gentlemen of standing, whom he called in to answer for him — not the seedy citizens of squalid Bohemia — when he was attacked by one of them, quite unjustly though characteristically. His patron may well have been one of those who stood by him, for we find him saying in a sonnet later:

> Your love and pity doth the impression fill
> Which vulgar scandal stamped upon my brow ;
> For what care I who calls me well or ill,
> So you o'er-green my bad, my good allow ? [4]

His was a personality of singular charm and appeal : as Ben Jonson said of him, in one of the most generous tributes ever made by one of the writing tribe to another, he was 'indeed honest, and of an open and free nature'.[5] Ben went on to say, as of no one else, 'I loved the man, and do honour his memory — on this side idolatry — as much as any'. Unlike Marlowe, he was well-adjusted to life, while at the same time being more responsive to it and more sensitive, not less. This is what is so remarkable, for he was a normal man in his tastes, with his 'sportive blood', his out-of-doors disposition, his addiction to sport, his perfect fixation on deer-hunting as a young man, his intense responsiveness to women. Then he had the double advantage of being a talented actor, with his instinctive ability to put himself in other people's places, get inside their skins, mimic them with his loving observation of their follies and humours. The penetrating understanding of Dr. Johnson perceived that Shakespeare's natural bent — again, so unlike Marlowe — was for comedy, that comedy came naturally to him where tragedy, at any rate in his earlier work, was a matter for labour. Can one doubt that with this combination of qualities and talents — the good humour and merriment, the jests, the sheer unforced cleverness, the sensibility and instinctive good breeding — he made an irresistible companion for a youth much younger than himself, whenever the 'separable spite' that divided them, the radical difference in their social status and circumstances, allowed them to come together ?

We know quite well what Shakespeare looked like, though our one authentic portrait of him comes from years later. Aubrey tells us, what we can easily believe, that he was 'a handsome, well-shaped man : very good company, and of a very ready and pleasant smooth wit'.[6] The dominant impression given was that of the fine dome of the head — a perhaps self-conscious reference in *The Comedy of Errors* corroborates the likelihood that he was already going bald ; beneath the broad capacious forehead were the alert, luminous eyes, full of intelligence and observation, ready to brim with mirth. Cheeks full and well-liking, with long, fleshy, sensual nose ; the lips with rather a feminine curve, sensuousness and sensibility alike in them and the discriminating nostril. One sees that the well-rounded features are easily mobile, the expression changeable, as an actor's should be. The whole impression of the countenance corroborates Jonson's words, 'of an open and free nature' — nothing mean and reserved, or lean and hungry, malevolent or envious : we perceive that he put the whole of himself into his work, as he was no less ready to give himself to life.

Such was the man, now 28, who recommended himself to the service of a promising new patron of letters, just coming before the notice of the world at nineteen. In Sonnet 26 Shakespeare ties up the first section of the Sonnets, the persuasions to marry, with an *envoi* to his young lord :

Lord of my love, to whom in vassalage
Thy merit hath my duty strongly knit,
To thee I send this written embassage,
To witness duty, not to show my wit.

He goes on to promise something better to prove himself worthy of patronage :

Till whatsoever star that guides my moving
Points on me graciously with fair aspect,
And puts apparel on my tattered loving
To show me worthy of thy sweet respect.
Then may I dare to boast how I do love thee ;
Till then not show my head where thou mayst prove me.

This shows that Shakespeare, much encouraged by being received as the young peer's poet, naturally has more ambitious endeavours in mind : it was Southampton's patronage, and the support that went with it, that enabled him to write his two long poems, *Venus and Adonis* and *The Rape of Lucrece*, in these years. When he published them, one in 1593, the other in 1594, he dedicated them in the same terms of duty, and with the word 'duty' itself thrice-iterated, as it is in this *envoi* to the first section of the Sonnets.

Nothing could have exceeded the importance of his reception, of this patronage, for Shakespeare or of its consequences for our literature : after much ill luck and many cross-blows of fortune, it turned out in the end that he was providentially fortunate in this. What made it indispensable, a matter of practical urgency, was that these years, 1592 and 1593, were plague-years — there are many references to plague in the Sonnets — during most of which the theatres were closed and the actor was without visible means of support for his family. They were hard and cruel years, which saw the theatre-folk dispersed, their struggling companies fractured, fragments of them coming together and trying to combine for a tour in the country — as we find Edward Alleyn, most famous of Elizabethan actors, the star of the Lord Admiral's men, touring with

Strange's men in 1593, while London is decimated by the plague. Another of the companies, Pembroke's — with which Shakespeare may have acted, for they owned plays of his — came back from the country broken and bankrupt. In London the whole family of Robert Browne, the actor, for example, was wiped out. The hardships of the time bore cruelly, in one way and another, upon those who depended upon writing for the theatre. In September Robert Greene died, in poverty and debt, charging his deserted wife to see that the couple who had sheltered him were paid, 'for if he and his wife had not succoured me I had died in the streets'.[7] At about the same time Thomas Watson, Marlowe's friend, obscurely perished; next year, at the end of May, Marlowe was killed. In the winter of 1593–4 Kyd disappeared, and not long after, Peele. Shakespeare was lucky to have come through these years: no wonder he expresses himself grateful again and again for the protection he received from his patron. The Sonnets express gratitude, duty, obligation along with friendship and love.

The anxiety of this time deepened with the second successive year of plague, and this is one element in the increasingly sombre tone of the Sonnets. However, what would transpire was not evident at the beginning of the period; what is clear is that it provided the actor-playwright with just the opportunity to fulfil his ambitions as a poet and write the two long poems with which he achieved success and recognition as such — in addition to writing most of the Sonnets. Then, too, there is reason to think that *The Taming of the Shrew* was written in the country at this time, with its Cotswold background; while we move forward with 1593–4 to *A Midsummer Night's Dream* and *Love's Labour's Lost*, with their visible connections with the Sonnet-period and their decipherable associations with the Southampton circle.

What better to do in these years than to go home to Stratford and write? The very next Sonnets find the poet travelling away into the country, absent from his young patron — a

situation all the more stimulating to the imagination in the
first stages of awakened love.

The summer of 1592 found Southampton beginning to take
an interest in his inheritance and seeking to shore up the roof
of one of his houses. In June he wrote to Lord Burghley's
secretary to draw his attention to the fact that 'my manor-
house at Beaulieu with divers parcels of my inheritance there
are like to fall in great decay and danger to be lost through
want of means to supply the charge of reparations during my
wardship'.[8] He enclosed a note of what was necessary, hoping
that Burghley would take appropriate action. He wrote
'from my lodging in the Strand'. Why was he not under Lord
Burghley's roof? — he was still his ward ; and why did he not
approach him directly, rather than through a secretary? We can
only suppose that relations were awkward through Southampton's hanging back from marrying Burghley's granddaughter.

In August Southampton was incorporated Master of Arts at
Oxford, in time for the Queen's visit at the end of September.
She was accompanied by the French Ambassador, Burghley,
and a number of peers : the Earls of Worcester, Cumberland,
and Pembroke, the last with his son Lord Herbert, a boy of
twelve ; Lord Admiral Howard, Lord Buckhurst, and Ferdinando, Lord Strange ; together there also were Essex and
Southampton. In the Latin poem celebrating the visit and the
visitors Southampton is singled out for the characteristics by
which Shakespeare describes him : his physical beauty and
the cheeks hardly yet adorned with down :

> quo non formosior alter
> Affuit, aut docta juvenis praestantior arte ;
> Ora licet tenera vix dum lanugine vernent.[9]

Whether Shakespeare was present we do not know, but in *A
Midsummer Night's Dream*, written not long after, we have a
tell-tale description of just such an academic scene in the
Queen's presence :

> Where I have come, great clerks have purposèd
> To greet me with premeditated welcomes;

> Where I have seen them shiver and look pale,
> Make periods in the midst of sentences,
> Throttle their practised accent in their fears,
> And on conclusion dumbly have broke off.

While in *Love's Labour's Lost*, written about the same time and also closely associated with the Southampton circle, we have a term of art from the university :

> Proceeded well, to stop all good proceeding!

This is the term for proceeding to one's M.A., as Southampton had done at Oxford that summer.

In September we learn that Southampton, like others at Court, was investing in privateering, which came very much to the fore in these years between the great expedition to Lisbon in 1589 and that to Cadiz in 1596. Southampton had a share with Ralph Bowes, one of the Gentlemen Pensioners, the Queen's personal guard, in the *Galleon Dudley*. This privateer had captured a St. Malo ship laden with sugars from Brazil and brought her into Portsmouth. Southampton and Bowes claimed title to some part of the prize, as against the Crown. The matter came before the Privy Council, which evidently thought their claim excessive ; ultimately it went to the High Court of Admiralty for decision.[10]

Here we see something of the two sides noted at the time as characteristic of Southampton : the interest, and desire to take part, in martial enterprises ; the relish for literary celebration by the poets. Shakespeare, when he got to know him better, commented on his eagerness for praise :

> You to your beauteous blessings add a curse,
> Being fond on praise, which makes your praises worse.

But Shakespeare himself ministered to this desire in the golden youth, both in the rhetorical language proper to such a youthful deity (or old, or timeless, when it was a question, with the poets, of the Queen), and in the direct and personal language of his own feelings. Here is the one :

> What is your substance, whereof are you made,
> That millions of strange shadows on you tend ?
> Describe Adonis, and the counterfeit
> Is poorly imitated after you ;
> On Helen's cheek all art of beauty set,
> And you in Grecian tires are painted new.

Observe that Shakespeare is already thinking, in 1592, of Adonis and, moreover of Southampton as Adonis. Here is the more personal note, of what Shakespeare himself feels for the peer who has become his friend :

> Thou, best of dearest and mine only care . . .

> All days are nights till I see thee,
> And nights bright days when dreams do show thee me.

The relationship has already taken an acutely personal turn, so far as Shakespeare is concerned : it is clear that he has fallen for the young man, and his imagination become possessed by him. Poets also fall in love with the idea of being in love ; but we may be sure that nothing quite like this had happened to Shakespeare before, nor was to do so again. It was an unique experience, to be uniquely enshrined in the Sonnets ; for there is nothing else quite like them in our literature, and none that have made so ineffaceable an impression upon men's minds. This is why : they are not *literary* sonnets, in the way that so many sonnet sequences were — Daniel's and Drayton's and Constable's, even Spenser's — they were intensely autobiographical, speaking directly in every accent of feeling from the poet to his youthful patron. This is also why they were not published till long after : they were not written for publication.

The relationship has its ups and downs, as is the way with such, and soon there comes a cloud over it. This springs, in the nature of things, from the incursion of a woman into this paradise. We know Shakespeare's extreme, almost abnormal, susceptibility to women : he has a mistress, who is a lady of no very good character or repute, known in this circle. Shakespeare's own reputation is spotted, and he is afraid therefore to besmirch his patron with it (we must not forget the tutorial element in his attitude to the youth) :

> I may not evermore acknowledge thee,
> Lest my bewailèd guilt should do thee shame,
> Nor thou with public kindness honour me,
> Unless thou take that honour from thy name.

The poet had got his lord to write to the lady on his behalf, in the Elizabethan manner :

> He learned but surety-like to write for me,
> Under that bond that him as fast doth bind.

For, of course, such a woman would take the opportunity to get hold of the young peer, a much better catch than an indigent poet. Shakespeare is forced to accept the situation : beggars cannot be choosers :

> Take all my loves, my love, yea, take them all ;
> What hast thou then more than thou hadst before ?
> No love, my love, that thou mayst true love call ;
> All mine was thine before thou hadst this more.

In this unhappy imbroglio *à trois* Shakespeare suffers much anguish of spirit : not common, vulgar jealousy, be it noted, such as has led murder to be committed for less. The poet shows his quality of spirit in nothing so much as the way in which he reacts to this situation. He is chiefly grieved on the young man's account : Shakespeare feels his responsibility in the matter acutely ; but what adds to it is the uncertainty he is in with regard to the relations between his mistress and his friend. Has she got hold of him ? Has she seduced him ? — we get the impression that the Dark Lady is a woman of Shakespeare's age, much older than the youth :

> Two loves I have of comfort and despair,
> Which like two spirits do suggest me still :
> The better angel is a man right fair,
> The worser spirit a woman coloured ill.

What were they up to ? —

> And whether that my angel be turned fiend
> Suspect I may, yet not directly tell ;
> But being both from me, both to each friend,
> I guess one angel in another's hell.

Anyone who knows Elizabethan usage will know the bawdy implication of that, and the worse implication of venereal infection — all too frequent in Elizabethan society — that follows :

> Yet this shall I ne'er know, but live in doubt,
> Till my bad angel fire my good one out.

And what was the young man's attitude in all this ?

We have no evidence, but we may legitimately infer from what we know of his nature that the lady had no such hold on him as she had on the all too inflammable poet. It is not until several years later that his name is mentioned in connection with a woman at all, and then only with one, Elizabeth Vernon, by whom he was at last caught in the usual way and had to marry. But this was not until 1598, and no other woman comes into his life, excepting always his mother.

And what was his attitude towards Shakespeare ?

Here we have more evidence, if indirect, both internal and external. He must have had something in him, besides physical beauty, his wealth and position, to inspire the world's poet so strangely and so strongly. We know that he had charm, intelligence, generous impulses. Shakespeare tells us, in so many words, what it was : it was the open candour of his nature, something innocent and unspotted about it, without guile, above and beyond anything mean. That must have had an instinctive appeal for the poet, so much older and wiser in the ways of the world, who yet retained an open and free nature too. After an exceptionally prolonged adolescence, misled and spoiled by his adoration of Essex — though it was yet another sign of a generous nature that he was capable of adoration, unlike mean spirits — after the ordeal of his trial and imprisonment, Southampton emerged into the spotted atmosphere of James's reign singularly uncorrupt and incorruptible, much looked up to and respected in that venomous time. Though it is out of fashion in our own age to say such a thing, Southampton in the end was a good man. It is somehow consoling, and also right, that Shakespeare should always have seen this in him.

There was above all his youth : Renaissance sensibilities were so much more excited by the beauty of youth, when people visibly aged so much more rapidly, lost hair, complexion, teeth. Shakespeare is constantly conscious of the disparity of age between them —

> That time of year thou mayst in me behold
> When yellow leaves, or none, or few, do hang —

in addition to all the other disparities.

Nevertheless, on the other side, all too evident, are characteristics of youth familiar enough in such a relation, especially to anyone with the experience to understand it. The youth was, above all, wrapped up in himself (Proust, with his infallible intuition, perceived that well). We cannot think that the youth felt about the elder as the poet felt about him — such is the way of life. The surprising thing is that he responded as well as he did, and for that the poet was eternally grateful : it inspired his verse. On the other hand, the recognisable evidences are there : the familiar casualness of the young towards those older, of a so much superior socially towards an inferior, of a lord towards the poet who is his servant. As usual, so much is taken for granted. Here is Shakespeare dancing attendance upon the young man :

> Being your slave, what should I do but tend
> Upon the hours and times of your desire ?
> I have no precious time at all to spend,
> Nor services to do, till you require.

There is an element of sadness in that, a shade of irony, a sigh :

> Nor dare I chide the world-without-end hour
> Whilst I, my sovereign, watch the clock for you,
> Nor think the bitterness of absence sour,
> When you have bid your servant once adieu.

There is the situation, the dependant kept waiting by his lord, or dismissed perhaps casually enough. But Shakespeare's feeling was not a casual one, nor merely external : it was internal, and searched the crevices of the heart :

> Nor dare I question with my jealous thought
> Where you may be, or your affairs suppose,
> But, like a sad slave, stay and think of nought
> Save, where you are, how happy you make those.

It is a familiar enough reaction in such situations, but with a certain reproach under the beautifully turned compliment. This becomes explicit — and the dependent relationship to a patron — in the next sonnet :

> O, let me suffer, being at your beck,
> The imprisoned absence of your liberty ;
> And patience, tame to sufferance, bide each check,
> Without accusing you of injury . . .
> I am to wait, though waiting so be hell,
> Nor blame your pleasure, be it ill or well.

There is the relationship of aristocratic patron to the poet who is his servant, at his beck and call, perfectly clear.

We must not blame the young man too much — it is so like youth at all times ; this particular youth in the end proved constant, and proud of his poet, by a signal act of generosity which had the most fortunate consequences for Shakespeare and for our literature.

CHAPTER V

The Poet and the Patron

IT was only natural that such a youth should want change;
and in Sonnet 76 we find the poet asking,

> Why is my verse so barren of new pride ?
> So far from variation or quick change ? . . .
> Why write I still all one, ever the same . . .
> That every word doth almost tell my name ?

Shakespeare's answer is,

> O, know, sweet love, I always write of you.

He always insists on this :

> Since all alike my songs and praises be
> To one, of one, still such, and ever so.

That is to say, Shakespeare writes to and for his patron alone
— and no one else.

But there is the competition of other poets for his patronage
and support in this anxious worsening time. Before Southampton had taken Shakespeare into his service, already in 1591
John Clapham had dedicated his Latin poem 'Narcissus' to
Southampton — observe the Narcissus theme, it is glanced at
in *Venus and Adonis* and in an even more accomplished poem
written, as we shall see, in competition with it. Southampton
was a Narcissus, much in love with himself, and, as we know,
'fond on praise'.

There now appears on the scene a rival for his patronage,
whom Shakespeare, with his characteristic candour of spirit, at

once confesses to be his superior. He admits, with engaging modesty, that his lord

> Deserves the travail of a worthier pen ;

but he is discouraged when he reflects :

> O, how I faint when I of you do write,
> Knowing a better spirit doth use your name,
> And in the praise thereof spends all his might,
> To make me tongue-tied, speaking of your fame !

What is characteristic of the rival poet is his rhetoric — where Shakespeare pleads for himself only the simple sincerity of his devotion. The rival is a more powerful spirit, a grander figure with more prestige :

> But since your worth wide as the ocean is,
> The humble as the proudest sail doth bear,
> My saucy bark inferior far to his,
> On your broad main doth wilfully appear.

This proud spirit has evidently been received and welcomed : what would happen if he should oust Shakespeare and take his place in Southampton's favour ? The rival is already an established figure, Shakespeare not :

> Or, being wrecked, I am a worthless boat,
> He of tall building and of goodly pride.
> Then if he thrive and I be cast away,
> The worst was this : my love was my decay.

Shakespeare expresses himself as somewhat daunted by so formidable a competitor, whose

> comments of your praise, richly compiled,
> Reserve their character with golden quill,
> And precious phrase by all the Muses filed.

Courteous and polite as Shakespeare always is, he is acknowledging a real superiority : he can only say Amen

> To every hymn that able spirit affords,
> In polished form of well-refinèd pen.

All these sonnets describing the rivalry with the other poet have been in the present tense — it is the current, continuing situation. Suddenly, with Sonnet 86, standing out amid all those before and after, a sombre peak, we have a sonnet in the past tense : [1]

> Was it the proud full sail of his great verse,
> Bound for the prize of all-too-precious you,
> That did my ripe thoughts in my brain inhearse ?

Was it the proud pomp of his rival's great verse, this says, directed to capture Southampton, that had daunted Shakespeare and chilled his inspiration ? This can refer only to Marlowe, famous for his 'mighty line', his achievement of marrying splendid poetry to the drama, to which all that came after him, but Shakespeare in particular, owed so much. Only a few sonnets before, Sonnet 66, we find Shakespeare echoing a line from *Tamburlaine*,

> And captive good attending captain ill :

it is the phrase, the words, that catch Shakespeare's ear (as Valéry told Dégas, it is with words that one makes poetry, rather than ideas). In this case the actor's memory had caught the clang of 'captain . . . captive' from Marlowe's,

> And all his captains bound in captive chains.

From first to last Shakespeare's mind was influenced more by Marlowe than by any other of his contemporaries, all the more remarkably considering the sharp contrast between their nature and temperament. But there was every reason why Marlowe should have been unforgettable for Shakespeare. Now, in this Sonnet 86, when something decisive has happened to put the rivalry in the past — it ends with this sonnet :

> Was it his spirit, by spirits taught to write
> Above a mortal pitch, that struck me dead ?
> No, neither he, nor his compeers by night
> Giving him aid, my verse astonishèd.

The suggestion is that the rival poet trafficked with spirits, and, if so, there is nothing to surprise us in that. *Dr. Faustus* itself shows Marlowe's familiarity with the formulae for conjuring up spirits ; while his verse reveals a leaning to night-imagery, of the stars and planets, as against the flowers and pastures, the country sports, of the poet who was a countryman all through. There follows a sentence in the present tense, perfectly in place since the rivalry is over :

> He nor that affable familiar ghost
> Which nightly gulls him with intelligence,
> As victors, of my silence cannot boast.

Might not the 'affable familiar' be Mephistophilis, who certainly gulls Faustus nightly with intelligence ? — in the night-scenes of the play being currently performed that year, in an interval when plays could be performed. Then, back to the past tense, with

> I was not sick of any fear from thence.
> But when your countenance filled up his line,
> Then lacked I matter ; that enfeebled mine.

This means that Southampton had given countenance to the rival and that Shakespeare had felt discouraged by that fact.

Now Marlowe had been killed on 30 May 1593. We do not need to go in detail into his personality here. It was a sufficiently striking one — far more so than the easy, gentle, courteous Shakespeare. We know from the tone of Edward Blount's references to him that Marlowe was much loved by his friends ; we also know that he was hated by his enemies and a good many people who did not know him. His was a divided, perhaps a schizophrenic, nature : he must have had the fascination, the originality, of genius ; his conversation was audacious, not to say shocking ; on the other hand, he was impetuous and passionate, given to 'rashness in attempting sudden privy injuries to men'.[2] As against Shakespeare, for Southampton's favour, he had the advantages we have seen : far greater fame and prestige in the world of the theatre, more brilliance as a poet as yet, if — as Shakespeare implies — more rhetorical than sincere. For the ambivalent young peer, with his prolonged adolescence, Marlowe had had another re-commendation : his inclination to homosexuality.

Now he was gone ; the rivalry was over — there is nothing more about it in the Sonnets. But Marlowe left behind him an unfinished poem, *Hero and Leander*, of an accomplished rhetorical kind, superior to anything of Shakespeare's up to this date, a masterpiece. With any sense, we have no difficulty in perceiving who sat for the portrait of Leander. There is the ambivalent youth, who is at first reluctant as to the love of women :

> Some swore he was a maid in man's attire,
> For in his looks were all that men desire . . .
> And such as knew he was a man would say,
> Leander, thou art made for amorous play :
> Why art thou not in love — and loved of all ?
> Though thou be fair, yet be not thine own thrall.

Here is, from Marlowe, the young man of Shakespeare's Sonnets and the argument of their first section. Where Shakespeare was more general in his appreciation of the youth's beauty, Marlowe was quite specific :

> His dangling tresses that were never shorn,
> Had they been cut, and unto Colchos borne,
> Would have allured the venturous youth of Greece
> To hazard more than for the Golden Fleece. . .

with a graceful compliment to the young peer, whose long tresses had indeed been never shorn, and were to remain a distinguishing characteristic of all his portraits for some years beyond his (belated) marriage and into his imprisonment in the Tower. Nor is the remainder of the description any less recognisable — no dark Greek youth, but the fair, white-skinned Englishman :

> His body was as straight as Circe's wand ;
> Jove might have sipped out nectar from his hand.

78

Even as delicious meat is to the taste,
So was his neck in touching, and surpassed
The white of Pelops' shoulder : I could tell ye,
How smooth his breast was, and how white his belly,
And whose immortal fingers did imprint
That heavenly path with many a curious dint
That runs along his back . . .

When Leander at last confronts love — the love of women in the person of Hero, he uses the same arguments, and much the same language, to persuade her to yield up her virginity as Shakespeare's Venus uses with the reluctant Adonis :

The richest corn dies, if it be not reaped ;
Beauty alone is lost, too warily kept.

This line is very close to Shakespeare's in his poem :

Beauty within itself should not be wasted.

Indeed, the two poems, *Hero and Leander* and *Venus and Adonis*, are full of echoes of each other, theme, arguments, turns of thought and phrase : one has the impression that the poems were read aloud in Southampton's circle, or that each poet at least knew what the other was writing. Not only that, but there are echoes that reverberate between Shakespeare's Sonnets and Marlowe's poem. Where Shakespeare had written in an early sonnet :

Seeking that beauteous roof to ruinate
Which to repair should be thy chief desire ;

Marlowe writes,

Who builds a palace and rams up the gate
Shall see it ruinous and desolate . . .

One is no number : maids are nothing then,
Without the sweet society of men.

The phrase, 'one is no number', is also echoed by Shakespeare in a sonnet :

Among a number one is reckoned none.

There are other similarities and comparabilities — the well-known passages in both poems describing the horse on fire with desire snapping his bridle to go to the mare. Altogether, there can be no reasonable doubt that both these poems belong with the Sonnets, and that they all relate to Southampton whose situation, personality, and temperament at this very time are clearly reflected in them.

Marlowe was now dead, his splendid poem only half done. Shakespeare was beforehand with his *Venus and Adonis*, for in April 1593 it was registered for publication. He may have had some sense that it was inferior, as a work of art, to Marlowe's, for in his dedication of it to his patron he speaks of it in terms of modest self-deprecation. But there is also an underlying confidence in his promise of 'some graver labour', and in fulfilment, by the way, of the promise he had made in the *envoi* to the first section of the Sonnets, Sonnet 26. Here is the dedication: from its courteous, gentlemanly, rather grand language our impression of the poet is corroborated, as also is his countryman's background.

> To the Right Honourable Henry Wriothesley, Earl of Southampton, and Baron of Titchfield.
>
> Right Honourable, I know not how I shall offend in dedicating my unpolished lines to your lordship, nor how the world will censure me for choosing so strong a prop to support so weak a burden; only if your honour seem but pleased, I account myself highly praised, and vow to take advantage of all idle hours, till I have honoured you with some graver labour. But if the first heir of my invention prove deformed, I shall be sorry it had so noble a godfather, and never after ear so barren a land, for fear it yield me still so bad a harvest. I leave it to your honourable survey and your honour to your heart's content, which I wish may always answer your own wish and the world's hopeful expectation. Your honour's in all duty, William Shakespeare.

We recall that the first Sonnet had addressed him as,

> Thou that art now the world's fresh ornament:

Shakespeare, in his rather tutorial frame of mind, had hopeful expectations of his young peer. We shall see how they were

fulfilled. As for the poet's style in prose, we may observe
how it fits the old tradition that as an actor he played 'kingly
parts'. For all the poet's expressed modesty he gave his work
a challenging motto from Ovid : *Vilia miretur vulgus* — let
the mob admire what is base, but for him let Apollo minister
water from the purest springs. It was a challenge from the
actor-dramatist to graduate into the ranks of the poets and to
be taken seriously as such. The poem had a pronounced and
lasting success, and in time the poet received due recognition.

Venus and Adonis bubbles over with vivacity and comic
spirit, even high spirits — too much so, perhaps, for a perfect work of art. Like *Hero and Leander* it is written, as it
were, in inverted commas ; but with Shakespeare the natural
spirits rather break the bounds, where with Marlowe the
more mature aesthetic control keeps perfect decorum. (How
curious, and significant, that in the conduct of their lives it was
precisely the converse.) We recognise their common point of
departure, the suggestion for both Adonis and Leander that
derives from Southampton :

> Stain to all nymphs, more lovely than a man,
> More white and red than doves or roses are ;
> Nature that made thee, with herself at strife . . .

Once more we have :

> The tender spring upon thy tempting lip
> Shows thee unripe ; yet mayst thou well be tasted ;
> Make use of time, let not advantage slip ;
> Beauty within itself should not be wasted.

This is followed by a glance at the Narcissus theme, as it is
glanced at in *Hero and Leander* :

> Is thine own heart to thine own face affected ? . . .
> Then woo thyself, be of thyself rejected . . .
> Narcissus so himself himself forsook,
> And died to kiss his shadow in the brook.

We need say no more about the poem, except that it was
licensed for publication by Archbishop Whitgift with his own

hand — perhaps the name of the patron was sufficient, or the patron gave it his personal guarantee. It was printed by Shakespeare's fellow-townsman and contemporary, Richard Field, now a successful printer in London. In Shakespeare's lifetime it went into ten or eleven editions, twenty before the deplorable Civil War — surely success commensurate with the poet's tenacious literary ambition, long thwarted by un-propitious circumstances ?

Nevertheless, the relation between poet and patron had undergone a double strain. There was that involved in the imbroglio with Shakespeare's mistress :

> Beshrew that heart that makes my heart to groan
> For that deep wound it gives my friend and me!
> Is't not enough to torture me alone,
> But slave to slavery my sweet'st friend must be ?

It seems, however — and it would be in the nature of things — that this young man was much less 'slave to slavery' of the other sex than Shakespeare himself was, and that he had been able to extricate himself : it is probable that he was much less at the mercy of the dark lady's charms than the poet feared. The strain left by the episode of the rival poet appears to have been more severe : Shakespeare expresses himself ready to give up his claim to his young lord's affection, if that is his wish, and that gives one to suppose that the youth may have been moving over to Marlowe when he died.

The very next sonnet, Sonnet 87, after the sudden end to the rivalry is a valediction, with a return to the present :

> Farewell! thou art too dear for my possessing . . .
> Thyself thou gav'st, thy own worth then not knowing,
> Or me, to whom thou gav'st it, else mistaking ;
> So thy great gift, upon misprision growing,
> Comes home again, on better judgment making.

This says, with an accent of sadness, that when the youth accepted the poet as his friend, he may have been too young to know his own value, or he may have mistaken his man in Shakespeare. Likely enough — complete understanding is difficult between human beings, and these, for all their improbable sympathy, were very disparate persons. The coldness between them came at a bad time for the poet — 1593, the second year of plague and closing of the theatres :

> Then hate me when thou wilt ; if ever, now ;
> Now while the world is bent my deeds to cross,
> Join with the spite of fortune, make me bow,
> And do not drop in for an after-loss . . .
> If thou wilt leave me, do not leave me last,
> When other petty griefs have done their spite,
> But in the onset come : so shall I taste
> At first the very worst of fortune's might.

This shows clearly Shakespeare's fear that his patron might desert him ; he goes on to contemplate what would happen to him if Southampton should :

> But do thy worst to steal thyself away,
> For term of life thou art assurèd mine ;
> And life no longer than thy love will stay,
> For it depends upon that love of thine.

Such is the seriousness of the situation for the poet, should he be deprived of support at this juncture, nakedly revealed :

> Then need I not to fear the worst of wrongs,
> When in the least of them my life hath end.
> I see a better state to me belongs
> Than that which on thy humour doth depend.

There is plain speaking from a dependant, the reproach is not concealed. His fate is, however, accepted with resignation, and, all characteristically, given a charming turn of expression :

> Thou canst not vex me with inconstant mind,
> Since that my life on thy revolt doth lie.
> O, what a happy title do I find,
> Happy to have thy love, happy to die !

We must attend to the literal sense of what Shakespeare is saying here : his life depends on a 'revolt' or change of mind on Southampton's part. We have already seen what a clearance of the poets and dramatists these ill years, covered by the Sonnets, were to accomplish : Greene, Watson, and Marlowe had already gone, Kyd and Peele were to go. It is a sombre thought that Shakespeare might easily have been one of them.

The relation between the patron and his poet survived the strain, though — as is the way with such things — it had lost its pristine innocence : the illusion of paradise was over :

> So shall I live, supposing thou art true,
> Like a deceivèd husband ; so love's face
> May still seem love to me, though altered new :
> Thy looks with me, thy heart in other place.

And now, too, rumours are beginning to circulate about the young man :

> How sweet and lovely dost thou make the shame
> Which, like a canker in the fragrant rose,
> Doth spot the beauty of thy budding name ! . . .
> Some say thy fault is youth, some wantonness . . .

Shakespeare's tutorial attitude towards the youth asserts itself;

> I love thee in such sort,
> As thou being mine, mine is thy good report.

So the relationship jogs on, with periodic absences — indeed absence may have been its normal condition, and much more stimulating to the imagination anyway — to the end of the year 1593 :

> How like a winter hath my absence been
> From thee, the pleasure of the fleeting year !
> What freezings have I felt, what dark days seen,
> What old December's bareness everywhere !

With the spring of 1594 we come to Sonnet 107, the notorious topical references of which give us a firm dating ; for there are two, and the two converge upon one point :

> The mortal moon hath her eclipse endured,
> And the sad augurs mock their own presage ;
> Incertainties now crown themselves assured,
> And peace proclaims olives of endless age.

The capitulation of Paris to Henri IV in March 1594 brought an end to the religious wars that had been going on all through Shakespeare's life hitherto, and the hope of permanent peace. At the same time the 'mortal moon' — who is always the Queen in Elizabethan parlance—had come through the threat to her life of the Lopez conspiracy : her personal physician, Dr. Lopez, was condemned to death on February 28 for being in correspondence with Spain with the idea of poisoning her. Whether he was guilty or no, he was an intelligence-man used by both sides, and could not clear himself : it was Southampton's admired leader, Essex, who pursued Lopez to his death — against the will and conviction of the Queen.

Thus we have arrived at 'this most balmy time' — the spring of 1594, the two years of plague over, a time of release for the spirit, of hope and, as we shall see, of crowded creative accomplishment for the inspired poet. At some time in this year the Lord Chamberlain's company was formed, and Shakespeare was enabled to purchase a share in it. That gave him economic security at last : henceforward he never looked back. But who enabled him to make the purchase ? An authentic tradition coming down from Sir William Davenant, who had known Shakespeare and was in a position to learn, tells us that Southampton gave his poet at one time a large sum to go through with a purchase he had a mind to. It is generally thought that it was this that gave Shakespeare his share in the company which was to become so famous, with him as its dramatist, and the dramatist along with it. The clearance from the ground of his rivals and competitors gave him a tremendous advantage ; for the next four years, until the appearance of Ben Jonson in 1598, there was no one to compare with him. And with what creative energy he leaped forward to make the most of the ascendancy he took over from Marlowe, pouring out play after play, giving himself wholly to the theatre!

In the Sonnets of this time a conjunction of references points to his having *A Midsummer Night's Dream* in mind. Sonnet 98 says,

> Yet nor the lays of birds, nor the sweet smell
> Of different flowers in odour and in hue,
> Could make me any summer's story tell;

while Sonnet 106 suggests that he was reading Chaucer:

> When in the chronicle of wasted time
> I see descriptions of the fairest wights,
> And beauty making beautiful old rhyme
> In praise of ladies dead and lovely knights.

We recall that Chaucer's *Knight's Tale* is one of the sources of the play. It is clear from its nature that it was performed to grace some wedding ceremony; that it would not have been any wedding at which the Queen was present is obvious from these lines in deprecation of the unmarried state in the very first scene:

> To live a barren sister all your life,
> Chanting faint hymns to the cold fruitless moon . . .
> But earthlier happy is the rose distilled
> Than that which, withering on the virgin thorn,
> Grows, lives and dies in single blessedness.

We recognise this for what it is — a reference to the young Earl's refusal to enter on the married state, with its duties and responsibilities.

Since he would not, his mother the Countess made up her mind to do what she could to repair the damage, and protect the family's interests in the highest quarters. The Southamptons, as Catholics, could do with some reinforcement, especially since the Earl had alienated his guardian and protector, the Lord Treasurer. So the Countess, having kept her word not to marry again now for over twelve years, decided to marry the elderly and rich Sir Thomas Heneage, an influential Privy Councillor, Vice-Chamberlain of the Household, a reliable Protestant and close confidential servant of the Queen. It seems, however, that in the early months of this year Heneage was temporarily out of favour with the Queen [3] — a reason for her not gracing his marriage with her presence. We do not know whether the marriage was the reason for her disapprobation.

In *A Midsummer Night's Dream* the Duke, Theseus, is a grave and reverend personage, a governmental figure, who conducts his Hippolyta in dignified fashion, through the fooling of the youthful couples, to their bridal ceremony. Towards the end of the play we learn that the wandering lovers, lost amid the fairies in the wood, have been out observing May Day. The Countess's marriage to Sir Thomas Heneage took place on 2 May 1594. It is fairly clear that the play was produced to grace that occasion.

At the end the fairies wend their way through the chambers of a great house at night — 'the iron tongue of midnight hath told twelve' — to bless the bride-bed and the rooms of the house. We do not know where the wedding ceremony took place, but most likely at Southampton House, where the Countess lived. The house stood on the site of the present Southampton Buildings at the angle of Chancery Lane with Holborn — one can still observe the irregular rectangle formed by the property, with the garden skirting the Lane occupied by the large new Chancery House. In Shakespeare's time the house with which he was familiar was a typical late medieval house, a series of chambers and galleries around an open court. As late as the Victorian age there were still remains of the chapel amid the congeries of buildings. Next door is the still-existing Staple Inn ; across Chancery Lane from it is Lincoln's Inn ; indeed it is in the midst of the Inns of Court, whence came so many of the young 'termers' who were addicts of the theatres, and where so many plays were performed to grace the festivities in their halls.

Other, more suspect, persons too haunted the great house at

the top of Chancery Lane, and indeed the whole vicinity, at just this time. We learn that Robert Gray, a Catholic priest, with his questionable books and tracts, frequented Southampton House, and was kept in touch by letters from Jane Goodman, in the Countess's service.[4] The Catholic informer, Benjamin Beard alias Tichborne, reported that a couple of priests lived for eight years in the house, in the chamber next to Robert Gage — one of the Countess's cousins — who had been executed for his part in the Babington conspiracy. Beard also reported that Philip Roper, of that sainted, if not wholly saintly, family had lodged a couple of priests with him in his lodging near Southampton House, where they frequently consorted with other priests.

That spring also the poet fulfilled his promise to his patron to honour him with 'some graver labour' than *Venus and Adonis*. On 9 May *The Rape of Lucrece* was entered for publication, printed by Richard Field though published by John Harrison, 'to be sold at the sign of the White Greyhound in Paul's Churchyard'. Once more the dedication stands :

> To the right honourable Henry Wriothesley, Earl of Southampton and Baron of Titchfield. The love I dedicate your lordship is without end, whereof this pamphlet without beginning is but a superfluous moiety. The warrant I have of your honourable disposition, not the worth of my untutored lines, makes it assured of acceptance. What I have done is yours, what I have to do is yours, being part in all I have, devoted yours. Were my worth greater, my duty would show greater ; meantime, as it is, it is bound to your lordship : to whom I wish long life still lengthened with all happiness. Your lordship's in all duty, William Shakespeare.

Once more, as in the Sonnets, we have Shakespeare's re-iterated 'duty', expressed in courteous, stately language — indeed, there is a certain lordliness of language. Everyone has noticed the warmth — and we may add, the confidence — with which Shakespeare expresses his devotion. I know of no Elizabethan dedication that gives one more the sense of intimacy. But more important are the words, 'what I have done is yours, what I have to do is yours, being part in all I have, devoted yours'. This corroborates what Shakespeare says in the Sonnets,

> Since all alike my songs and praises be
> To one, of one, still such, and ever so.

It is beyond dispute that the work of this period, the narrative poems, the Sonnets, and, as we shall see, three plays, are all associated with Southampton. It is merely obvious that the Sonnets were written to and for the patron, and for no one else.

The Rape of Lucrece offered a marked contrast to *Venus and Adonis*, was in fact its perfect foil — one more evidence of the immense literary ambition released, perhaps even only made possible, by Southampton's patronage and support. Think what we owe to this golden youth's intelligence and discernment, no less than his generosity! Where the earlier poem had been skittish and amusing, full of naughty high spirits, the country in brilliant sunlight, the later is a night-poem, the action takes place in a darkened chamber, the atmosphere heavy-laden with guilt, moral torment, reproaches, and foreboding. It is the climate, sometimes the turns of thought and phrase, of the sonnets about Shakespeare's mistress : *The Rape of Lucrece* is allied to those as *Venus and Adonis* is to the early sonnets to Southampton. Perhaps we may observe, too, that the stanza about the legend of Philomel and Tereus, indeed the whole theme, allies the poem with *Titus Andronicus*, which must belong to these years of intermission from acting, which gave such a chance for writing.

Shortly, along with *A Midsummer Night's Dream*, and so in 1594, there came another play for Southampton and his friends, *Love's Labour's Lost*. Not only does its theme relate it to the period of the Sonnets, but also its form, for it incorporates a number of sonnets in the play. It is a skit on the circle by its poet and intimate : hence the private jokes and references not all of which are decipherable, and the characters to not all of whom have we a complete key. But the theme is recognisable as a variation on the Southampton theme : the young men at the Court of Navarre who, under the inspiration of their leader, the King, are going to abjure the society of women for three years and give themselves up to their books and studies. Very recognisable is Berowne, who thinks all this to be nonsense and speaks up for the natural life of the senses and the love of women : he speaks for Shakespeare. No less recognisable is his opposite number, Rosaline, with whom he ultimately pairs off, for she is described in the closest possible language to that which describes Shakespeare's mistress in the Sonnets, the same turns of phrase, whole lines almost interchangeable. We are at liberty to conclude, indeed we must conclude, that the Dark Lady, whose name we are never likely to know, was a lady well known in that circle.

Moreover, since John Florio was Italian tutor to the Earl, it is probable that the fantastic Don Armado in the play owes some strokes to him — it is all fantasy, high spirits and good-humoured fooling. At any rate, we do not have far to look for the Italian background and colouring, the Italian phrases, of these plays : Shakespeare would have known Florio in the Southampton entourage. We find John Florio appearing at a rather sinister conjuncture in October this year, when Southampton was giving all the aid he could to his friends, Sir Henry and Sir Charles Danvers, after their murder of Henry Long — the culmination of the feud between the Danverses and the Longs. This touched off the inspiration, in the suggestible mind of the poet, for his next play : he found a subject in Arthur Brooke's *Romeus and Juliet* that placed the familiar themes of love and friendship, dominant in these years, in the environment of family feud, duelling, and death. Out of this came *Romeo and Juliet*.

With the formation of the Lord Chamberlain's company and the actor-dramatist's leading part in it, with all this dramatic activity after the intermission of 1592–3, Shakespeare must have been — for all the speed and facility with which he worked — extremely busy. And, sure enough, in the last section of the Sonnets we find him having to apologise to his patron for neglecting him : the closeness of the relationship perhaps was coming to an end with the dependence. Sonnet 109 says,

> O, never say that I was false of heart,
> Though absence seemed my flame to qualify . . .
> If I have ranged,
> Like him that travels, I return again,
> Just to the time, not with the time exchanged.

The next sonnets continue the theme of the actor's absence, on tour in the country, and give us a precious insight into his feelings about his profession, his resentment at the necessity he was under to earn his living in this manner.

> Alas, 'tis true I have gone here and there
> And made myself a motley to the view,
> Gored mine own thoughts, sold cheap what is most dear,
> Made old offences of affections new.

There follows a bitter outburst at his lack of luck in life that has put him under the necessity of earning his living thus :

> O, for my sake do you with Fortune chide,
> The guilty goddess of my harmful deeds,
> That did not better for my life provide
> Than public means which public manners breeds.

From Sonnet 117 it seems that he felt that his patron had reason to reproach him :

> Accuse me thus : that I have scanted all
> Wherein I should your great deserts repay ;
> Forgot upon your dearest love to call,
> Whereto all bonds do tie me day by day ;
> That I have frequent been with unknown minds,
> And given to time your own dear-purchased right . . .

All this is a clear and generous recognition of the obligation he was under to the young patron — the bonds that tie him day by day, the 'dear-purchased right', which seems an obvious reference to what he owed to Southampton's handsome generosity.

From this Shakespeare moves to the trouble of mind he was in over his infatuation with his mistress —

> What potions have I drunk of siren tears,
> Distilled from limbecks foul as hell within —

and the rumours and scandal it gave rise to. No less revealing is to learn how he thinks of himself — no moral cant, the recognition of himself for what he is, with the frailties natural to one of his susceptible temperament.

> 'Tis better to be vile than vile esteemed,
> When not to be receives reproach of being . . .
> For why should others' false adulterate eyes
> Give salutation to my sportive blood ?
> Or on my frailties why are frailer spies,
> Which in their wills count bad what I think good ?

And so we come to the last sonnets in the Southampton sequence, the latest in time, which have a valedictory note, looking back over the relationship.

> Thy gift, thy tables, are within my brain
> Full charactered with lasting memory
> Which shall above that idle rank remain
> Beyond all date, even to eternity . . .
> Till each to razed oblivion yield his part
> Of thee, thy record never can be missed.

Shakespeare ends by affirming that his affection — as, we may be sure, his gratitude — will not change :

> No, Time, thou shalt not boast that I do change . . .

There follows Sonnet 124, which, with its topical references gives us a firm terminal date for the end of the special relationship, of which we have the record in the Sonnets. Shakespeare

affirms that his devotion was not a matter of policy, or changing
with the chances :

> No, it was builded far from accident ;
> It suffers not in smiling pomp, nor falls
> Under the blow of thrallèd discontent,
> Whereto the inviting time our fashion calls.
> It fears not Policy, that heretic,
> Which works on leases of short-numbered hours,
> But all alone stands hugely politic . . .
> To this I witness call the fools of time,
> Which die for goodness, who have lived for crime.

This is a plain reference to the government's severe campaign
of 1594-5 against the Jesuits and seminary priests, the severest
between the Armada period and the end of the reign. Their
position was that they were martyrs for their religion ; the
government's that they were traitors, operating against the
laws of the state in time of war. As usual we find Shakespeare in conformity with government and country at large on
the matter. It should be added that Southampton and his
mother, though Catholics, were not political Catholics involved
in any treasonable activities — unlike the father during 1569-
1572. And this gives us a definite date for the Sonnets : as
they had begun in 1592, so they came to an end in 1595.
Everything is in conformity with, everything supports, that
dating; it is impossible to impugn either the internal coherence
of the story or its consistency with the known and public
facts of Shakespeare's dedications of his poems to his patron
and all the other associations and evidences.

Sonnet 125 begins,

> Were't aught to me I bore the canopy,
> With my extern the outward honouring . . .

The image is that of holding the canopy over a person of
state — in case anyone supposes that the Sonnets were not
written for a patron who was a peer. The poet goes on to say,
looking back over the relationship, now with confidence and

achieved security, that his attitude had not been one of rendering merely outward honour. He concludes :

> No, let me be obsequious in thy heart,
> And take thou my oblation, poor but free,
> Which is not mixed with seconds, knows no art
> But mutual render, only me for thee.

It is appropriate that at this moment of leave-taking the poet
should go back in mind to his country origins — 'simple
savour', and an offering which is not mixed with 'seconds',
what is left over when the best flour has been taken. And after
all the deference and courtesy, the dependence and obligation,
how right that in the end he should stand on their equality
together, 'only me for thee' !

It was likely enough during this period, with Shakespeare as
Southampton's recognised poet and with another for a brief
spell a great rival, that the patron should have plenty of
flatterers, 'pitiful thrivers'. We have evidence of the way the
poets pursued his patronage. In May 1593 Barnabe Barnes
inscribes a dedicatory sonnet of his *Parthenophil and Parthenope*
to him :

> Vouchsafe, right virtuous lord, with gracious eyes,
> Those heavenly lamps which give the Muses light,
> Which give and take in course that fire
> To view my muse with your judicial sight.

What a difference from the Sonnets of Shakespeare, with their
convincing poetic reality ! — but this verse at least gives
evidence of Southampton's patronage of the Muses.

Next year appeared Thomas Nashe's novel, *The Unfortunate
Traveller*, with its long prose dedication to the Earl. The tone
is somewhat jaunty : 'Prize them as high or as low as you list,
if you set any price on them, I hold my labour well satisfied'.
For all its echo of Shakespeare's dedication of *Venus and
Adonis*, 'only if your honour seem but pleased, I account myself

highly praised', how different a tone! Nashe goes on, 'long
have I desired to approve my wit unto you . . . Incompre-
hensible is the height of your spirit both in heroical resolution
and matters of conceit. Unreprievably perisheth that book
whatsoever to waste paper which on the diamond rock of your
judgment disasterly chanceth to be shipwrecked. A dear lover
and cherisher you are, as well of the lovers of poets, as of poets
themselves . . .' And so on. What a contrast with the dignity
and control of Shakespeare's dedications!

Nashe does not seem to have been received, or at least
retained, for the dedication was subsequently dropped. Meanwhile he made an attempt in verse, inscribing a bunch of
lascivious valentines to the young man :

> Ne blame my verse of loose unchastity
> For painting forth the things that hidden are,
> Since all men act what I in speech declare.

He ends with an allusion to Shakespeare's Ovidian poem :

> Thus hath my pen presumed to please my friend :
> O, mightst thou likewise please Apollo's eye!
> No, Honour brooks no such impiety,
> Yet Ovid's wanton muse did not offend.

This seems to be suggesting — Shakespeare's poem had been
received, why not his, Nashe's ?

And this was but a beginning. As the years went on more
and more writers, poets, prose-writers, dramatists, divines,
voyagers, what not, poured out their offerings to this most
generous of men, ardent in the twin pursuits, martial glory and
the arts. He proved much more successful in the one than in the
other, with such a poet as Shakespeare to provide him the
monument in literature he promised :

> Your monument shall be my gentle verse,
> Which eyes not yet created shall o'er-read,
> And tongues to be your being shall rehearse,
> When all the breathers of the world are dead.

You still shall live — such virtue hath my pen —
Where breath most breathes, even in the mouths of men.

And what did Shakespeare owe to Southampton ?

It was a world of refinement and sophistication, of culture and aesthetic sensibility that was opened to the country-bred actor by his entrance into the Southampton circle. One scholar has preceptively noticed one simple change in his tastes, from a study of his imagery : 'Shakespeare's extreme sensitiveness about the quality, freshness, and cleanliness of food developed rather late — possibly after experience of more delicate fare than at Stratford, at the tables of his London friends. Up to about the age of 30, we get little sign of it, and his references to hunger, appetite and surfeit are such as might be made by any healthy youth. From 30 onwards there is increasing evidence of fastidiousness.' This may be paralleled by his growing awareness of the art of painting, or of the greater social assurance and ease in moving from *A Comedy of Errors* and *Two Gentlemen of Verona* to the world of *Romeo and Juliet* and *A Merchant of Venice*.

Even more significant is the breath of inspiration that blows in these latter plays, and immediately in *A Midsummer Night's Dream* and *Love's Labour's Lost*, compared with those earliest comedies. It was the experience of friendship and love — which are indeed their themes — recorded in the Sonnets that made the difference. Then, too, in the ill years 1592 and 1593, there is the opportunity, the challenge, that the young peer's patronage provided to write for him the two splendid poems, *Venus and Adonis* and *The Rape of Lucrece*. There are, altogether less 'literary' in their nature, the Sonnets themselves : too intimate, too autobiographical for publication, they have lasted much longer than the contemporary sonnet-sequences, for they speak, in their own phrase, to 'the hearts of men'. We are at liberty to accept the authentic tradition going back to Davenant and conclude that it was Southampton's bounty that enabled his poet to purchase his share in the Lord Chamberlain's company, which rescued him from the insecurity of a mere actor and made him part of the famous partnership that came to dominate the stage for the rest of his life. Nor was this the end of the relationship, though the period of dependence was over.

Altogether, we may say that Southampton well deserves his monument in our literature.

CHAPTER VI

The Follower of Essex

IN his Diary for 1594 Lord Burghley entered under the date 6 October, somewhat ominously, 'the Earl of Southampton at full age'.[1] Now the young man would be called to account, made to pay for going back on his word to marry the great man's granddaughter. Instead, the Earl's name was being bandied about as one of the most eligible young peers at Court. There was the Countess of Rutland's daughter, Lady Bridget Manners, to marry. Her waiting woman reported to the Countess, 'if your ladyship ask Mr. Manners's advice, he will speak straight of my lord of Bedford, or my lord of Southampton, which is exceeding unlikely. If they were in her choice [Lady Bridget's], she saith she would choose my lord Wharton [a widower with all his children] before them, for they be so young and fantastical and would be so carried away that . . . she doubteth their carriage of themselves.'[2]

Sage young lady! They were, indeed, both carried away into the folly of the Essex conspiracy, one of them nearly losing his head, the other a fortune. But this was some years ahead yet.

Meanwhile, Southampton was involved in a sorry affair, which can have done him no good with the Queen and her Lord Treasurer and aligned him more closely with Essex's followers.

In the neighbouring county of Wiltshire a feud was raging between two of the leading families, the Danverses and the Longs. Sir John Danvers, head of the family at Dauntsey with

large estates, was 'of a mild and peaceable nature', according
to John Aubrey, who was a kinsman.³ His wife was of
'prodigious parts for a woman. I have heard my father's
mother say that she had Chaucer at her fingers' ends. Knew
how to manage her estate as well as any man ; understood
jewels as well as any jeweller. A great politician ; great wit
and spirit, but revengeful.' Of her sons Sir Charles, now about
25, had fought in the Netherlands, where he had been knighted.
Sir Henry, Southampton's exact contemporary and especial
friend, had been page to Sir Philip Sidney and went on to fight
under Count Maurice of Nassau. In 1591 he fought in the
Normandy campaign under Essex, to whom he owed his
knighthood.

It is difficult to say how the feud began, but the Longs were
at fault for the killing of a Danvers man, and, according to
Lady Danvers, 'the cunning contriving of the saving of his
life that did it'.⁴ There were mutual charges : Sir Walter
Long with his faction indicting Sir John Danvers at assizes ;
Sir John indicting a Long retainer for robbing a church. From
this flowed 'derisions and foul abuses offered to my husband's
chief officer, and open scorns of him and his in saying they had
knighted him with a glass of beer ; last of all, letters addressed
to my son Charles, of such form as the heart of a man indeed
had rather die than endure'. The Danvers brothers decided
to bring the Longs to signal account ; Aubrey, always attentive to omens and coincidences, tells us of Somerford Magna
that the 'assassination of Harry Long was contrived in the
parlour of the parsonage here. Mr. Atwood was then parson ;
he was drowned coming home. . . . My great-grandfather, R.
Danvers, was in some trouble about it, his horses and men being
in that action. His servants were hanged . . .'

Southampton was at Titchfield, with his sister and her
husband, for his birthday. Some days before the younger
Danvers visited him there, so that he would be apprised of the
situation. On Friday 4 October the Danverses gathered their
party together and made for Corsham, where it may have been

Justices' day; for there were gathered for dinner at Mr. Chamberlain's house Sir Walter Long and Henry Long, Anthony Mildmay and divers other J.P.s and gentlemen. The Danvers party pressed into the house; there was a violent altercation between Sir Charles and Henry Long, swords were drawn and Henry Long was killed, apparently by Henry Danvers's dagger. Aubrey tells us that 'R. Wisdom was then lecturer and preached that day, and Henry Long expired in his arms'.

The hue and cry up, the Danvers party made off across country to Titchfield for aid from the Earl in making their escape. Here Thomas Dymoke makes his reappearance upon our scene as the Earl's chief agent in aiding his friends. The fugitives were secreted from Saturday to Tuesday under Dymoke's roof at Whitley Lodge; the Earl took their horses into his park to rest and graze — a stableman remembered Sir Henry's 'maidenhair-coloured velvet saddle' all bloody. (The fine saddle was afterwards disputed between Dymoke and Robinson, gentleman of the Earl's stables.) Victuals were sent over from the great house, and John the cook to dress their meat for them. A Danvers retainer came over to Titchfield to arrange a passage across Channel. Dymoke's servant girl washed the brothers' shirts for them, one of them covered with blood. Southampton spent his birthday at home, but on Monday rode over to Whitley with seven or eight of his followers, supped there and stayed all night with the brothers. Next day he conducted them to Burseldon ferry to make for Calshot Castle, commanded by a friend.

Dymoke took the party across; a soldier gave evidence subsequently that 'the lesser knight, whose name was Sir Charles Danvers, as he thinketh, was hurt in one of his hands, and he saw one of their men, a surgeon, being a little man and young, dress the said knight's hurt'.[5] When the Deputy Keeper of the Castle arrived, it was arranged to give out that the knights were going into Brittany for service. 'And the knights, Dymoke and the Deputy, with the rest of the com-

pany, did sup in the Deputy's chamber with such victuals as
they brought with them, beef, mutton, and cold pasty of
venison. And this examinate, going and coming amongst
them, did perceive the said knights to be very sad.' Thus they
remained till Friday, more victuals being sent from Titchfield,
dressed by the Arundells' cook.

On the Friday Southampton sent an urgent message that the
authorities were on their trail and that the party would be
apprehended that night : 'upon which message delivered they
all departed suddenly, in a great hurly burly', almost over-
setting the boat. The boatman set them ashore at Bald Head ;
one of them 'asked Mr. Dymoke if he knew the way to Titchfield, who answered he knew the way very well if it were at
midnight'. They seem to have gone back to Whitley Lodge.
The Porter of Calshot Castle was of the opinion that the knights
remained in the country two or three days more, 'because the
weather was foul, and the wind altogether against them'. By
then a passage was arranged for them across Channel and they
were safe ; the others remained to face belated and obstructed
justice. Dymoke returned to the Castle with four pieces
of gold, 'to be divided amongst the soldiers for their
pains'.

On Saturday, 12 October, when Lawrence Grose, the Sheriff,
was passing over Itchen ferry to inquire into the affair, 'one
Florio an Italian, and one Humphrey Drewell, a servant of the
Earl of Southampton, being in the said passage-boat, threatened
to cast Grose overboard, and said they would teach him to
meddle with their fellows, with many other threatening
words'.[6] Among their fellow-servants who should be
examined appear the names of some thirteen, Hennings, the
Earl's steward, Payne, keeper of his wardrobe, Robinson,
gentleman of his horses, Nashe, the Earl's bailiff, and we hear
of the Earl's falconer, his barber, stablemen, grooms, what
not. We see something of the scale on which the young
peer lived.

For himself, he hurried off to London, away from the scene.

In France the two brothers were well received by Henri IV, always friendly to Essex and his following, and the King interceded with Elizabeth and Robert Cecil on their behalf. For some years in vain. Aubrey tells us that the father, Sir John Danvers, died of grief : 'his sons' sad accident broke his heart'. And this is corroborated by the widow, in one of her passionate letters to Cecil : 'and if a life notwithstanding must be answered with a life, what may be trulier said than that my son slew Long with a dagger, and they have been the cause of slaying my husband with dolour and grief ; and if Sir John Danvers were a worthier man, and his life of more worth than Harry Long's, so much odds the Longs have had already of our good name and house'. Nor was this the end of the story : it bound Southampton and the Danvers brothers together in the bond of danger shared. After, this led one of the trio to the scaffold and another to the verge of it, Bacon tells us that Sir Charles was 'exceedingly devoted to the Earl of Southampton, upon affection begun first upon the deserving of the same earl towards him when he was in trouble about the murder of one Long'.[7]

The affair made a great sensation at the time. Feud and challenges, death and exile, John Florio, the Earl's tutor, in the foreground — it all made its impression on the mind of the Earl's poet, quick to catch suggestions, take up hints from everywhere. For his very next play he looked up a plot, Arthur Brooke's old poem, based on a familiar Italian story. And so, placed safely in its Italian setting and with its Italian atmosphere, next year we have *Romeo and Juliet*.

Lord Burghley, disappointed of his hopes of Southampton for his granddaughter, found a more promising match for her in the new Earl of Derby, William, who succeeded his brother this year, better known as Ferdinando, Lord Strange, patron of the theatre. But it transpired that his widow, the celebrated Alice Spencer, was pregnant. The wary Lord Treasurer thereupon postponed concluding the marriage until the child were known to be boy or girl : if a boy, the new earl would be no earl at all. The Cecil luck held : the child turned out to be a girl. At last the Lady Elizabeth Vere could go forward to a marriage of the grandest, performed at Court at Greenwich, 26 January 1595, graced by the presence of the Queen. The sulky Southampton was made to feel the draught of disapprobation from on high. Father Garnet, the Jesuit, who was in a position to know everything, tells us that 'the young Earl of Southampton, refusing the Lady Vere, payeth £5,000 of present payment'.[8] He would have done far better to marry the girl and be done with it.

Garnet's actual figure sounds unconvincingly large ; nevertheless now that Southampton came into the management of his estate for himself, he found it considerably embarrassed — and he had not the Lord Treasurer behind him to help. In fact he could not get full possession of his lands from the Crown. In 1596 he had to bring a case 'for the inheritance of all his lands — 2,000 marks per annum', i.e. some £1,660 a year at a conventional valuation; but this would not take account of the benefit of occasional large fines, and the general upward trend of returns on land. Elizabethan estates are a highly complicated matter, and there is no point in going into Southampton's in detail, even if his affairs were clear — which they were not to him, so how can they be to us ? One important consideration was that one-third of the revenues would go to his mother — a condition always liable to be a source of dispute. His father had left large debts as yet uncleared. We find the son plunging into prize ventures at sea in the hope of making some spectacular return. In addition, he was extravagant, generous, and of a gambling disposition — like his leader, Essex. This led both into financial difficulties ; these aggravated their political discontents and led them into political gambles that were even more dangerous.

In September 1595 we hear the first rumour of Southampton paying attention to Elizabeth Vernon, one of the Queen's maids of honour. Sir Robert Sidney's agent at Court writes, 'my lord of Southampton doth with too much familiarity court the fair Mistress Vernon, while his friends, observing the Queen's humours towards my lord of Essex, do what they can to bring her to favour him ; but it is yet in vain'.⁹ Elizabeth Vernon, was one of the four orphaned daughters of Sir John Vernon of Hodnet in Shropshire. Left unprovided for, she was preferred to the Queen's service by the favourite Essex, who was her first cousin. The Queen's relations with Essex grew more and more unsteady and temperamental ; there were faults on both sides, though his temper was chiefly to blame. It looks here as if Southampton's friends were at this point trying to mollify the Queen's hardening attitude towards Essex. Elizabeth Vernon, born in January 1573, was some nine months older than Southampton.¹⁰

Meanwhile, the letters of Southampton's mother show her well-contented with her elderly husband, Sir Thomas Heneage, and both of them on the best of terms with Sir Robert Cecil. (This relationship was of considerable advantage to her son, who seems to have remained always on friendly terms with the younger Cecil and to have relied on his good will in his troubles.) But already Heneage was ailing. The Countess wrote to Cecil on 29 July 1595 — it was the custom for widows of superior social rank to retain their title on marrying someone of lesser rank : 'You do well to comfort those that love you, specially when with one labour you can comfort us both ; Master Heneage taketh your sending and I your saying very kindly. This hath been a painful night to him ; I hope better of the day.' ¹¹ We perceive from her letters that the Countess was not only a charming woman, but an intelligent and stylish one. She concludes, with a Tudor turn of humour : 'I pray you commend me to that wicked woman that loves you and likes me : they call her my lady Catherine'. The Queen intended to visit the couple at Copt Hall on her progress in August. 'Your letter showing her Majesty's liking to continue her purpose in coming to our poor lodge at Copt Hall hath given him [Heneage] more comfort than anything else, the rather for that he esteems it grows from her own goodness. That he most desires is to know the certainty of her time of coming, without the which he shall be evil able to do that he desires and shall become him.' [12] 'Our poor lodge', indeed! — this was Elizabethan cant for the splendid mansion Heneage had been enabled to raise by his remunerative offices and the Queen's bounty.

A week later : 'Master Heneage was much revived by your letter, as indeed he is ever glad to hear from you, believing in your love ; and of his desire to see her Majesty well content in Copt Hall I think you are sufficiently persuaded, but that we may have certainty is that we wish'.[13] Meanwhile, duty compelled her to report that smallpox had reached Epping and Waltham, and was approaching Copt Hall. 'That I received now I have thought good to send you herewith, to impart to her Majesty.' Heneage's health showed no amendment, and the Queen came not to Copt Hall. He wrote himself once more to Cecil to deliver his last remembrance to her in 'this long, weary, and most painful sickness of mine. . . . Yet never man was more cared for by a most kind companion, that cares not to kill herself to cure me. God reward her, for I cannot, but by the favour of that grace which upon earth is the fountain of our grace.' [14]

When Heneage died in October, he showed his confidence in the Countess by making her his executrix and did his best to reward her in his will. She was left Copt Hall for life, with much of the household stuff ; for we find her handing on in her will in turn to her son, tapestries and hangings with wrought gold and Heneage's arms on them, 'a ring of gold with a fair table diamond in it, which Sir Thomas Heneage had of Sir Walter Ralegh', and 'I leave my dear son all the pictures in the little gallery at Copt Hall'.[15] Heneage left her the large and valuable manor and rectory of Epping with its possessions in various parishes as her jointure ; £500 a year out of the late monastery of Watton in Yorkshire, and Heneage House in Bevis Marks in London.[16] Altogether she had done extremely well by her second husband, and out of her sixteen months of married life with him.

The moment the news of his death was certain, the kites and crows flocked round for the pickings of his offices : 'the places that live are many, and many great suitors for them. . . . The Queen is not now to be seen, she takes his death somewhat heavily.' [17] She and Heneage were precisely of an age ; she had made a confidential servant of him from the time of her accession and made his fortune. The same report from Court concludes thus : 'my lord of Southampton, offering to help the Queen to her horse, was refused ; he is gone from Court, and not yet returned'. This was a deliberate, a public, mark of disapprobation ; evidently he was not approved of in that quarter.

However, at the jousts at Court to celebrate the Queen's accession day, 17 November, when a bevy of earls tilted in her honour — Cumberland, Essex, Sussex, Bedford — Southampton made a fifth, running as Bevis of Southampton, that famous hero of medieval romance. And when Gervase Markham published his poem this year in memory of Sir Richard Grenville of the *Revenge*, he prefaced a sonnet to it, among others, inscribed to Southampton :

> Thou glorious laurel of the Muses' hill
> Whose eyes doth crown the most victorious pen —

from which we see the absurdity of fancying Markham as the rival poet of Shakespeare's Sonnets.

In 1596 the war at sea leaped into activity again. Since the Lisbon fiasco in 1589 there had not been a major expedition against Spain. Now it was decided to undertake one on the largest scale, another example of combined operations under the joint command of Lord Admiral Howard and Essex, against Cadiz. All the young men of spirit at Court were agog to go, among them Southampton.

Preparations were well advanced when suddenly there came

news, at the end of March, of a surprise attack upon Calais by the Spanish forces, when Henri IV was engaged too far away to be able to come to its rescue. England was particularly sensitive to having the Spaniards in control of Calais athwart the Channel. Elizabeth herself had never given up hope of recovering Calais and recompensing the disgrace her sister's feeble government had brought upon the nation by its loss. The sea-forces gathering for Cadiz were deflected to intervene at Calais, if possible. Essex went down to Dover : 'it is the greatest scorn in the world to lie here', he wrote, 'in sight of a French king that stays but to join with us, and of a place that imports with us and all our friends in these parts of Christendom so much, and to have an expectation of doing somewhat, and yet to have our hands tied'.[18] There we see his tendency constantly to gird against the Queen for looking before she leaped, for considering all the politic aspects of a course of action instead of following his precipitancy. She was not behindhand : she wrote him from *The Due Repulse*, the flagship in the Thames, 'as distant as I am from your abode, yet my ears serve me too well to hear that terrible battery that methinks sounds for relief at my hands. Wherefore, rather than for lack of timely aid it should be wholly lost, go you, in God's blessed name, as far as that place where you may soonest relieve it, with as much caution as so great a trust requires. But I charge you, without the mere loss of it, do in no wise peril so fair an army for another Prince's town. God cover you under his safest wings, and let all peril go without your compass. Believe Cecil in the rest. From *The Due Repulse*, where this day I have been.'

There we have them both : youth, eagerness, gallantry, impolitic rashness on one side ; age, experience, politic consideration, not without kindness, on the other. 'Crabbèd age and youth cannot live together.'

Southampton was ardently hoping to follow his leader on the great expedition. On March 17 the Lord Admiral had written to Cecil, 'my Lord Thomas Howard and the Earl of

Southampton was with me when your letter came. There came to us, being aboard of *The Due Repulse*, the Earl of Cumberland, and he seemed to me to be much grieved with that he is stayed ; but I dealt so with him as he knoweth how it must be.' [19]   When the expedition's purpose was diverted to Calais, among Essex's instructions appeared this : 'to take with him only such nobles as have leave to go, namely, Sussex, Rich, Herbert, and Burgh ; but not Derby, Southampton, Mountjoy, Compton, Windsor, nor Sheffield'.[20]   These young peers had as yet, for the most part, no heirs ; the Queen thought of herself as a nursing mother of the nation over which she presided : hence her prohibition, in her watchful care of them. Meanwhile Southampton went down to Dover.   Essex reported on April 15 : 'I know not whether Lords Southampton and Compton, who are here, have licence to go.   I have charged them to return else, and if they come on board without it, will send them back.'   Back they had to come.

In the meantime Calais was battered into submission : Henri IV, as excellent a politician as Elizabeth, had calculated that he would rather have the Spaniards in possession, who would surrender it at the peace, than the English, who would not.   This kind of calculation — of which Essex's mind was incapable — had not been lost on the Queen : it had been present to her mind all along.   The expedition to Cadiz went forward.

But Southampton was not on it.   He thus missed the most splendid triumph, the finest exploit, of the whole long war — the capture of Cadiz.   Among the instructions to the joint commanders, the Lord Admiral and Essex, were 'a series of enlightened and humane prohibitions of unnecessary slaughter of their enemies or the killing under any circumstances of women and children and aged men'.[21]   The Queen wrote a prayer for the happy success of the expedition : 'we humbly beseech thee with bended knees prosper the work, and with the best forewinds guide the journey, speed the victory, and make the return the advancement of thy glory, the triumph of their fame and surety of the realm, with the least loss of English blood'. This was a characteristic note from the famous old woman.

All worked together *à merveille*. The capture of the heavily fortified Atlantic port was a resounding triumph in which Ralegh and Essex, and their respective followings, pulled together — though the successful plan of attack was the older man's, not the younger's. In addition to the capture and sack of the city, all the merchant shipping with which the harbour was crowded, and a number of the king's fighting galleons, were captured or destroyed ; in the inner harbour the treasure-fleet scuppered itself with the loss of millions. All the fame of the action accrued to Essex, whose signal gallantry and humanity made an immense impression on the Spaniards, who were not used to behaving with such restraint themselves, either in Europe or America. War-weariness spread throughout Spain, though Philip plodded fixedly on, pushing forward preparations for yet another Armada.

In the cathedral at Cadiz, 27 June, there was an unprecedented creation of knights, no less than fifty-three — much to the Queen's disgust, when she heard of it. Among them was Captain William Harvey, a gallant young fellow of a good Kent family, who as a youth had served against the Armada and, boarding a Spanish ship, was said to have killed the captain. We shall hear more of him. What infuriated the Queen was that, when she had undergone such charges for the expedition, everyone conspired to cheat her of the returns upon it. Her own Clerk of the Council, Anthony Ashley — knighted for his services — attempted to embezzle a valuable catch of jewels. Though an official, he was interested in prize transactions. Just prior to the expedition we find him writing to Cecil : 'albeit I might have gotten above £1,000 clear by this booty unseen, yet are you witness that I preferred my duty to her Majesty before all private. I do find that some parties interested have been earnestly dealt with from the Earls of Derby and Southampton to buy the thing with warrant to save harmless from all danger.'²² After Cadiz he protested too much ; he was not allowed to get away with his swag.

Essex, after Cadiz, stood at the apex of his career, a famous figure both at home and abroad. He was now in his thirtieth year, a familiar presence, with his fine carriage of himself, his spade-shaped auburn beard, the noble forehead, the pale-blue luminous eyes, with plenty of intelligence but with a haunted expression as if with some fore-knowledge of his fate. To his natural intelligence and cultivation — for Burghley, whose ward he had been, had had him well-educated at Cambridge — Essex added the gift of style. It is present in everything he did or said, not only in the verse that he wrote but in the natural rhythms of his speech revealed in his letters : there is always poetry in them. It shines forth no less in the gestures of the man — the invincible generosity, the carelessness of himself (where others, with much less to give, were so wary and cautious), the innate courtesy that everyone noticed. He improved on this by his cult of popularity. Therein lay danger : for if he was Bolingbroke, as people increasingly thought of him — with the monarch growing old and the succession still unsettled — who then was Richard II ?

Southampton's poet, now the popular dramatist, has several touches of Essex in his portrait of Bolingbroke, notably in *Richard II*, written and performed just at this time : here he is

> Mounted upon a hot and fiery steed
> Which his aspiring rider seemed to know,
> With slow but stately pace kept on his course,
> Whilst all tongues cried, 'God save thee, Bolingbroke ! . . .'
> Whilst he, from the one side to the other turning,
> Bareheaded, lower than his proud steed's neck,
> Bespake them thus, 'I thank you, countrymen'.

It might be Essex, returning from Cadiz, or on any of his appearances in the city : the kind of welcome that neither Burghley nor his son could command, for all their far greater services to the country. Nor, increasingly, could the Queen :

Essex was stealing from her the popularity for which she had worked and schemed for a lifetime.

For, to all the gifts the fairies had bestowed at his christening, one quality was added that wrecked all the rest : he was unstable. Through his mother, the beautiful and intolerable Lettice Knollys, he was a cousin of the Queen ; of oldest Norman stock, with royal blood in his veins, he never forgot that he was as well-descended as she. And he thought himself as good. This was where he was wrong : though he had glimpses, he never had the full illumination of her subtle, politic brain. As a very masculine man, with an irresistible way with women (and well-practised among her frail maids of honour, to her lively disapprobation), he thought himself superior. He would never accept his stepfather, Leicester's, somewhat undignified rôle of a mere subordinate. This was precisely the rôle the Queen intended him for : she needed someone to take Leicester's place in this last decade of her reign. Essex's proud spirit, inherited from his mother, could break but not yield. Hence the increasing disaccord, the constant jarring, between the Queen and her Prince Charming, getting more and more on each other's nerves, until the final, fatal breach.

One of Essex's temperament simply could not take telling, though he had warnings enough. At this very moment Francis Bacon offered him the politic advice for which he was paid — at all costs to keep the Queen's good opinion, thus to avoid military offices and building up a military following, to stand for civilian office and peaceful courses, and to give always the appearance of yielding his inclinations to the sovereign's will. Essex rewarded the giver of the advice, and took the course clean contrary to it. (Bacon drew his own conclusions : regarding Essex as hopeless, he prepared to move over to the other side.) In 1597 Essex secured the military office of Master of the Ordnance, and then insisted on being made Earl Marshal — all more and more imprudent. Essex's triumph at Cadiz appeared as a set-back to Burghley's policy aiming at peace ; Anthony Bacon, Essex's intimate adviser, wrote that it 'hath made the old Fox to crouch and whine'.[23] This was the language these young men held about the old man who had guided the state so long and so successfully — and kept them out. All those who were *out* looked more and more to Essex as their leader : Puritans on one hand, Catholics on the other, all the young swordsmen who were not Ralegh's followers, a number of young peers, all the discontented and all who expected to gain by change on the death of the Queen. It grew into a dangerous and powerful, if motley and incoherent, opposition.

Southampton's own discontents riveted him to it, though, as we have seen, he had given himself to Essex from the first. Thwarted of the chance to serve, to win renown, even to follow his leader — this had no good effect on a young man anxious to make his mark in action and win some share in the glory of the age. The next thing we hear of him, early in 1597, is a quarrel with the remarkable, and difficult, Earl of Northumberland, who was Essex's brother-in-law but who lived on bad terms with his wife. Southampton thought that Northumberland had spoken ill of him, and, since his left arm had been hurt at ballon, sent his rapier to Northumberland as a challenge.[24] The Queen stepped in to prevent a duel between two of her peers, and they were called before the lords of the Council, who composed the quarrel and made them friends. Already in February we learn, more agreeably, that Southampton was asked by Sir Robert Sidney, head of the family at Penshurst, then absent as Governor of Flushing in the Netherlands, to be godfather to his little daughter. Southampton 'did take it exceeding kindly that he was desired . . . and will most willingly do it'.[25] For the christening there was a grand gathering at which he welcomed the guests, who included his mother and the dowager Countess of Derby.

This year was signalised by another attempt to break the war-will of Spain with a powerful expedition against the Spanish coast, this time Ferrol. The Queen was against it, but the two

factions in favour of an offensive war-policy, Essex's and
Ralegh's, came together to force her hand and carried Cecil,
now in the key position as Secretary of State, with them.
Southampton, in some disgust, had got leave to travel abroad
for a year ; but now Cecil obtained licence for him to serve
as an independent adventurer on the new expedition, the
Islands Voyage, on which he got command of the *Garland*.
His letter, taking leave of Cecil, gives us a glimpse of his state
of mind : 'though my fortune was never so good as to enjoy
any favour from her Majesty that might make me desire to
stay in her Court, yet should I account myself infinitely unhappy if, with the loss of serving her, I should likewise lose
her good conceit of me. Wherefore I pray you to study to
preserve that, and I will direct the whole course of my life to
do her service.' [26] We shall see how he kept to this promise.

The fleet was to go in three squadrons under Essex, Lord
Thomas Howard, and Ralegh, with a Dutch squadron as
fourth. Early in July they were concentrating at Plymouth.
Southampton reported to Cecil, 'we find ourselves in a far
worse case than we expected, the fleet being altogether un-
furnished of good mariners, and we almost left destitute of any
means to supply it. . . . There is such a general want that all
the captains complain ; although my experience is very small
in these matters, yet my lack is so apparent that I can easily
discern it. I have already been driven to set thirty sick men
on shore, besides some that have run away, and those that
remain are for the most part unable to perform any labour that
belongs to them.' [27] Here was the obverse to the medal of
Elizabethan glory, or, rather, we have brought home to us the
conditions out of which they snatched their achievements.

No sooner did the fleet get to sea but a tempest bore down
upon them, dispersing it and doing considerable damage.
Essex staggered back to Plymouth with most of his squadron,
to be joined shortly by Ralegh. Lord Thomas Howard, a
better sailor, held on his course, and so did Southampton and
Mountjoy, who came on board his ship when the weather

improved and all decided to make for their rendezvous at the Northern Cape of Spain.[28]   They arrived in sight of the Spanish coast, but found no English fleet ; instead they were summoned back to Plymouth.   There they remained a month, repairing damage and eating up their provisions, while they waited for favourable weather.   Sickness spread among the men, so that the land forces had to be disbanded.   Hence, when they arrived off Ferrol again, it was impossible to attack it or the armada that Philip was yet again assembling — his third — within.   It was decided to make for the Azores and lie in wait for the treasure-fleet.

Bad weather and ill luck continued to dog them this year. On the second voyage out to the Spanish coast Sir George Carew's ship had got into difficulties.   He reported that 'we shot off our ordnance and hanged out our lights, but the tempest was so great as the ships which were ahead me could not hear or discern it, the *Garland* excepted, who an hour after day came unto me and did not leave me until the evening.   At which time my lord of Southampton, seeing no possibility for my ship to follow the fleet, and understanding from us that we were in great peril to be lost . . . sent his pinnace to me to come aboard his ship.   Although the danger I was in were inducement enough unto this, yet . . . I resolved to take the fortune of my ship.   The Earl, fearing to be embayed and to lose the fleet which all that day was never in sight, headed on his course.' [29]   Concentrated off Finisterre, Essex had summoned his captains on board *The Due Repulse* to send home a message that they were all well and hoped to do something yet.   There are their signatures in order : Essex, Rutland, Southampton, Lord Thomas Howard, Mountjoy, Grey, Sir Christopher Blount, Sir Francis Vere, Sir Anthony Shirley — several of them names which were to come together in more sinister circumstances another day.

In the Azores the only exploit of note, the capture of Fayal, was performed by Ralegh, greatly to Essex's disgust who attempted to cashier him.   This led to an outbreak of all the old enmity between them. Essex next made the mistake of stretching much too far to the eastward for an anchorage, thus missing the chance of intercepting the treasure-fleet on its way to Terceira. In the night Sir William Monson found himself cheek by jowl with the Spanish fleet slipping by. He gave chase and was followed by Vere and Southampton, whose *Garland* captured a prize, though not one of the treasure-ships. These managed to get into the safety of the heavily-fortified Angra Roads. Thus the grand opportunity of the campaign, and of the war, was missed. At Court the rumour was that Southampton had 'fought with one of the King's great men-of-war, and sunk her',[30] but it seems that this was no more than the prize he had captured. The fleet came home full of mutual recrimination and bitterness ; while the Queen, elo-quent with reproaches, determined to have no more such expeditions for the rest of her days.

All that autumn the weather continued stormy : a large part of Philip's third Armada foundered off Finisterre with the loss of many hundreds of lives. At home the Countess was worried for her son, and carried her trouble of mind, as every-body did, to Cecil : 'I wish I might hear of his speedy home-coming ; which, if you think I may hope for, I pray you give me a little light'.[31] And again, 'yesterday's storm filled my heart with sourest thoughts. I purpose to send presently to him, whereto I beg a warrant for post horses for better speed. I purpose on Thursday to thank the Queen for her favour, and hope you may have some fresh news for me then.' No inquiry for Sir William Harvey, who had also served on the expedition — it was already rumoured in May of that year that she would marry him.

As for Southampton's other close relations, his brother-in-law Thomas Arundell made a fool of himself, while his sister quarrelled with her father-in-law. We see why the couple were so much under Southampton's roof, in London or at Titchfield : old Sir Matthew would not have them at War-dour. The son had got leave to go abroad and offer his services to the Emperor Rudolf, who was only too appreciative of young Englishmen, and Arundell returned with the title, if nothing more, of Count of the Holy Roman Empire. On his arrival back in England he sent his cousin Cecil his news : 'had I not suffered a shipwreck, and so lost all my apparel, linen, horses, money and whatsoever else I had, and withal gotten an extreme cold with tumbling into the sea for the safety of my life, I would myself have been the deliverer of these salutations'.[32] It seems that his patent as Count was swallowed up by the sea, too, though it was genuine enough.

The Queen was not going to have any of this nonsense. She regarded it as an impertinence that one of her subjects should have accepted a foreign title without her permission, and she well knew the annoyance that claims to the precedence of an earl, on the part of a mere untitled gentleman, would give to everyone. The fatuous Arundell, quite unaware, went on to outline to the Secretary of State the confidences he thought he had received as to negotiating peace. Perceiving some coldness in his welcome, he fell back on asserting his kinship to the Queen, his close relation to Cecil. She put him in custody to cool his head and deflate his pretensions ; and on his release rusticated him from Court. The title became something of a fool's cap on his silly head, for ever writing long, self-important letters to his busy cousin. Nor did Sir Matthew want him at Wardour — the son had constantly spurned his father's advice — and threatened to disinherit him. Lady Mary was in no better favour : on her last visit to Wardour she too had displeased her father-in-law. Now she also carried her complaint to Cecil, taking a somewhat lofty tone. Sir Matthew was willing to receive his son and family, 'only excepting against myself, upon some unkindness that passed between us at my last being there ; neither (as I understand) is he otherwise to be wrought in this matter than by the advice of some special friend'. In return for a letter from Cecil, 'one on whose friendship he doth rely above any other', she promised that 'I will not behave myself otherwise towards him than as shall become a kind and respective daughter-in-law. I am persuaded that your persuasions will effect as much as I require of him.' [33]

While Southampton was at last making a beginning of his public career, his dramatist was going forward to make the most of the opportunity afforded him by his fellowship in the Lord Chamberlain's company. The Lopez affair appealed to the anti-Semitic feelings of the mob — though in that the sixteenth century hardly disgraced itself as the twentieth has done — and led to a revival of Marlowe's *The Jew of Malta*. Powerful, and successful theatre as that was, Shakespeare now went beyond the master in poetic beauty, as always in humanity, with *The Merchant of Venice*. Shylock is its most memorable figure — a human being, as Barabas is not. In this play the friendship between Antonio and Basanio is perhaps more important than the latter's love for Portia. At Cadiz one of the galleons captured had been the vice-admiral, the *St. Andrew*. This is reflected in

> But I should think of shallows and of flats,
> And see my wealthy *Andrew* docked in sand,
> Vailing her high-top lower than her ribs
> To kiss her burial.

The name of Gobbo — old Gobbo with his son Launcelot — sounds Italian enough in this Italianate play, but in fact it was a name well known in the parish of Titchfield and turns up in the registers there.[34] (There is no reason why the Earl's poet should not have been there with him.)

In these last years of the reign people were conscious of a comparison with that of Richard II, with its favourites, and with Essex as a potential Bolingbroke. While on the Islands Voyage in 1597 Ralegh wrote back to Cecil that Essex was 'also wonderful merry at your conceit of Richard II'. We do not know what the esoteric joke among them was, but it was a dangerous subject to joke about. When Shakespeare's play was printed in 1597 the deposition scene had to be left out. In his next play, *King John*, it seems that the Cadiz expedition is glanced at :

> And all the unsettled humours of the land,
> Rash, inconsiderate, fiery voluntaries,
> With ladies' faces and fierce dragons' spleens,
> Have sold their fortunes at their native homes,
> Bearing their birthrights proudly on their backs . . .
> In brief, a braver choice of dauntless spirits
> Than now the English bottoms have waft o'er
> Did never float upon the swelling tide,
> To do offence and scath in Christendom.

While there is a specific reference to the dispersal of Philip's Armada in the stormy autumn of 1596 :

> So, by a roaring tempest on the flood,
> A whole armado of convicted sail
> Is scattered and disjoined from fellowship.

Southampton continued to be the target of dedications from hopeful authors. Thomas Wilson brought out his translation of Montemayor's *Diana*, dedicated to him 'now upon the Spanish voyage with my lord, the Earl of Essex' — evidently the author thought that Southampton was on the Cadiz expedition. In 1597 Henry Lok inscribed a sonnet to him, in a volume printed by Richard Field :

> By blood, by value, noble we you see,
> By nature, and by learning's travail wise,
> By love of good, ill's hate, you virtuous be :
> Hence public honour, private love doth rise . . .
> Of honour, wisdom, virtue, I dilate,
> Which (you pursuing) will advance your state.

We shall see.

CHAPTER VII

Marriage and Discontentments

SOUTHAMPTON had earned the disapprobation of the Queen; it was unlikely, upon the course he was following, that he would be able to reinstate himself in that easily exhausted treasury of merit. In this year 1598 he was to fall further into disfavour, and that in turn propelled him into still more unsatisfactory courses.

In January we find his brother-in-law, Arundell, pestering cousin Cecil for some employment abroad — sententiously as usual. 'It hath been ever a policy among princes to work their own good out of all sorts of men by employing every man to what he is most fit. From me there can no good be expected by keeping me at home in disgrace ; but if I went to sea (especially seeing the art of navigation and the mathematics have been the chiefest part of my studies) it is unlikely but I should effect as much as some other. . . . And to the end the world may see how highly I prize the grace and sight of my sovereign, I am contented never more to importune that sight till I have, at mine own charges and with the adventure of my life, brought into England either a carrack or the worth of a carrack.' [1] No notice was taken.

Meanwhile the Earl was hanging about the Court in a very discontented frame of mind. Peace was being negotiated at length between France and Spain, and Sir Robert Cecil was being despatched to France with the aim of delaying it and exploring the possibilities of a general peace that should include both England and the Netherlands. Southampton was anxious to get away from his discontents and difficulties, also from the entanglement with a woman in which he had at last been caught, and embark on the continental tour which was an indispensable part of the education of a cultivated nobleman who hoped to serve his country. The news at Court in mid-January was that he would accompany Cecil into France and thence onwards on his travels, 'which course of his doth exceedingly grieve his mistress, that passes her time in weeping and lamenting'.[2] The next we hear is of a quarrel between Southampton and Ambrose Willoughby that seems to have been over gossip about Southampton's mistress, Elizabeth Vernon.

One night there was a scene in the Presence Chamber itself, after the Queen had gone to bed. Southampton, Sir Walter Ralegh, and Mr. Parker were playing at primero late, dan young Willoughby 'as squire of the body required them to give over. Soon after he spake to them again that, if they would not leave, he would call on the guard to put down the board : which Sir Walter seeing put up his money and went his ways. But my lord of Southampton took exceptions at him and told him he would remember it ; and so, finding him between the Tennis Court wall and the garden, struck him and Willoughby pulled off some of his locks. The Queen gave Willoughby thanks for what he did in the Presence and told him he had done better if he had sent him to the porter's lodge to see who durst have fetched him out.'[3] The Queen followed this up by commanding the Earl to absent himself from Court.

In February the news was that 'my lord of Southampton is much troubled by her Majesty's strangest usage of him. Somebody hath played unfriendly parts with him. Mr. Secretary hath procured him licence to travel. His fair mistress doth wash her fairest face with too many tears. I pray God his going away bring her to no such infirmity which is, as it were, hereditary to her name.'[4] This is a reference to the famous elopement of Dorothy Vernon with a young Manners, and the love-match that followed, by which Haddon Hall came to the Manners family and name.

We have portraits of Elizabeth Vernon, from which we can tell what she looked like — the earliest at Boughton in the possession of her Buccleuch descendants. Her face is a regular pretty oval, hair drawn back from rounded forehead, hardly decipherable eyebrows — evidently a blonde — lively alert eyes, an aristocratic nose, tiny, child-like mouth and small chin. The whole gives a rather *mignonne* impression. In one portrait in which she is making her toilet, jewel-box open on a table beside her, little lap-dog at her feet, she is holding up to her hair falling long over her shoulders a comb on which is inscribed *Menez-moi doucement*. There is no evidence that Southampton treated her any otherwise than in accordance with that. We know that she was much in love with him. After she had got him, her later portraits show her a contented, satisfied matron with a certain sweetness of expression.

The next we hear before Southampton's leaving is the rumour that he will marry his 'fair mistress', but that, as before over Lord Burghley's granddaughter, he asked for a little respite. He was not ready, even yet, to undergo the yoke. A few days later he received his licence to travel beyond seas for a couple of years, with ten servants and six horses ; from his father's executors he raised £300 to be taken up at Rouen. Cecil, Lord Brooke and Southampton with all their train set out on 10 February, the Earl leaving behind him 'a very desolate gentlewoman, that hath almost wept out her fairest eyes. He was at Essex house with Essex and there had much private talk with him in the court below.' [5] The father-less gentlewoman was Essex's cousin and in a sense under his care ; Essex and his ardent follower must have come to an understanding in case of an accident.

When the ambassadorial train arrived in France Henri IV was far away at Angers, and thither they all proceeded, not arriving until well on in March. Cecil presented Southampton to the King, who 'then very favourably embraced and wel-comed the Earl. And so, suddenly took me [Cecil] by the hand, contrary to my expectation, saying he would walk with me down into his garden *en qualité d'ami*, where he entertained me an hour and a half with many pleasant and familiar discourses.' 6 This was the prelude to some candid talk between the allies, though from the first it was evident that Henry of Navarre was bent on making peace with his old enemy, Philip. The question remained whether the Netherlands, and by consequence England, could be included in it. In April Cecil returned, having accomplished nothing. While these questions remained unresolved, and with some private anxieties on his mind, Southampton did not know whether to proceed on his Italian tour or not. He followed up a present to Essex with a letter in June : 'if I were not somewhat acquainted with the slowness of your proceedings [i.e. the government's] often used in things of small moment and therefore much more to be expected in a matter of this consequence, I should now hope to be soon out of doubt what will become of it ; but knowing with what advisement the affairs of our country are managed, I am resolved to expect with patience the end of this matter'.7

Such was the impatient tone that prevailed among these young men.

While these affairs remained unsettled Southampton's plans for his Italian tour received a blow from an unexpected quarter. The Queen suddenly pardoned the Danvers brothers, with whom he had expected to make a party for Italy, and this necessitated their returning home. For some time they were delayed in Paris by illness. Meanwhile we find the cultivated Earl forwarding the latest French songs to his friend, Sir Robert Sidney. In August, with the Danvers brothers back in England, Southampton wrote to Cecil : 'for the return of him and his brother I cannot but rejoice with you ; though, in respect of myself, I find more reason to mourn the loss of so pleasing companions. But such is my affection to them as I do prefer their good before the satisfaction of myself. If it had not been for their departure I should ere this time have written unto you out of Italy ; but now by means of that my journey is stayed until I hear out of England. For if, after the despatch of his business there, I may not have the company of the younger, my voyage will be infinitely unpleasing unto me, being to pass into a country of which I am utterly ignorant, without any companion. I cannot here imagine what may hinder him, but if any let should happen, I beseech you if you can remove it, for I protest it will be an exceeding maim unto me if I miss him.' [8] We see how keen Southampton was on the companionship of Sir Henry Danvers, a very agreeable young man who never married but went on to a career of public service and philanthropy. He became an eminent benefactor of the university of Oxford, to which he presented the beautiful Botanic Garden opposite Magdalen College. Later on, in Ireland, we learn that Southampton was Danvers's 'shadow', always with him.

However, it was not Southampton's male friendships that got him into trouble at this point, but his female : the news from England in August was that Mistress Vernon had had to leave the Court and take refuge at Essex House. Meanwhile, relations between the Queen and Essex had worsened, and he was in acute disfavour. The same newsletter that tells us this informs us of the disappearance of the greatest figure in England, architect of the greatness of the reign, Lord Burghley. Only the Queen remained of her generation ; the game was in the hands of the younger men now — if they knew how to play it.

John Chamberlain specially went up to London from Oxfordshire to see 'the solemn funeral . . . with all the rites that belong to so great a personage. The number of mourners one and other were above five hundred, whereof there were many noblemen, and among the rest the Earl of Essex, who . . . methought carried the heaviest countenance of the company. Presently after dinner he retired to Wanstead, where they say he means to settle, seeing he cannot be received in Court, though he have relented much and sought by divers means to recover his hold. But the Queen says he hath played long enough upon her, and that she means to play a while upon him, and to stand as much upon her greatness as he hath done upon stomach.'⁹ As for poor Mistress Vernon : 'some say that she hath taken a venue [a fencing term, meaning a thrust] under the girdle and swells upon it. Yet she complains not of foul play but says the Earl of Southampton will justify it ; and it is hinted, underhand, that he was lately here four days in great secret, of purpose to marry her, and effected it accordingly.'

This turned out to be true ; and on 3 September Cecil wrote to Southampton, who had stolen back to Paris, in the stiff terms proper to noble offenders on such occasions. 'I am grieved to use the style of a Councillor to you to whom I have ever rather wished to be the messenger of honour and favour, by laying her Majesty's command upon you. But I must now put this gall into my ink, that she knows that you came over very lately, and returned very contemptuously ; that you have also married one of her maids-of-honour, without her privity. For which, with other circumstances informed against you, I find her grievously offended, and she commands me to charge you expressly (all excuses set apart) to repair hither to London, and advertise your arrival, without coming to the Court, until her pleasure be known.'¹⁰ At the same time Cecil wrote to the English ambassador in France, informing him of the order, signed personally by the Queen in her grand style at the head of the Signet letter : 'you know the nature of his offence, and what it is like to prove, which makes me wish that his lordship should take heed [not] to make it worse with any contempt, being the first day it is known — a matter that cannot danger his fortune further than the cloud of her Majesty's favour, who punisheth the form rather than the substance'.¹¹ This enclosed the official Privy Signet letter commanding Southampton 'in our name precisely and upon his duty to return presently [i.e., immediately] upon the sight hereof . . . Elizabeth R.'.

The news ran round at Court that when the Queen had been informed of the new Lady Southampton and her adventures, 'her patience was so much moved that she came not to chapel.

She threats them all to the Tower, not only the parties but all
that are partakers in the practice. It is confessed that the Earl
was lately here and solemnised the act himself, and Sir Thomas
German accompanied him on his return to Margate. . . . I now
understand that the Queen has commanded that there shall be
provided for the new Countess the sweetest and best appointed
Chamber in the Fleet.'[12] The writer was a punster, playing
on the fact that young Mistress Vernon had been a lady of the
Queen's Privy Chamber. He now ended with a poor Greek
pun : 'these are but the beginning of evils : well may he hope
for that merry day *en thanato* [in death] which I think he did
not find *en thalamo* [in the marriage-bed]'.

All this was grist to the mill for Court gossips, and merrily
they clacked. Here is the inveterate Tobie Mathew : 'Mistress
Vernon has spun a fair thread, as fair as I hold her a better
spinner than a painter'. Tobie had a point here : Mistress
Vernon had caught her evasive young Earl in the only way in
which he could be caught. She had allowed herself to be got
with child early in March, before the Earl left on his travels,
thus spinning a thread to keep him attached to her. Just as her
colleague in the Privy Chamber, another Elizabeth, the more
formidable Elizabeth Throckmorton, had, by risking everything, caught Sir Walter Ralegh, to the ruin of his favour with
the Queen. To the Queen it was not merely a personal
matter, personally offensive as the conduct of these young
people was : she was responsible for the honour of her Court
and for the wellbeing of the well-born, if frail, young ladies
in her charge. She had to keep order in the nursery, and she
behaved generously to them if they kept the rules and were
married properly. Elizabeth Vernon, like Elizabeth Throckmorton, had done very well for herself. The man in each case
was the loser, for neither of these girls had any dowry to bless
herself with. Southampton would have done far better to
marry the Lord Treasurer's granddaughter years before.

In Paris Southampton was for some time unaware how his
misadventure would be taken. He wrote to Essex that he had

reported his marriage to Cecil, hoping that he would procure of the Queen 'a favourable toleration of that which is past . . . for I assure you only the fear of having her Majesty's displeasure is more grievous unto me than any torment I can think of could be. I trust therefore that as my offence is but small, so her anger will not be much and so consequently it will not be very difficult to get my pardon.' [13]

Meanwhile, in England Essex had been ill — always a way of recommending himself to the sympathy of the Queen, who was not without heart. She had sent him her personal physicians, and, now recovering, he was working his way back to favour. He was entertaining foreigners — the brother of the Governor of Calais, a Frenchman who greatly pleased the Queen by his bearing and language. 'There were divers Almains with him, whereof one lost 300 crowns at a new play called *Every Man's Humour*.' [14] This was Ben Jonson's brilliant comedy, with which Shakespeare had welcomed his junior to the Lord Chamberlain's company and in which he acted.

At last, by 22 September, Southampton received the Queen's command to return, which gave him a double reason for anxiety. There was not only her displeasure, but his own financial embarrassment. On leaving England he had farmed out his estates to pay his creditors and meet his debts, reserving only a small portion to maintain himself and 'a very small train in my time of my travel'. He could not afford now to return home. (Did he reflect that a good dowry would have helped matters at such a juncture?) What was he to do? The young man besought his leader, now his cousin by marriage, 'how to direct my course, for according as you shall think fit I will not fail to do'.

From his London house in Blackfriars, next the private theatre, Lord Cobham wrote him the advice to return at all costs, and the Queen's displeasure would not long continue. 'The exception that is now taken is only your contempt to marry one of her maids and to acquaint her withal. But for any dishonour committed by your lordship, that conceit is clean taken away, so that your lordship hath no manner of cause to doubt any disgrace, but for some time absence from Court. . . . If you should forbear to come, I assure you it would aggravate the Queen, and put conceits [suspicions] into her which at this present she is free of.' Cobham, who was something of a favourite with the Queen at this moment, assured the young man of 'that love which I have ever professed to you'.[15]

In this unsatisfactory state of affairs, and in this discontentment of mind, the young man took to making high wagers on his game of tennis in Paris — no doubt with the hope of recouping his fortunes. Instead, he lost. A French agent of Cecil's suggested to him, kindly enough, that he should pass the word to Essex that if his protégé were not brought home soon he would ruin himself. For he was wagering two, three, and four thousand crowns at tennis, and Marshal Biron (Henri IV's favourite) had won 3,000 crowns from him in a few days. Everybody was laughing at him, and the best service Essex could do for him would be to bring him back since he loved him.[16]

At the end of September Southampton came over secretly to England and sought an interview alone with Essex, pledging him not to let anyone know of his presence. Essex sent his confidential secretary, Henry Cuffe — Fellow of Merton and excellent classical scholar — to meet Southampton and give him the advice 'to solicit kissing of the Queen's hand by Mr. Secretary [Cecil], and to spend some of your first time in that suit. I did also note down of your being so good a husband as to make a journey down to Leez.' [17] This means Leez priory in Essex, the home of Essex's sister, Penelope, Lady Rich — the 'Stella' of Sir Philip Sidney. There Southampton's wife had taken refuge for her *accouchement*.

After his brief secret visit Southampton returned to France, for on 16 October he wrote to Essex from Rouen, apologising for having brought blame upon him by his actions, begging his pardon with the grace everyone knew to be in his nature, and dedicating himself anew to Essex's service. 'For myself, I assure your lordship the thought of her Majesty's indignation conceived against me is much more grievous than the fear of whatsoever punishment can be laid upon me.' He was preparing to return and accept what was coming to him, 'hoping that when I have once abid penance sufficient for the offence committed, I shall be restored to her former good opinion'.[18]

Early in November he came over, about the time of the birth of a daughter, who was named Penelope after Lady Rich, her godmother. Gossip Chamberlain reported, 8 November, 'the new Countess of Southampton is brought abed of a daughter and to mend her portion, the Earl her father hath lately lost 1,800 crowns at tennis in Paris'.[19] A day or two later he was committed to the Fleet for his misdemeanour; but his confinement, as Cecil had promised, was more for the form than the substance, and within a fortnight he was out again. It cannot be said that the Queen had been hard on him; there is justification for her point of view in the unkind comment of a Catholic exile to the traitor Sir William Stanley on Southampton's marriage: 'maids of the Court go scarce twenty weeks with child after they are married, and every man has liberty of conscience to play the knave'.[20]

Southampton's mother had done so well out of her second marriage, to Sir Thomas Heneage — the 'Master Heneage' of her letters — that she was now contemplating a third marriage, to the spirited young soldier of her son's age, Sir William Harvey. He was a gentleman of good Kentish family, whose grandfather, Sir Nicholas Harvey, had been gentleman of the Privy Chamber to Henry VIII. On his mother's side he had attractive Welsh blood. As we have seen, as a youth he had signalised himself in fight against the Spanish Armada; in 1596 and 1597 he had served on the Cadiz and Islands expeditions. One of Essex's knights, he had also been rewarded for his services with the keepership of St. Andrew's Castle in Hampshire — the Calshot where the Danvers party had taken refuge on their flight from justice. This was in February of this year, 1598. In May it was rumoured that he and the Countess were married ; it was not so, but they were thinking of it. In September, when Sir Fulke Greville was made Treasurer of the Navy, it was thought that Harvey might be Comptroller, but he did not get the job. However, he was getting the Countess.

This added greatly to Southampton's worries this year while he was in France and in no position to stop it. For, of course, his mother's marriage to a young man of his own age and with no means of his own, might be very prejudicial to him financially. His mother was very well off, himself financially distressed. He was not on good terms with his mother — a part of his inheritance from his father, along with Thomas Dymoke, his mother's old enemy, whom he trusted and liked as had his father before him. His mother, poor lady, had had plenty of reason to disapprove of his conduct, and now she much resented his affair with Elizabeth Vernon and his secret marriage. There was plenty to go into on both sides, and both resorted to Essex as arbiter between them.

On her son's twenty-fifth birthday, 6 October 1598, the Countess replied to Essex's overture. Evidently he had made a plea on behalf of his kinswoman, the new Countess. The Countess Senior, as she signed herself, would willingly receive Essex at the Savoy when he came to town and hear what he had to say on behalf of the offending couple. 'In the mean, your kinswoman shall find your favour in me, and more should, if she were not his that never was kind to me ; but in this matter and manner, unnatural, undutiful, God grant not unfaithful. To your lordship's heart I leave it, that is a parent, but I hope shall never find that I have felt for ever and ever.' [21]

Southampton's mother was an emotional woman ; but she was a charming one and had a good heart. This was the worst thing anyone had yet had to say about her son — evidently he had inherited something of his father's disaccord with the mother. This may well have contributed something to the ambivalence of his make-up, for on the other side he had inherited her looks and charm.

In this complex personal negotiation between mother and son Essex enlisted the help of the courtly, insinuating, artful Lord Henry Howard. A son of Elizabeth's cousin, the executed Duke of Norfolk, Lord Henry was immensely aristocratic, learned, devious, secretive. A crypto-Catholic and a crypto-homosexual, religious-minded and well-read in the Church Fathers, he had been a partisan of Mary Stuart ; he had his great days to come, as a leading minister of James I, under whose lax ways he made a vast fortune, ruined Sir Walter Ralegh and destroyed Sir Thomas Overbury. The only thing to be said for this odious man must be that he was profoundly conservative and sincerely hated the new deal in England and everything it stood for. This honest broker took up the negotiation with relish.

Essex reported to Southampton that he had spoken with his mother in the Privy Chamber : 'the apartment served not for long conference or for private . . . but she saith she told the Queen enough to make her see that I and she were kind one to the other'.[22] Essex enclosed Lord Henry's characteristically long and intricate account of the affair, which this unemployed busybody — the Queen had no use for him — evidently enjoyed. Here are the main points out of a mass of involved verbiage. 'Upon acquainting her with your demand of me . . . whether she were married, as many thought, or at the very point of marriage, as some gave out, she did assure me on her honour that the knot of marriage was yet to tie — although she would be stinted at no certain time, but ever reserve her own liberty to dispose of herself when and where it pleased her.' Lord Henry had passed on Essex's advice 'not to give any scandal to the world by matching during her son's disgrace ; for the greater pause and leisure she took in the last match, the greater hazard she would run in this by marrying unseasonably'.[23]

The Countess stood up for her choice of Sir William Harvey, and said that 'her son could take no just exception to the party, who had been more plain with her in his defence during this time of separation and unkindness than any man alive'. She went over to the offensive in the matter of her son's marriage, as to which she had been kept completely in the dark. But she promised that Sir William Harvey would speak with Essex before the marriage took place.

Lord Henry had been successful: he had wormed out everything. He was very good at that.

Next, Essex saw the Countess on her son's return and 'told her how sad I found you, how the grounds of it were her un-kindness, the discomfort and discontentment you took in her marriage, and scorn that Sir William Harvey should think to offer any scorn to you'. Essex aligned himself with her son and his point of view : 'I made her see what a certain pillar and bulk she had to lean to in having so noble and worthy a son, what a fire would be kindled in her house if she did not satisfy you, and what need she was like to have of you, if she divide herself from you how dangerous and miserable a life she was like to lead. I do assure myself this has taken great impression.'

Next day, 5 November, Sir William Harvey came to call on Essex, who told him plainly that a certain mischief would fall upon Southampton by the match. Harvey replied, with point, that that was no argument against himself, 'for, if my lady should not marry him, she might marry another, and that were all one'. Essex replied that that was true enough, yet any such marriage was disadvantageous to the son, 'and you could not love him that were cause of it'. Essex added that Harvey had not shown proper respect to Southampton since his return, and did not seem to care whether he were angry or pleased. Harvey replied that he had been going to visit Southampton, but that the Countess bade him to wait awhile. He denied having spoken disrespectfully of Southampton, but 'when he was threatened . . . they that were angry without cause must be pleased without amends'. It must be allowed that this retort was as effective as it was eloquent.

Nevertheless, more reasonable than her son, the Countess postponed her marriage ; during the interval, in drawing up the marriage-settlements, her son's objections could be met, his apprehensions allayed.

At the moment of Southampton's return his brother-in-law, Thomas Arundell, was in trouble again. We hear from John Chamberlain that 'the Imperial Count Arundell is in keeping of Dr. Herbert, on account of communications had with Stanley on his arrival'.[24] This John Stanley had arrived from Spain, with one or two other scoundrels, with a madcap scheme for poisoning the pommel of the Queen's saddle, and with this they managed to besmirch the name of Father Henry Walpole (who had been executed in 1595) and other Jesuits. In December Arundell wrote to Cecil that his father was dying, and complained that he was leaving him no interest in land or goods but only the use of the estate for life, 'and that so limited by a lease he has made to feoffees that he does not see how he may be able to pay his debts'.[25] With his lack of confidence in his son, it is perhaps not surprising that Sir Matthew was leaving unduly large sums for public purposes, for making a causeway about Sherborne, and an exorbitant sum to the poor.

At last the Imperial Count was able to report, in his own inimitable terms, that his parent was dead. 'My most worthy, most dear father is dead, whose continual prayers, whose last breath ending in the name of Jesus may sufficiently proclaim the mercy that our Saviour showed him, and the eternal state of bliss wherein He hath now placed him.' More to the point, 'his love and care towards his friends and country, his many legacies and his excessive largesse bequeathed to the poor, do manifestly declare'.[26] To her Majesty he bequeathed 'two presents, of little worth, yet the best (as he thought) that his present state afforded : the one a little table carpet wrought in

China, a thing well esteemed of himself yet unworthy of so high a Majesty ; the other my more unworthy self, both which being to be recommended to the intercession of yourself his dearest friend, shall ere long be brought to your hands'. And so on for pages : one sees what a fool Thomas Arundell was, and expects that the busy Secretary had no compunction in denying him his door when he turned up.

Nothing would choke off the Imperial Count. On the last day of the year he is again writing to Cecil : 'Mr. Donnington, sometime servant to my lord of Southampton, in his return from Spain was here this present Sunday, whom myself refused to speak withal or to see. Though this might seem sufficient for my clearing, yet bearing an ever careful zeal to the safety of her Majesty's sacred person, and not knowing how far the poison of the Spanish practices may have infected his otherwise not unhonest disposition, I thought good to inform you hereof. . . . I hope that my well-meaning to my sovereign shall not get me the hateful name of a promoter.' [27]

After his own escapes and escapades perhaps it was only natural that he should thus hope to ingratiate himself ; but in so far as it might reflect on his brother-in-law, it was not very nice of him.

In 1598 John Florio produced his Italian dictionary, *A World of Words*, admirable for its scholarship — the best Italian dictionary to date — and to us fascinating for its Elizabethan English, the light it throws on their world. [28] Under *framponato*, for instance, it tells us 'a kind of high horse-shoe, such as the brewers' horses use in London'; under *arrochiare* — 'to tell incredible tales, as we say to lie for the whetstone'. *Zuccata*, we learn, is 'a meat made of pompions or gourds. Also a flim-flam tale, a tale without rhyme or reason, or without head or foot'; *zuccone*, 'a shaven pate, a knotted poll, a polled pate, a ninny, a dolt-head'. We see the expressiveness of the language at this moment of expansion, and can appreciate Florio as a companion to the plays of Shakespeare.

They clearly would know each other well in Southampton's service, for Florio had been in the Earl's household at least since 1594, and perhaps before. He had probably been recommended to the Earl by Burghley, who had been a good friend to Florio's father. John Florio, some twenty years older than Southampton, was his Italian tutor and taught the language to other cultivated persons among the nobility. For the book was dedicated to Southampton, along with his friend Rutland and Lucy Harington, the blue-stocking Countess of Bedford who became Donne's patron. The book was printed by Arnold Hatfield for Edward Blount, Marlowe's publisher-friend — who had in that same year brought out his *Hero and Leander*, with its touching evocation of the dead poet — 'to be sold at his shop over against the great north door of Paul's church'.

Young Rutland had returned early that year from his three years' travels abroad, during which he had spent some time in Italy ; Southampton was still abroad when the Epistle Dedicatory was written. 'In truth I acknowledge an entire debt not only of my best knowledge but of all, yea of more than I know or can, to your bounteous lordship, most noble, most virtuous and most honourable Earl of Southampton, in whose pay and patronage I have lived some years, to whom I owe and vow the years I have to live. But as to me and many more the glorious and gracious sunshine of your honour hath infused light and life, so may my lesser borrowed light, after a principal respect to your benign aspect and influence, afford some lustre to some others.'

After more of this kind of thing one respects all the more the dignity and restrained expression of Shakespeare's dedications of *Venus and Adonis* and *The Rape of Lucrece* to Southampton. But, if one has any perception, one perceives something more. Florio lived in Southampton's household as a servant, and his language is in keeping. The language of Shakespeare's dedications is more dignified, but also more familiar and affectionate. And that is quite right, for the Southampton of the public dedications was the young man of the Sonnets ; and also, though Shakespeare was on terms of affection with him, he was only in a formal sense his patron's servant : he remained essentially, through his profession, independent.

Florio continues, 'I might make doubt lest I or mine be not now of any further use to your self-sufficiency, being at home so instructed for Italian as teaching or learning could supply that there seemed no need of travel ; and now by travel so accomplished as what wants to perfection ?' And so we come to Southampton's friend, young Rutland, who is described as 'well-entered into the tongue ere your honour entered Italy, there therein so perfected as what needeth a dictionary ?' But it is when we come to the Countess of Bedford that we feel we have heard such language before : 'your excellent ladyship (my most-most honoured, because best-best adorned Madame), who by conceited industry, or industrious conceit, in Italian as in French, in French as in Spanish, in all as in English, understood what you read, write as you read, and speak as you write' . . . and so on. Surely one hears the accents of Don Armado in *Love's Labour's Lost*, that skit on the Earl's entourage by his poet ?

Florio's friend Matthew Gwynne supplied him with three sonnets, signed Il Candido — for Gwynne is the Welsh for white. That to Southampton begins,

> Brave Earl, bright pearl of peers, peerless nobility,
> The height of arms and arts in one aspiring . . .

and continues,

> Now liv'st in travel, foreign rites inquiring . . .
> Though there your honour see what here we hear,
> And hear what here we learn at second hand . . .

From which we appreciate the gulf that separated Southampton's acknowledged poet from all the others, save only Marlowe ; while the line —

> The height of arms and arts in one aspiring —

reminds us again of Southampton's twin aspirations : to shine in action as well as in literature, in arms as in the arts.

CHAPTER VIII

Soldiering in Ireland

Two questions dominated these last years of the reign : the war in Ireland, which flared up into something approaching a national resistance movement, under the politic leadership of the great O'Neill ; and the question of the succession upon the Queen's death. These highly inflammable issues came to be interconnected, particularly through the inflammable personality of Essex, who meant to dominate both and make himself the decisive person in the English state at the take-over by King James of Scotland.

The summer of 1598 had witnessed the worst disaster to English arms that there had been in Ireland, when a force of over a thousand well-equipped troops had been cut to pieces at the Yellow Ford, near Armagh, with the loss of their commander, Marshal Bagnal. This gave the signal from Ulster, which was entirely at O'Neill's command, for the resistance to spread into Munster. It was thus that Edmund Spenser was driven from his little peel-tower at Kilcolman, put to the flames behind him, to seek refuge in Westminster, where he died of exhaustion. The same letter that tells us that at Court 'the Queen danced with the Earl of Essex upon Twelfth day', also says 'Spenser, our principal poet, coming lately out of Ireland, died at Westminster on Saturday last'.[1] On the last day of that month of January 1599 we learn further that 'Sir William Harvey's marriage with the Countess of Southampton that hath been smouldering so long comes to be published'.

The English government was gripped with a sense of crisis, and it was resolved to send the largest army that had yet been sent into Ireland — some 15,000 troops and 1,000 horse — to finish the job. But who was to be given the task and the command of these large forces? The Queen wanted Knollys or Mountjoy, the able young soldier who ultimately accomplished it. But in Council Essex made it impossible to appoint him, as too inexperienced; and he blocked the appointment of anyone else to so crucial a post, virtually the second person in the state. In the end there remained no one but himself, and he undertook the command with heavy misgivings. Ireland had been the grave of so many men's reputations; his own father had died there, worn out, while yet a young man. Later he complained that he had felt 'a natural antipathy against this service'. He made all kinds of difficulties, raised objections and brought forward new demands. In the end these were met and he had to go. By mid-March we hear, 'the Earl of Essex hath all his demands, the Queen showing herself very gracious and willing to content him. . . . The Earls of Southampton and Rutland (who hath lately married the Countess of Essex's daughter), the Lords Grey, Audley, and Cromwell do accompany him.'[2] On 27 March Essex took horse with his companions and rode through and out of the City on his way along Watling Street, 'in all which places and in the fields the people pressed exceedingly to behold him, especially in the highways, for more than four miles space, crying out saying, "God bless your lordship! God preserve your honour."'[3] In the City the skies had been calm and clear, but at Islington there suddenly arose a storm of thunder and lightning, which people took as a bad omen.

Arrived in Ireland, Essex by his own authority appointed Southampton Lord General of the Horse. Meanwhile, he had been proposed for election as a Knight of the Garter. Lord Henry Howard, who had accompanied Essex's party along the road as far as Stony Stratford, hurried to tell his young friend the tales from Court — tale-telling was his peculiar forte.

Northumberland, Worcester, and Mountjoy had spoken up for him, 'notwithstanding the Queen's special bar with injury. But there was another [he means himself] that was not afraid to run upon the pikes of some that will be thought to be very special friends of his, to show that he valued your friendship and noble virtues more than other men's caprices and partialities. But hereof you must never take notice, because I tell tales out of school and would not impart so much to any other than yourself.' ⁴ Lord Henry added, 'the Queen begins to storm exceedingly at my lord of Rutland's incorporation into Jason's fleet, and means, she says, to make him an example of contemning princes' inhibitions to all that shall come after him'. Rutland had been forbidden to go, had slipped away and was now ordered back.

Sir Henry Danvers was with Southampton, and in a cavalry charge had received a severe wound in the face ; Penelope Rich was anxious for his 'good face', so evidently he was good-looking. Southampton's women-folk were naturally anxious for him. His mother wrote in May, 'this is the third letter of mine to you, since I received from you. Though Wiseman and Tracy came from you, it made me a little doubtful of your well-doing till they did assure they left you well ; so we presume for certain you are before now in the field and some service undertaken. You may believe I carry a careful heart whilst you are in these dangers.' ⁵ It seems that Southampton's wife had preceded him along the road as far as Chartley, Essex's castle in Staffordshire, where she took up residence with his sister Penelope. The following letter would seem to have been written before he left London ; the portrait of him being painted before he went may be that with a breast-plate on, a corselet on the ground, a plumed helmet on the table beside him. There are the familiar long tresses over the left shoulder, longer than ever, with at last the light traces of a moustache on the upper lip. 'My dear ,ord and only joy of my life, being very weary come to this house with my long journey, I was very quickly healed of that pain with the reading your kind letter. . . . I most infinitely long for you, and my dear and only joy I beseech you love forever most faithfully me that everlastingly will remain your faithful and obedient wife'.[6] There follow two postscripts, which I give in the original spelling for their flavour and to catch the sound of her voice :

'Sweet my lord let your man Foulke bye me a stumiger [stomacher] of scarlet haulf a yeard brode and as long at least, lined with plush, to kepe my body warm a days which I must ride. I send you word I groe bigger and bigger every day.

I pray you remember to send wane to your dafter before you come hether that I maye sartantly hear by you howe she dos whoe next yourselfe I will ever love most, and loke that your pickter be very finly done and brot hither so soon as may be, or else I wil do nothing but chide with you when you come to me.

The promise of a son and heir is borne out by a letter from Lady Rich : 'your lordship's daughter is exceeding fair and well, and I hope by your son to win my wager'. The next letter to him is from Essex's wife, Frances — Walsingham's daughter and widow of Sir Philip Sidney : 'I do infinitely long to hear of my lord's happy proceedings against the proud rebels, which to acquaint me with, you shall do me a great favour. . . . Pray commend me to Sir Harry Danvers, and bid him take heed of the saffron smocks. I think he means not to write to any of his friends till he may write in Irish, which is more eloquent than the English.'[7] In June we learn that Southampton's wife is disappointed of her hope of having another child as yet : 'the witness you give me in your letter that you are not troubled for my not being as, I protest unto you, I infinitely desired to have been is much to my content. And though I be not now in that happy state, yet I doubt not but that in good time and for the infinite comfort of you and myself God will bless me with bearing you as many boys as your own heart desires to have. And I beseech him now and ever to preserve you from all dangers and soon to bring you perfectly well to me and, my only joy, I pray ever let me enjoy your love as I now assure myself I do, to the infinite joy and contentment of my heart.' 8

There can be no doubt that, with his good looks, his charm and good nature, Southampton had the capacity of arousing love, and in many quarters. The next we hear, however, is of a military quarrel which had unfortunate consequences for him.

Lord Grey of Wilton, who was Southampton's senior, was serving under him as Colonel of Horse. He was the son of Spenser's Lord Deputy, Arthur, Lord Grey, the bright Artegal of the *Faerie Queen*. The son inherited his father's Puritan proclivities, and improved on this with a choleric, quarrelsome temper ; he was a thoroughly unpleasant man. In a skirmish with the Irish in June, determined to act independently and win glory for himself, he 'did charge without direction' from his general. Southampton reproved him and committed him to the charge of the marshal for the night. Grey never forgave this humiliation and for the next two years pursued Southampton with challenges and insults. He really was a man of one idea and a desperado. But the political consequences were more important : Grey took Cecil's side in the faction-fighting with Essex that was dividing the English state, and later left the service in Ireland to come over with his tales. And the Queen's disapprobation of Southampton was aroused : she took offence at Essex's promotion of him as Lord General of the Horse, ordering him to displace him and appoint someone else.

Essex replied to the Council : 'that her Majesty, in the Privy Chamber at Richmond, I only being with her, showed a dislike of his having any office, I do confess. But mine answer was that, if her Majesty would revoke my commission, I would cast both myself and it at her Majesty's feet ; but if it pleased her Majesty that I should execute it, I must work with mine own instruments, and from this profession and protestation I never varied. Whereas, if I had held myself barred from yielding my lord of Southampton place and reputation someway answerable to his degree and expense, no man, I think, doth imagine that I loved him so ill as to have brought him over.' [9] We see in this Essex's intractable self-will, and he went over into the eloquence and passion into which he could always work himself up. 'Was it treason in my lord of Southampton to marry my poor kinswoman, that neither long imprisonment [he had been in the Fleet only a matter of days], nor no punishment besides that hath been usual in like cases can satisfy or appease ; or will no kind of punishment be fit for him but that which punisheth not him, but me, this army, and poor country of Ireland ?'

This letter was of course intended for the Queen's eyes, in the constant bickering between them to which his self-will led. And in fact we know, what we might have guessed, that Essex had intended to have his own way over the Queen in the matter. Before leaving he wrote to Southampton : 'of you nor of any particular friend of mine or place in the army, there hath been no mention. Which I was content to let pass, because when my commission is once passed, it will give me authority in direct words to bestow all places, and then if she quarrel with me, her wrong is the greater and my standing upon it will appear more just.' [10] As if she had not understood that perfectly ! Now she took up the pen herself and replied very much to the point, anger making her eloquent :

> For the matter of Southampton, it is strange to us that his continuance or displacing should work so great an alteration either in yourself (valuing our commandments as you ought) or in the disposition of our army, where all the commanders cannot be ignorant that we not only not allowed of your desire for him, but did expressly forbid it, and being such a one whose counsel can be of little, and experience of less, use. Yea, such a one as, were he not lately fastened to yourself by an accident, wherein for our usage of ours we deserve thanks, you would have used many of your old lively arguments against him for any such ability or commandment. It is therefore strange to us, knowing his worth by your report, and your own disposition from ourselves in that point, will dare thus to value your own pleasing in things

unnecessary, and think by your private arguments to carry for your own glory a matter wherein our pleasure to the contrary is made notorious.[11]

One hardly knows whether to admire more in this missive the political sense and experience, or the nerve of expression of the ageing woman who wrote it. One cannot mistake the accents of a real animus that had developed in her mind against Essex. When he was present in person his charm melted her heart — and he always presumed upon that to put emotional pressure on her. But when she considered his self-will, setting it up against hers, her unrivalled experience and services to the state, she could not forgive him. Essex had used the argument that Southampton's dismissal would discourage the gentlemen who had volunteered their service. This infuriated her: she regarded the suggestion as impertinent, and came back with:

And where you say further that divers or the most of the voluntary gentlemen are so discouraged thereby as they begin to desire passports and prepare to return, we cannot as yet be persuaded that the love of our service, and the duty which they owe us, have not been as strong motives to these their travails and hazards as any affection to the Earl of Southampton or any other. If it prove otherwise (which we will not so much wrong ourselves as to suspect) we shall have the less cause either to acknowledge it or reward it.

There was sarcasm, with a royal threat as a sting in the tail. What a woman! — and what a fool Essex was to oppose her: the only way was submission, co-operation, understanding. As for Southampton, she clearly had no use for him.

Actually, at this moment, the poor young man was rendering her good service to the best of his ability. At Arklow in July he was risking his life in a cavalry skirmish — 'a very brave charge given on the rebels by our horse under the leading of my lord of Southampton', Essex's secretary reports, 'where Captain Constable was hurt and Mr. Cox was slain'.[12] A number of gentlemen of quality were in the action. Southampton kept up correspondence with his friends in England and was able to inform Sir Charles Danvers that his brother's severe head-wound was on the mend. Sir Charles replied, 'I doubt not by this time you have received the verdict which has passed against you here, wherein as you will find sufficient cause of discontentment in that it is a proof of your Prince's displeasure, so have you this cause of comfort, that your greatest enemies, by the proof you have given of yourself, are forced to confess you to be more worthy of the place you hold than any that can be named, and unto your deserts and government are not able to take the least exceptions'.[13] This was a comforting testimonial.

Lord Henry Howard, however, under the familiar guise of offering consolation was able to pour oil upon the flames of resentment. 'It grieves me very much to call to mind how just cause you shall have rather to increase your complaint of wrongs offered to you without cause or colour before this come to your hand, but against that supreme force that wieldeth actions by sovereign predominance, opposition availeth not.'[14] However, as might be expected, we learn a good deal as to the inwardness of the affair from this shrewd observer : that Secretary Cecil had kindly held up the messenger bearing the Queen's injunction five days in the hope that she might relent. Secondly, 'the truth is, howsoever flaws be coloured, the main blow is not stricken at yourself. The most worthy gentleman that lives [i.e. Essex] is pierced through your side. . . . This fury began first upon the speeches between Lord Grey and your lordship, which makes men more sorry that, since right was on your side, revenge should be the reward of good consideration.'

Essex had to back down and dismiss his friend from his post as Lord General. Southampton took it in good part and went on serving as a volunteer captain of a company. No doubt Lord Grey had hoped for the post ; he did not get it. Consolatory letters arrived from Southampton's adoring wife. Lady Rich was being pressed by her difficult — and openly cuckolded

— husband to leave Chartley to join him in Essex. Lady Southampton submissively wrote her spouse for permission to accompany her : 'let me, I pray you, know your pleasure. What I shall do, which no earthly power shall make me disobey and what you dislike in this letter, I beseech you, lay not to my charge. . . .' [15] It is clear that Elizabeth was not only very much in love with her husband but also was determined to make him an obedient wife — very much in contrast with the beautiful Penelope, who lived openly with Lord Mountjoy and bore him a family of children, in addition to her horrid husband's. Elizabeth added a pleasant postscript : 'all the good news I can send you that I think will make you merry is that I read in a letter from London that Sir John Falstaff is, by his mistress Dame Pintpot, made father of a goodly miller's thumb, a boy that's all head and very little body. But this is a secret.'

From which we see at least that this creation of Southampton's poet was becoming a household word.

The Queen had no confidence in Essex, was utterly dissatisfied with his conduct of the campaign — and with every reason. Instead of marching against the main centre of resistance, native Ulster, when his army was fresh and force undiminished, he frittered his resources away by a subsidiary campaign in the south. When the Queen was expecting him in high summer to march north, he wasted time in attacking pockets of resistance around Dublin. By early September he was too late and, in spite of the reinforcements he had received, his army was in no condition to tackle the wily O'Neill in his natural fortesss.

The Queen wrote to express, bitterly, her 'expectation that you would proceed as we have directed you ; but your actions always show the contrary, though carried in such sort as we were sure to have no time to countermand them'. She passed over to sarcasm, which he could least bear. 'Before your departure no man's counsel was held sound which per-

suaded not presently [i.e. immediately] the main prosecution
in Ulster, all was nothing without that, and nothing was too
much for that.' She then recounted all that had been done for
him, the largest army ever yet sent into Ireland, the reinforcements and supplies sent over. 'Of all which courses, whoever
shall examine any of your arguments used for excuse shall find
that your own proceedings beget your difficulties. . . . If sickness of the army be the reason, why was not the action undertaken when the army was in better state ? If winter's approach,
why were the summer months of July and August lost ? If
the spring were too soon, and the summer that followed
otherwise spent ? If the harvest that succeeded were so
neglected as nothing hath been done, then surely we must conclude that none of the four quarters of the year will be in season
for you and that Council to agree of Tyrone's prosecution, for
which all our charge is intended.' [16]

This was a blow levelled at the Council in Dublin, which
Essex had gathered, with Southampton at his right hand, to
support him in the decision against undertaking an expedition
to the far north at this late date. The fact was that only a war
of attrition — such as Mountjoy ultimately carried through —
could reduce O'Neill in his impregnable Ulster fastness, and
Essex was not the man to carry through such a campaign.

With his usual bad judgment Essex now took a fatal step :
he listened to O'Neill's proposals for a parley and a truce —
extremely damaging to the English cause, after the big effort
that had been put forth. He went north with the army, and
at a ford on the Ulster border had a couple of meetings with
the wise and politic O'Neill, the only Irish adversary in the
Queen's reign to approach her in craft and statesmanship.
Essex was no match for him, but by now, driven to despera-
tion, his own intentions already bordered on treason. At the
ford in the river Lagan Essex was accompanied by Southampton, who was given the charge of keeping everyone out of
earshot. Nevertheless they were overheard — and what was
discussed with the Irish leader, a proclaimed traitor at war

against the Crown, was what should happen at the Queen's death. Essex was already in touch with James, whom he hoped to use to bring pressure on the Queen ; here in O'Neill, whose resistance he had been expressly sent to quell, was a third figure in the pattern he was forming to checkmate his sovereign.

Having accomplished nothing with all that had been done for him, Essex decided to leave his government in this unsatisfactory posture of affairs and without permission come over to cast himself at his sovereign mistress's feet. Gone were all the hopes their dramatist had expressed, in *Henry V*, of a triumphant return :

> Were now the general of our gracious empress —
> As in good time he may — from Ireland coming,
> Bringing rebellion broachèd on his sword,
> How many would the peaceful city quit
> To welcome him !

His return was very different : a bedraggled body of his personal followers, Southampton with him, posting along the roads to Westminster to surprise the Queen. It was the morning of Michaelmas Eve and the Court was at Nonsuch. At the crossing of the Thames to Lambeth it was found that Lord Grey was ahead of them, hurrying to alert Cecil what to expect. When Essex arrived he rushed up, all bemired as he was, to the Queen's bed-chamber to that famous scene with him at her feet, her with her hair about her face, not yet attired. He was kindly received ; but it was the last time she saw him. Political sense, sense of duty, asserted itself ; he was placed in the custody of the Lord Keeper, in honourable confinement, to be examined on his misconduct of his government and never again resume his place in the state.

In the absence of its owner Essex House in the Strand, with its garden going down to the Thames, was occupied early in October by the Southamptons — their own house being leased out with his estates — and Lady Rich. There was much sympathy with Essex, and his friends were becoming a faction in the state. So many of them came to express their condolences that the Queen — not far away at Whitehall — was offended, and the ladies of the family thought it prudent to withdraw into the country. 'My Lord Southampton and Lord Rutland come not to the Court ; the one doth but very seldom ; they pass the time in London [i.e. in the City] merely in going to plays every day.' [17] What plays were there for them to see ?

Well, that autumn there was a new play by Southampton's dramatist at the Globe — *Julius Caesar*, with its political theme and overtones, the wisdom of its moral, if only it had been taken notice of. A Swiss tourist describes his visit : 'after dinner . . . at about two o'clock, I went with my companions over the water, and in the thatch-roofed house saw the tragedy of the first Emperor Julius with at least fifteen characters, very well acted. At the end of the play they danced together, as is their custom, marvellously well and gracefully : two men in men's clothes and two in women's gave this performance.'[18] There was a goodly number of other new plays to choose from. At the Rose the Admiral's men were putting on *Sir John Oldcastle*, which was doubtless suggested by the Chamberlain's men's triumph with Falstaff. The Children of Paul's were playing Marston's *Histriomastix*, which so provoked Ben Jonson and began a series of exchanges between the private theatres and the public, the boys' companies and the men's. Then there were Marston's *Antonio and Mellida*, Dekker's *Old Fortunatus*, Chapman's *All Fools*, among numerous others.

On 16 October Southampton stood godfather at the christening of Essex's daughter, with Lady Cumberland and Lady Rutland as godmothers. This took place 'without much ceremony', naturally enough in the circumstances, and later we hear of Lady Essex appearing all in black at Court as a suitor on behalf of her husband. The charges that were being brought against him were not the important ones — the first being his appointment of Southampton against the Queen's express wish. The real charge against him was what he had discussed with the traitor O'Neill — the change-over at the Queen's death and how these circumstances might be controlled. These *arcana imperii* could never be made public ; so the Queen's case went by default, and the darling of the people garnered sympathy, while her treatment of him lost her some popularity in London.

Essex, like other people in adversity, found religion, and now wrote to his younger friend :

> I have ceased to be a Martha, caring about many things, and believe with Mary that one thing is needful. In the leave-taking of friends, it is a duty to try to further each other's welfare. Happiness is only to be found in the favour of God. I hope you will employ your talents to God's glory and your own honour, remembering that all is received from God and must be accounted for to him. . . . You may think this but the vapour of a prisoner, and believe I would do as before, if my fetters were taken away. I should be an apostate, hypocrite, and atheist, if I did. I was long a slave to the world, in spite of many callings of grace, and therefore recognise God's justice in calling me to the marriage-feast and afflicting me in this world to give me joy in another. I wish you the joy of unfeigned conversion. I was only called upon by divines, but your lordship now has the call of one who knows the end of all this world's contentments. I have explained the way of salvation, and will never go to sleep nor wake without prayer for you.[19]

We shall see what little good, alas, these considerations did either of them. On the other hand, to quote at length what these people wrote, in their diverse situations of grief or passion, repentance or mere hysteria, enables us to put our hand on their pulse, to feel the very rhythms of their feeling, so long since stilled.

Southampton was bent not on conversion but on action. The Queen was determined that Mountjoy should take Essex's place in Ireland, and her choice turned out the right one. The rumour was that Southampton would have charge of a company of horse with two hundred foot. Upon this Lord Grey

148

PALACE HOUSE, BEAULIEU

PLACE HOUSE, TITCHFIELD ABBEY

SIR EDWIN SANDYS

SOUTHAMPTON'S
GRANDFATHER:
THE FIRST EARL
From Palace House, Beaulieu

QUEEN ELIZABETH I
*From the portrait
at Corsham Court*

KING JAMES I
*From the National Gallery
of Scotland*

SOUTHAMPTON'S WIFE:
ELIZABETH VERNON
From Boughton House

SOUTHAMPTON IN
THE TOWER
From Boughton House

THE EARL OF ESSEX
From Woburn Abbey

SOUTHAMPTON AS A SOLDIER
From Welbeck Abbey

TO THE RIGHT HONORABLE
Henrie VVriothefley, Earle of Southampton,
and Baron of Titchfield.

Ight Honourable, I know not how I shall offend in dedicating my vnpolisht lines to your Lordship, nor how the worlde vvill cenfure mee for choofing fo ftrong a proppe to fupport fo vveake a burthen, onelye if your Honour feeme but pleafed, I ac-count my felfe highly praifed, and vowe to take aduantage of all idle houres, till I haue honoured you vvith fome grauer labour. But if the firft heire of my inuention proue deformed, I fhall be forie it had fo noble a god-father : and neuer after eare fo barren a land, for feare it yeeld me ftill fo bad a harueft, I leaue it to your Honou-rable furuey, and your Honor to your hearts content, vvhich I wifh may alvvaies anfvvere your ovvne vvifh, and the vvorlds hope-full expectation.

Your Honors in all dutie,

William Shakefpeare.

TO THE RIGHT
HONOVRABLE, HENRY
VVriothefley, Earle of Southhampton,
and Baron of Titchfield.

HE loue I dedicate to your Lordfhip is without end:wher-of this Pamphlet without be-ginning is but a fuperfluous Moity. The warrant I haue of your Honourable difpofition, not the worth of my vntutord Lines makes it affured of acceptance. VVhat I haue done is yours, what I haue to doe is yours, being part in all I haue, deuoted yours. VVere my worth greater, my duety would fhew greater, meane time, as it is, it is bound to your Lordfhip; To whom I wifh long life ftill lengthned with all happineffe.

Your Lordfhips in all duety.

William Shakefpeare.

A 2

SHAKESPEARE'S DEDICATIONS
TO SOUTHAMPTON

SOUTHAMPTON AT THE PERIOD
OF THE SONNETS

From the miniature by Nicholas Hilliard

SOUTHAMPTON'S MOTHER: MARY BROWNE

From Welbeck Abbey

SOUTHAMPTON AS A BOY
From the tomb at Titchfield

THE SOUTHAMPTON TOMB
AT TITCHFIELD

— who also wanted to command the army there — sent Southampton a challenge : out of England they would be able to meet. Grey sent him some very offensive letters : 'as the chief impediment why you refused France, you alleged the Deputy's [Mountjoy's] speedy departure. He is gone, you are here, and yet I hear not of you. But to conclude all wordy disputations, worthy rather of women than of men of war', etc. — from which we see the kind of fire-eater Grey was.[20] Southampton wrote, with moderation and style, 'though I love disputation in this kind as ill as any, yet understand I so well how to maintain my right as I shall not lose the least part of it. . . . Ireland therefore is the fittest and only place I can now appoint to meet you in ; the country you know is large, and there are in it many port towns, far off from either Deputy or governor, to any of which I will not fail to come, according to our agreement.'[21]

Disappointed of his hope of the command in Ireland, Grey went into the Netherlands hoping to oust the able soldier, Sir Francis Vere, from his command there. Southampton remained on in London, hoping to kiss the Queen's hand — the importance of which was that it meant restoration to her good books, pardon for his offence. Cecil was, as always, a good friend to him, but the honour could not be obtained. Instead, the order came down from on high, that the Southamptons, Lady Leicester — the beautiful and odious, Lettice Knollys, Essex's mother, whom the Queen justly detested — and Anthony Bacon, Essex's confidential secretary, were to remove from Essex house, to which Essex was now sent in the charge of two keepers, 'and none to come to speak with him but by her Majesty's leave'. She knew, what hardly anyone else did, that his thoughts, whether religious or not, were turning to treason.

In mid-April Southampton deferred his departure a week longer, 'hoping to have access to her Majesty's presence, but it cannot be obtained'.[22] In her last years the famous and much-tried old woman was getting more autocratic than ever ; however, before Southampton left she sent him a gracious message wishing him safe going and returning. Sir Charles Danvers accompanied him along Watling Street as far as Coventry ; Sir Robert Sidney's agent reported of the young Earl, 'he is a very fine gentleman and loves you well'. Mountjoy was engaged in pressing O'Neill back into Ulster and hemming him in with his main forces at the Newry. The Lord Deputy commanded Southampton to follow him north, sending a convoy to see him through the dangerous pass of the Moyry, where O'Neill purposed to catch him. Here in June there took place a skirmish in which the Earl distinguished himself and won commendations from the Deputy : 'in the Moyry I protest he saved our honour ; for, suddenly apprehending that some of our troops began to brandle [take alarm] that being in the rear were left somewhat naked, he charged Tyrone [O'Neill] himself (being in the head of six score horse) — with some seven in his company, and by that assured our men and beat Tyrone back to musket shot'.[23] The Lord Deputy hoped that Southampton's valour and service would expiate his offence in the Queen's mind, and proposed him as governor of Connaught. Southampton wrote to Cecil, 'it is a place, I protest unto you, I am nothing greedy of, neither would I at all desire it, but in hope by that means to effect somewhat whereby to recover her Majesty's good conceit, which is my only end and all the happiness I aspire unto'.[24]

This, however, was out of the question : the Queen would never extend to him a mark of her approbation, and Cecil was able to assure the loyal (and local) Earl of Thomond that 'he should never have come under him', i.e. Southampton. In some annoyance Southampton thereupon decided to leave Ireland for the Low Countries. He wrote to Cecil, 'since I have here nothing to do but as a private man, which condition cannot afford me means to perform aught worth the thinking of, and that I do desire to spend my time so as I may best be enabled to serve her Majesty, I do intend, God willing, to go hence into the Low Countries to live the rest of this summer in the States' army, where perhaps I may see somewhat worth my pains'.[25] There Grey was now making a name for himself. At once he challenged Southampton with obvious vindictiveness : 'your coming hither includeth repentance of your former cool answers. Now neither advantage of time's peril, or your promise may be pretended. I call you to right me and your own letters.' [26]

The Queen imposed a direct prohibition upon these fighting fools. 'Her Majesty, understanding that your lordship hath withdrawn yourself out of Ireland into the Low Countries, where the Lord Grey is also at this present, because it is publicly known there is unkindness and heartburn between you and him, and that you are noblemen of valour who are fit to reserve yourselves for her Majesty's service, and not to hazard them upon private quarrels, it has pleased her Majesty, from her own mouth to give express directions unto us to command your lordship in her name (upon your allegiance) in no sort to offer, accept, or hearken to any challenge or meeting with the Lord Grey.' [27]

However, honour demanded some kind of reply to Grey. Southampton wrote, 'you are acquainted with the commandment I have received which forbids me to answer you, which, however you respect not, I must obey, and therefore do directly refuse your challenge. But because you shall not think I dare not walk alone for fear of you, I will tomorrow in the morning ride an English mile out of the ports [i.e. the gates of Middleburg], accompanied by none but this bearer, and a lackey to hold my horse who shall bear no weapons.'

Nothing seems to have transpired, and both returned, when the season's campaigning was over, to London for the winter. On 9 January of the new year, 1601, Southampton was riding alone with only a page, when outside Durham house — Sir Walter Ralegh's residence — he was set upon by Lord Grey and his attendants. Southampton defended himself until help arrived, but the poor page lost a hand in the fray. Grey was sent to the Fleet for his assault, but was soon out ; for Essex had reached the end of his tether, and was gathering his party together for an open *coup* against the state.

CHAPTER IX

The Essex Catastrophe

THE great reign ended with a tragic fiasco.

It all hinged upon the personality of Essex, gifted, appealing to people, but unstable. He had been raised, by his birth and the Queen's favour, to a position in the state beyond that which his gifts and character merited. The stepson of Leicester, the one man whom Elizabeth had really loved, she spoiled Essex both as youth and man ; the woman in her could not resist him : he was the handsome son that might have been hers. He constantly took advantage of this to bring pressure on her as ruler, to wring concessions, gifts, posts, policies out of her. And he would never back down to take a subordinate position as servant of the state, which she designed for him and which Leicester had always been prepared to accept at her hands.

In the end they got on each other's nerves, with their constant jars ; but it was Essex who was broken. The Queen retained a personal kindness for him, perhaps a last lingering hope that he might amend. Even in these final miserable months of 1600, when she, almost alone, knew that he was harbouring thoughts of treason, when one of his friends at Court interceded for him, her eyes filled with tears as she turned away and left the room. When he was ill she sent her personal physicians to him, or sent round some nourishing broth. One day in a masque at Court one of her maids of honour besought her to dance — it was young Pembroke's mistress, Mary Fitton. What character did she represent, Elizabeth asked. 'Affection', replied the girl. 'Affection!'

sighed the Queen. 'Affection is false.' And so Mary Fitton herself found before her time was up.

Elizabeth was right. At the same time as Essex was suing her all through these months with letters protesting repentance and passionate devotion, he entertained wild speeches of her to those who gained access to him. One day he said, of the ageing woman who had poured gifts and honours upon him, that 'the Queen, being now an old woman, was no less crooked in mind than she was in carcass'.

He was himself hardly in his right mind, not right in mind or body. He was ill and overstrained ; he might have been suffering from some amatory disease (it was for saying this that he had driven Dr. Lopez to his death). He was certainly in two minds — on the surface protesting love and submission, at the back of his mind plotting treason ; perhaps a touch of schizophrenia, easily passing over into hysteria. In August of the year 1599 in Ireland, a few days before going north to meet O'Neill, he had come into Southampton's chamber in Dublin Castle with a proposition to him and Sir Christopher Blount that he should land in Wales with an army of two or three thousand and march to bring pressure on the Queen. Perhaps he had Bolingbroke or Henry Tudor at the back of his distracted mind. Southampton dissuaded him from the madcap scheme. Nevertheless, when he returned from Ireland, a lot of knights and captains, officers and soldiers, came back after him — so great was his pull with military men. Sir Robert Sidney's agent had reported, 'this town is full of them, to the great discontentment of her Majesty. Most of the gallants have quitted their commands, not wishing to stay after him : so that the disorder seems greater than stands with safety.' [1]

All the discontented elements in the state were looking to Essex as their leader, and that made a large party. Queen and Cecils had held power and kept to a middle course now for forty years. A lot of people had accumulated grievances, particularly on both wings, Puritan and Catholic, particularly too among the younger generation that felt itself kept out.

Essex appealed to all these sections, to which he offered the promise of toleration and promotion. It was indeed an incoherent platform, for all their resentments and recriminations did not add up to a policy — a position as incoherent as their leader, against the central and experienced body of the English state. Unimportant in itself, it may yet appear symptomatic that Essex now that he had found religion, leaned to the Puritans, while Southampton was a Catholic.

Mountjoy himself, who came of a Catholic family — the Blounts — and was now in command of the army in Ireland, belonged to Essex's faction. When Southampton went over to join him in April 1600, he had carried letters from Essex urging Mountjoy forward with contacts with King James in Scotland and to bring his forces over into Wales. But Mountjoy was now a man with a job to carry through in Ireland; the Queen knew of his contacts but said nothing and left him to go forward with the task over which Essex had so disgracefully fallen down. By the end of August he was freed from constraint : what was he to do with his liberty ? Mountjoy and Southampton suggested that he should go abroad and wait for better times. This Essex refused to do ; in any case, he was a broken man financially, all his estate was pledged, he would find it impossible to raise the money. This was a further factor in impelling him towards more desperate courses.

That autumn Essex House was thrown open to his followers who flocked there ; so did the London citizens to hear popular Puritan divines who preached there daily. Excitement mounted in London ; people were expecting the Earl to be restored to favour, or something dramatic after Christmas. It seems that he summoned Southampton home from the Netherlands. A few indications left in the state papers tell their tale. Some followers of Southampton, the Giffords down in Hampshire, made ready their armour.[2] In mid-January 1601 Essex's steward, the Welsh swordsman, Sir Gelly Meyrick, was down at Itchell conferring with Southampton.[3] Essex was drawing his followers around him for a *coup* in early February : Sir Ferdinando Gorges was summoned up from his command at Plymouth ; Sir Charles Danvers and Sir Christopher Blount, both secret Catholics, took up their posts at Essex House. From subsequent lists of those inculpated we glimpse how extensive the support for Essex was : besides Southampton were the Earls of Rutland and Bedford, Lords Monteagle, Sandys, Cromwell, and Chandos, with numerous knights and gentlemen of family — Essex himself named some one hundred and twenty leading persons as strictly his followers who could be depended upon, apart from numerous sympathisers and the London mob who were with him.

The inner circle or 'knot', as the Elizabethan phrase was — it is the phrase for the conspirators in *Julius Caesar* — met at Drury House, Southampton's residence, in the absurd hope of averting suspicion. There their crazy plans were evolved, if that is the word. They were to make a *coup de main* on the Palace of Whitehall. Blount with his party was to hold the gates ; Sir Charles Danvers to take possession of the guard-chamber, Sir John Davies with his party possess the presence chamber. Only the two Earls, Essex and Southampton, were to penetrate into the privy chamber and the sacred presence of the Queen. And then what were they to do ? They meant to rid her of her ministers by *force majeure* and instal themselves in their places. Was it likely that this would be accomplished without opposition and without bloodshed ? So muddled were they that they do not seem to have contemplated this possibility — though Sir Christopher Blount at his execution confessed that they would have carried things to their conclusion, even to the shedding of the Queen's blood. Essex was not present at Drury House and nothing was concluded ; 'shall we resolve upon nothing then ?' said Southampton in a passion. All was left to Essex.

The Council was well-informed of what was afoot and was not letting itself be taken by surprise. It took the initiative and precipitated things by summoning Essex to its presence on

Saturday, 8 February. He refused on ground of sickness, and at once the messages went out for his supporters to gather round him. That evening there supped with him Southampton, Blount, Sir Charles Danvers, Sir Robert Vernon, and Lady Rich, the beautiful bitch who had all the while been egging him on. That noon Blount had dined at a tavern with Monteagle, Sir Charles Percy, and other Essex partisans. After dinner they crossed the Thames to the Globe theatre, to see *Richard II* and his 'deposing and killing'. Shakespeare's fellow, Augustine Phillips, afterwards deposed that they had not intended to play this play, 'as being so old and so long out of use that they should have a small company at it'.[4] But Monteagle and Percy had promised the players 40s. more to put on this play, with its scenes of rebellion and the deposition of a monarch.

Next morning, Sunday, the Council sent a deputation of its members to call Essex to account. They were shrewdly chosen — one recognises Robert Cecil's deft touch; for Knollys was Essex's uncle, Worcester a relative, Lord Keeper Egerton and Lord Chief Justice Popham 'ever my best friends', as Essex admitted. Essex House and its courtyards were now thronged with armed men, and the councillors were in some danger. Essex took them into the house, but proceeded to lock them in as hostages, while he and Southampton marched out with their following to raise the City. Lord Chandos took the opportunity to sneak away, muffling his face in his cloak (again, like the conspirators in *Julius Caesar*). The two Earls rode up Ludgate Hill and along Cheapside, to make for the house of Sheriff Smyth, whom Essex expected to call out the City apprentices for him. Instead of that, Cecil had sent timely warning to the Lord Mayor to call out the trained bands and had had Essex proclaimed throughout the City as a traitor. In the disciplined English state this was fatal — quite unlike Paris which the Duke of Guise had had at his disposition against his King. When Essex tried to make his way down Ludgate Hill again, he found it was barred and chained, and his company was repulsed. There was no hope of getting through to Whitehall, which in any case had been barricaded. With difficulty, and with a diminished following, he managed to regain the shelter of Essex House — to find that his hostages, the councillors, had been released by Sir Ferdinando Gorges, hoping to work his passage from the wreck.

As the February evening closed in so the government forces closed in on Essex House ; they were under the command of the Lord Admiral, while Lord Grey at last had his heart's desire as General of the Horse, Cecil's brother, Burghley, General of the Foot. Sir Robert Sidney gained possession of the gardens, Burghley of the courtyard, where a couple of soldiers were slain and a footman of Southampton's. Essex's following fortified themselves within the house. When the Lord Admiral sent Sidney to summon them to surrender, Southampton came out on the leads to parley with his cousin. The line he held was the regular one Essex had been putting forth and was to maintain for the rest of his brief days — that his life was in danger from 'the atheists and caterpillars of the commonwealth' around the Queen — this meant Ralegh and his friends — from whom they sought to deliver her. Southampton tried to make conditions for their surrender, and expostulated with his cousin — and Essex's brother-in-law — that they had no traitorous intentions. To this Sidney replied that the Lord Admiral was sending for ordnance and would blow the house up. Upon this they surrendered, Essex, with his usual gallantry, requesting that all the punishment might rest on his shoulders and the others diminished, who had entered into accord with him only out of friendship or as servants to their lord. Southampton requested that 'things doubtfully said or done might be construed to the best, which the Lord Admiral said should be done'.[5]

The Earls were then taken into custody and across the water to Lambeth for the night, since it was too late to shoot London Bridge. Shortly after they were sent down river to the Tower. It had been a futile demonstration rather than a rebellion. Nevertheless, there now remained to pay the price.

Ten days later, 19 February 1601, the trial of the two Earls was held in Westminster Hall. It was conducted with all the panoply and ritual, and with all the stage-play effects, of those solemn scenes of a Tudor trial for high treason. A large court was railed off in the sounding spaces of that raftered hall, where twenty-five peers under Lord Treasurer Buckhurst sat with the judges in judgment upon their fellow peers. There were the seven serjeants-at-arms with their maces, Buckhurst as Lord High Steward under a canopy of state, Sir Walter Ralegh as Captain of the Guard with forty of the Queen's Guard in attendance. Then the officials of the Tower brought the two Earls before the bar, 'the gentleman-porter with the axe standing before them, with the axe's edge from them'.[6] With the stateliness of the time the two Earls kissed one another's hands and embraced each other. The trial went forward.

We do not need to go into the exchanges back and forth in detail : more helpful to summarise in the words of an intelligent reporter, John Chamberlain, what it added up to. 'The only matters objected were his [Essex's] practice to surprise the Court, his coming in arms into London to raise rebellion, and the defending his house against the Queen's forces. To the two latter he answered that he was driven for safety of his life, to the former that it was a matter only in consultation and not resolved upon, and if it had taken effect it was only to prostrate himself at her Majesty's feet, and there manifest such matters against his enemies as should make them odious and remove them from about her person, and recall him to her former favour.'[7] We notice already that it was essentially Essex's trial, himself the central figure, with Southampton as accessory. When Ralegh was sworn, Essex said, 'What booteth it to swear the fox' ; when Lord Grey's name was called, Essex 'laughed upon the Earl of Southampton and jogged his sleeve'. All day from nine till five Essex bore himself with great bravado, playing to the gallery as he had always done, constantly and loudly protesting the loyalty of his intentions.

The impression they made is registered by honest John Chamberlain. Essex's defence of himself was delivered 'with such bravery and so many words that a man might easily perceive that, as he had ever lived popularly, so his chief care was to leave a good opinion in the people's minds now at parting. But the worst of all was his many and loud protestations of his faith and loyalty to the Queen and state, which no doubt caught and carried away a great part of the hearers. But I cannot be so easily led to believe protestations, though never so deep, against manifest proof. . . . At his coming to the bar his countenance was somewhat unsettled, but after he was once in, I assure you I never saw any go through with such boldness and show of resolution and contempt of death. But whether this courage were borrowed and put on for the time, or natural, it were hard to judge.'

The trial, dramatic enough in itself, was made notable by its unexpected and ironical confrontations. Essex's insinuations against Cecil's loyalty, that he was intriguing for a peace with Spain, gave him the chance to step forward from a private closet into the light of the public scene and make an eloquent justification of himself that was also a bid for popular sympathy. Francis Bacon, formerly Essex's protégé and adviser, had at last worked his passage to the government side and was able to make the case against his old leader : 'my lord, I spent more hours to make you a good subject than upon any man in the world besides'. No one loved Francis Bacon the more for this. Sir Ferdinando Gorges let his leader down once more by giving evidence for the Crown against him at one point. The rats were leaving a sunk cause.

Not so Southampton. The young man stood up well to the day's ordeal ; it was natural enough that he should plead that he had been led into the affair not by treasonable intent but by affection for his friend. Chamberlain reports, 'the Earl of

Southampton spake very well, but methought too much — as well as the other — and, as a man that would fain live, pleaded hard to acquit himself. But all in vain, for it could not be ; whereupon he descended to entreaty and moved great commiseration. And though he were generally well liked, yet methought he was somewhat too low and submiss, and seemed too loth to die before a proud enemy.' Southampton also had his revelation of the falseness of friends, for young Rutland testified against him as 'a persuader and inviter of my lord of Essex to these actions. He wrongeth me exceedingly ; for he was never the man that saw me once discontented.' Life has these surprises for one from friends ; Southampton was learning.

The trial was a fair one, in the terms of those days — much fairer than that accorded to Ralegh and Lord Grey a couple of years later, at a turn in fortune's wheel. There was no hope that Essex and Southampton would avoid condemnation to death ; at their sentencing, slowly and ceremoniously the edge of the executioner's axe was turned towards them. That night Essex's Puritan divine, Ashton, effected what all the peers and judges had not been able to do : in the silence of the Tower he broke Essex's nerve. To the councillors who were summoned to hear his confession he confided, 'yesterday at the bar, like a most sinful wretch, with countenance and words I imagined all falsehood. . . . I am the greatest, the most vilest and most unthankful traitor that has ever been in the land'.[8] He went further : he was ready to accuse his faithful secretary Cuffe — ambitious don that he was — of instigating his actions. (When Cuffe came to die, this commoner showed a better spirit and that he was made of sterner stuff.) Essex went on to blame his friends, not sparing his own sister Penelope or, himself become virtuous, her relations with Mountjoy. 'Would your lordship,' wrote the Lord Admiral to Mountjoy, 'have thought this weakness and this unnaturalness in this man ?'

For all his appeal to the populace Essex was not of the stuff of which real leaders are made.

However, he would not sue for mercy to the Queen, and that decided his fate. Alive, he was a danger to the state, and the old woman knew her duty, though it broke her heart. On 25 February he was led out to his execution in a courtyard of the Tower — Ralegh, in charge of the Guard, looking down on the scene from a window. No doubt the tramp of feet, the noises accompanying an execution, the sudden stillness as the executioner held up the head of a traitor, penetrated to the chamber of another condemned man within. What would become of him ?

Essex was not the only one to die. His confidential servants, the spirited Cuffe, and the horrid Sir Gelly Meyrick, his steward, were hanged, drawn and quartered at Tyburn. On the scaffold Cuffe said bravely, 'I am here adjudged to die for plotting a plot never acted, for acting an act never plotted. . . . Greatness will have the victory.' [9] Of those who had plotted at Drury House, Essex's stepfather, Sir Christopher Blount and Sir Charles Danvers, were beheaded like gentlemen on Tower Hill. Immense fines were imposed on the rich peers who were inculpated, though these were subsequently mitigated. Others served terms of imprisonment. Abroad it was held that England had given a notable example of bloodiness in punishing subversion ; but it was not long before Henry of Navarre's favourite, Biron, went the way of Essex.

From the examinations and confessions of prisoners we derive a few more touches. We learn that Essex himself advised Southampton to make a complete submission. It weighed in the younger man's favour that he had not consented to Essex's project of landing with part of his army in Wales and marching on London. Of this Sir Christopher Blount was a witness, that highly masculine person, 'who, the world knows, never loved me'.[10] On the other hand, there was a professional soldier, Captain Piers Edmonds, whom Essex made much of and took him riding in his coach with him. He had been made Corporal-General of the Horse under

Southampton in Ireland, and according to one witness, 'ate and drank at his table and lay in his tent. The Earl of Southampton would cull and hug him in his arms and play wantonly with him.'¹¹ Evidently there were consolations for service in the bogs.

This did not mean that Southampton was not attached to his wife — she was the only woman we hear of in his life, after the brief affair with the dark lady of the Sonnets. After the disastrous Sunday of 9 February — the rebellion *unius diei* as the Queen contemptuously called it — Southampton wrote a love-letter to prepare and console his wife for ill news. 'Sweet heart, I doubt not but you shall hear, ere my letter come to you, of the misfortune of your friends. Be not too apprehensive of it, for God's will must be done and what is allotted to us by destiny cannot be avoided. Believe that in this time there is nothing can so much comfort me as to think you are well and take patiently what hath happened, and, contrariwise, I shall live in torment if I find you vexed for my cause. Doubt not but that I shall do well, and please yourself with the assurance that I shall ever remain your affectionate husband.' ¹²

But Southampton was condemned to death. At once his wife and mother sued to Cecil to intercede with the Queen for mercy. The wife wrote distractedly beseeching him 'by whatsoever is dearest unto you ... to be my means unto her sacred Majesty that I may by her divine self be permitted to come to prostrate myself at her feet, to beg for mercy for my lord'.¹³ It is not to be supposed that the Queen wanted to see her former maid of honour at such a moment. Southampton's mother, no less distracted, wrote more to the point. 'God of heaven knows I can scarce hold my hand steady to write, and less hold steady in my heart how to write, only for what I know, which is to pray mercy to my miserable son. ... It appeared to me many times his earnest desire to recover her Majesty's favour, his doleful discontented behaviour when he could not obtain it, how apt despair made him at length to receive evil counsel and follow such company. I rather fear it than know certainly what bewitched him that he should not know of practice and conspiracy before the execution of it. . . .' Confused as this reads, poor lady, it summed up her son's course fairly well. Since the age of 18 he had followed Essex's star, 'bewitched' as his mother said, beglamoured as we might say. And the people of England with him — for there was a generosity about the personality of Essex that was wanting to wiser heads. The people long lamented him, and made the last months of the reign sad, singing about the streets :

> Sweet England's pride is gone,
> Well-a-day, well-a-day . . .

Or,

> All ye that cry Ohone, Ohone,
>   Come now and sing O Lord with me.
> For why ? Our Jewel is from us gone,
>   The valiant knight of chivalry.

Everybody was sorry for Southampton. We have seen something of this in the favourable impression he had made at his trial. He had made no attempt to turn round on his leader, or blame him, unlike Bacon or Gorges. His youth, or the impression he gave of youth — for he was no longer so young — made its appeal. Nowadays we should describe it as delayed adolescence ; what he now had to endure made a man of him. Nevertheless, not only the charm came through, but a certain nobility of spirit which Shakespeare had glimpsed in the youth and which was borne out later by the man.

The day after Essex's execution Cecil wrote a long account of these events to Mountjoy, Lord Deputy of Ireland — all very sedate and discreet, for the now all-powerful Secretary knew well how far Mountjoy had gone along the road with Essex. Like everything of Cecil's, it was a clever communication, making things easy for Mountjoy, since Cecil himself had cause for grief in the incrimination of Sir Henry Neville 'as he married my cousin german'.[14] And, 'I grieve for the young Earl of Southampton, who was drawn in merely for love of Essex ; but as most of the conspiracies were at Drury house, and he always chief, it will be hard to save him. Yet I despair not, he being penitent and the Queen merciful.' At the end of another month, 'I hope, seeing her Majesty has so satisfied justice in the execution of the principal conspirators, the Earl of Southampton shall be spared'.[15] It seems that there was almost a conspiracy between the Queen and Cecil to save Southampton, for had he not been a 'principal conspirator' ? Cecil argued that 'the poor young Earl . . . hath been drawn into this action', and that of 'those that would deal for him . . . I protest to God I am one as far as I dare'.[16]

The Queen, however, would not want to extinguish a peerage, and as yet Southampton had no heir. At Lady Day a correspondent reported, 'there were some looking for the Earl of Southampton this morning on Tower Hill, but it is otherwise, and so hoped'. Tobie Mathew, well-informed as usual, was able to opine, 'the Earl of Southampton is almost safe' ; and so it turned out. Southampton's life had really been saved by Cecil. Cecil emerged from this desperate challenge to the authority of the state, as well as to good sense, to pilot the country smoothly through the juncture between the last of the Tudors and the first of the Stuarts, the union of the two kingdoms that had been the objective of Tudor policy for the past century. Naturally his elevation made him the target of many jealousies, of which a clever and sensitive man was well aware — 'I that know so well the infinite injuries [i.e. insults] which the envy of this time hath often cast upon me' . . . he had grown well-nigh 'desperate of the constancy of any worthy man's love or friendship'.[17]

Nevertheless, so long as the Queen lived Southampton remained a close prisoner in the Tower. He was a condemned man, a dead man in the law — the documents refer to him as 'the late Earl'. He was closely attended by a keeper, Captain Hart, who found his 'long continuance in this manner' little better than being a prisoner himself and petitioned to be free of it. Southampton was already a sufferer from the 'quartern

ague' — periodic bouts of fever, probably malarial — and in
March had to be attended by his doctor, the celebrated Dr.
Paddy, for 'a swelling in his legs and other parts'.[18] In August,
in that foetid atmosphere, when plague was apt to appear, his
sickness grew worse. He petitioned that he might see his
mother and the other trustees of his little daughter, in hope to
obtain the Queen's favour 'towards his child, from whom his
great offence hath taken all which otherwise should descend
unto her'.[19] This was granted, though, it was made clear,
more at his mother's suit than his own. In October he was no
better, but 'grown very sickly'; in consideration of this the
Queen was pleased that 'for his comfort the Countess his wife
shall be permitted to have access unto him . . . at convenient
times'.[20]

The Earl's lodging in the Tower was next the Queen's
gallery, the east end of which was partitioned off to make a
withdrawing chamber for him, in addition to his bedchamber.
A well-known portrait of him, of which there are several
copies, was painted of him in the Tower. There is the familiar
long countenance, with the grey-blue eyes and arched eyebrows, looking paler and sadder now. The fair moustache
has grown, though the beard is still only beginning; the long
locks fall down on both shoulders. He is wearing a dark
cloak in the fold of which his left arm rests; the right hand,
gloved, carries the other glove, both embroidered with love-
knots. In the background is a gallery-window, its diamond
panes somewhat cracked; a window-seat and on the sill above
a finely bound book with the Wriothesley arms embossed
upon it. Behind the book sits the Earl's companion, a black-
and-white cat, head turned pertly, bright eyes watching the
painter. There were many rats in the Tower.

Southampton had plenty of time to read and reflect, before
he emerged a wiser, if not sadder, man.

Naturally books were not dedicated to a condemned person.
The last dedication to him had been made by Edward Blount,

Marlowe's friend and publisher, of a translation, *The History of the Uniting of Portugal to Castile*, in 1600. Blount writes evidently from some acquaintance with Southampton : 'in such proper and plain language as a most humble and affectionate duty can speak, I do here offer up on the altar of my heart the first-fruits of my long growing endeavours ; which, with much constancy and confidence I have cherished, only waiting this happy opportunity to make them manifest to your lordship. . . . Your honour's patronage is the only object I aim at ; and were the worthiness of this history I present such as might warrant me an election out of a world of nobility, I would still pursue the happiness of my first choice, which has since been confirmed to me by my respected friend the translator, a gentleman most sincerely devoted to your honour.'

Two years before, in 1598, Blount had published Marlowe's unfinished *Hero and Leander*, with a dedication in terms that make it clear that Marlowe was loved by his friends : 'we think not ourselves discharged of the duty we owe to our friend when we have brought the breathless body to the earth. For, albeit the eye there taketh his ever farewell of that beloved object, yet the impression of the man that hath been dear unto us, living an afterlife in our memory, there putteth us in mind of farther obsequies due unto the deceased.' This publication brought Marlowe vividly back to Shakespeare's mind — though in a sense Marlowe never ceased to live on in his memory, for there is no other contemporary poet whose phrases are so frequently echoed by him from first to last. In the play that he was writing in this year, *As You Like It*, there comes Shakespeare's only reference to a contemporary throughout his plays :

> Dead shepherd, now I find thy saw of might :
> 'Who ever loved that loved not at first sight ?'

And that it was *Hero and Leander* that set going these echoes from the past we can tell from the reference, 'Leander, he would have lived many a fair year, though Hero had turned nun, if it had not been for a hot midsummernight. For, good youth, he went but forth to wash him in the Hellespont and, being taken with the cramp, was drowned ; and the foolish chroniclers of that age found it was Hero of Sestos. But these are all lies : men have died from time to time, and worms have eaten them — but not for love.' It is a good joke, but there is also disillusionment in it. Shakespeare had reason to remember.

We have seen that there are flecks of Essex in Shakespeare's Bolingbroke, notably in his careful cult of popularity with the mob, and a direct expression of a hope of Essex's triumphant return from Ireland in *Henry V*. And there are more suggestions of contemporary circumstances in the plays than has been altogether realised. That this was so was understood quite well at the time from the insistence of the authorities that the deposition scene in *Richard II* should be omitted from the printing of the play in 1597, while all references to the deposition had to be left out of the *Henry IV* quartos until after James's safe accession. Queen and conspirators alike were aware of the suggestions given and taken from the public stage and the scene of public affairs.

It is indeed not likely that the most sensitive register of the age should fail to register, however discreetly and indirectly, the moods and experiences of the time. Something of Essex is reflected again in *Hamlet*, written in just this year of Essex's disgrace and occlusion, his eclipse and fall in this time of both solar and lunar eclipses to jar people's nerves.

> How dangerous is it that this man goes loose !
> Yet must we not put the strong law on him :
> He's loved of the distracted multitude,
> Who like not in their judgment but their eyes ;
> And where 'tis so, the offender's scourge is weighed,
> But never the offence.

This had been precisely Elizabeth's dilemma in dealing with Essex after she had learned of his meditated treason in Ireland.

On the other hand, the world thought of him as

> The courtier's, soldier's, scholar's, eye, tongue, sword,
> The expectancy and rose of the fair state . . .
> The observed of all observers.

In these years of bitterness when the light for so many people had gone out, men's teeth were on edge, factions still fought and jostled for position with their eye on the Queen's death, while Southampton was in the Tower, Shakespeare wrote his bitterly disenchanted play, *Troilus and Cressida*. With Shakespeare one must not look for too close a transcription of actual circumstances — in any case the circumstances of Essex's catastrophe were too dangerous for transcription ; nevertheless this play, placed safely in classical antiquity, cuts nearer the bone than any.

It is a deeply disillusioned play, disillusionment with war — and for that there was by this time overwhelming reason — and disillusionment with love : these are its themes. The war between Greeks and Trojans is mostly described, in searing and contemptuous terms, as mere faction-fighting. The play's message is 'a plague on both your houses', 'fools on both sides' its specific words. But what gives such an edge to these reflections is the experience that it is the follies of one's own side that are least bearable — 'their fraction is more our wish than their faction. But it was a strong composure a fool could disunite !' There is something of the relationship between Essex and Southampton reflected in that of Achilles and Patroclus : particularly in their skulking in their tent together, Essex's sulky withdrawals from public life, the younger man's emotional feeling for him. Recognisable characteristics of Essex are described :

> Things small as nothing, for request's sake only,
> He makes important.

That had been always Essex's way with the Queen.

> Possessed he is with greatness
> And speaks not to himself but with a pride

That quarrels with self-breath : imagined worth
Holds in his blood such swollen and hot discourse . . .

In the end,

He is so plaguy proud that the death-tokens of it
Cry 'No recovery.'

And when the catastrophe came the consequences are as closely
observed :

'Tis certain greatness, once fallen out with fortune,
Must fall out with men too.   What the declined is
He shall as soon read in the eyes of others
As feel in his own fall.   For men, like butterflies,
Show not their mealy wings but to the summer ;
And not a man, for being simply man,
Hath any honour, but honour for those honours
That are without him — as place, riches and favour,
Prizes of accident as oft as merit ;
Which, when they fall, as being slippery standers,
The love that leaned on them as slippery too,
Doth one pluck down another and together
Die in the fall.

The political sense that Shakespeare had always shown in his
plays dealing with public events, with monarchy, rebellion,
the mob, achieves in the plays of these years — particularly
with *Julius Caesar* and *Troilus and Cressida* — its most searching
and incisive analyses, in which layer upon layer of fond
illusion, sheer silliness, folly and insincerity is stripped away,
to reveal men simply as the things they are.   Yet at the heart
of human society, holding it together, understood only by
elect minds,

There is a mystery, with whom relation
Durst never meddle, in the soul of state
Which hath an operation more divine
Than breath or pen can give expressure to.

The peculiar tension that aches throughout *Troilus and Cressida*
comes from the fact that this is its author's comment on an

experience, part tragedy, part fiasco, in which his personal affiliations and affections were on one side, his intelligence on the other.

Writers write out of their experience, consciously or sub-consciously — experience illumined by imagination. *All's Well That Ends Well*, which also belongs to this sickening time — the last uneasy months of a great reign — is also a play that reflects strain. It is a curiously uncongenial play — perhaps this is why — and the strain is more personal, less public. The situation is that of a young Count, immature, adolescent, spoiled, who will not accept the obligations of his station and will not marry. The King designs a bride for him in the virtuous young woman, his doctor's daughter, to whom he is under great obligations, for she has healed him of a wellnigh fatal sickness. In the play the young Count has no redeeming qualities at all : petulant, filled with aristocratic pride, he refuses to marry. Where have we met this refusal to shoulder obligations, incurring trouble all round, before ? In the play the Count is made to marry the girl designed for him. She has the support and confidence not only of the King, not only her conspicuous virtue, but the affection and belief of the Count's mother. The Countess of Rosillion in the play is much like the Countess Shakespeare had known — wise and kind, tender and good, for all that neither husband nor son had treated her with kindness. Life had not spoiled her innate goodness of nature, such as we see it revealed in her letters to her son, her dealings with Cecil and Essex, Sir Thomas Heneage's expressed gratitude for her care of him, the Queen's confidence in her.

This was the aristocratic circle with which Shakespeare had been familiar, which he had had the fortunate chance to have had under close observation. Writers write about what they know. After these chastening experiences, from which there was so much to learn, a new note is observable in Shakespeare :

> From lowest place when virtuous things proceed,
> The place is dignified by the doer's deed.

Where great additions swell's and virtue none,
It is a dropsied honour.

And again,

Honours thrive
When rather from our acts we them derive
Than our foregoers.

This is a new emphasis. Earlier, he had perhaps been willing to take the aristocratic world on its own terms, understandably glamourised. Now he knew that there were as great fools there as anywhere else, and the more to be blamed for the sway they exercised, the responsibilities they defaulted upon. This led him back to essential human values, which nothing had led him to desert, to which no social glitter or brilliance of position had blinded him, which always remained the touchstone :

There is no shuffling, there the action lies
In his true nature.

CHAPTER X

A New Reign : the Rewards of Favour

WE have it on the authority of Dr. Johnson that 'the noblest prospect which a Scotchman ever sees, is the high road that leads him to England'. Certainly no one can ever have waited with such impatience to take that road as King James did to succeed to his inheritance on the death of the Queen. In these last two years of her life he could hardly contain himself. His ambassadors were on the way south to bring pressure in favour of Essex when he had made his premature outbreak ; Cecil had hurried on Essex's execution, and neatly took over these personal contacts with James, a private line to him. James owed his smooth and orderly accession to the English throne to Cecil more than any other man and was, within the bounds of reason, duly grateful. In the first years of the reign Cecil — supported by the Howards, with whom he allied himself, Worcester, Egerton and the moderate middle-of-the-road men — was all-powerful. But James's inclinations were with the dead Essex and his friends, a cause which also had the recommendation of being popular. Cecil tactfully sent Essex supporters to Scotland and Ireland to announce James's accession.

Privately he grieved for the Queen. Southampton's mother took this opportunity to write and console him for his loss :

I could now hate myself and sex that bars me from showing my love to you as most I would, yet as I can I desire to assure you that no alteration of time or fortune (that is far from you) can make me forget my bond to you for me and mine, who under God breathe by your means. God give him [i.e. her son] means, as I believe he hath mind, to be truly thankful to him and you. Grieve not yourself to hurt for that can not be recalled ; let it be your comfort, your own true worthiness has made you more happy, though for the present less great. All wise and honest give you due commendation for your exceeding wisdom and temper in the carriage of this great cause. God, I doubt not, will bless you and your services for that endeavour and I will remain while I have breath your true thankful friend.[1]

Already before the Queen's death Southampton had written to James for a warrant for his liberty immediately upon the news, and the last thing the King did before setting out from Holyrood was to write giving authority for Southampton's enlargement. In London, where Southampton had people's sympathies with him — while Cecil was hated for Essex's execution — men expected him to be set at liberty, while all longed to see the new King.[2] Three weeks after the Queen's death, on 10 April Southampton was freed and commanded to present himself, with Sir Henry Neville, according to their ranks — an indication that their restitution was on the way. Chamberlain reported that 'these bountiful beginnings raise all men's spirits and put them in great hopes, insomuch that not only Protestants, but Papists and Puritans, and the very poets with their idle pamphlets, promise themselves great part in his favour. So that to satisfy or please all, *hic labor hoc opus est*, and would be more than a man's work.'[3] And so James found. However, for the time, this spring-time, the month of April during which James moved south, being royally entertained all the way by his new subjects, pausing to hunt — while the press of people hurrying up the Great North Road to greet him grew ever larger — there was a feeling of euphoria all round.

A fortnight later, 25 April, Southampton and Pembroke met the King at Burghley, the immense country palace the old Lord Treasurer had built, about which he had spoken with such modest deprecation. Southampton was warmly welcomed ;

James took Essex's orphaned boy in his arms, kissed him and said that he was the son of the noblest knight the land had begotten. Sir Walter Ralegh got a very cold reception, and left on his way into conspiracy and to take Southampton's place in the Tower.

One day in June at Windsor there was a flare-up of the old quarrel between Grey and Southampton in the presence of Queen Anne.[4] She was asking Southampton why so many great men did so little for themselves at the time of Essex's rising. Southampton replied that once the Queen had been made a party against them, they were forced to yield. If the Queen had not been brought into it, none of their private enemies would have dared to oppose them. Lord Grey was standing by, at once contradicted Southampton and said that their opponents would have dealt with them. Southampton gave him the lie, and both were committed to their lodgings under guard. It was not long, however, before Grey was inculpated in the Bye Plot and brought to book. Condemned to death, along with Cobham and Ralegh, he was not executed, but spent the rest of his life in the Tower.

With this reversal of fortune all the crawlers came crawling round. Sir John Davies wrote to explain away his confession, in which he had touched Southampton. Francis Bacon wrote to him that 'I would have been very glad to have presented my humble service to your lordship by my attendance, if I could have foreseen that it should not have been unpleasing to you. And therefore, because I would commit no error, I choose to write, assuring your lordship (how credible soever it may seem to you at first) yet it is as true as a thing that God knoweth, that this great change hath wrought in me no other change towards your lordship than this, that I may safely be now that which I was truly before. And so craving no other pardon than for troubling you with this letter, I do not now begin, but continue to be, your lordship's humble and much devoted Francis Bacon.'[5]

Evidently they had known each other in the days before

Bacon passed over to Cecil's side and took part in bringing his former master to the block. This clever, shameless letter, in which the well-turned phrases do not conceal the effrontery, did not succeed in working his passage back into Southampton's favour. There is no evidence of any friendship, or even contact, between them throughout James's reign, until towards the end, when Southampton took a leading part in the Lords in bringing Lord Chancellor Bacon to book.

James dripped benefits and bounty upon his new subjects, not forgetting the press of Scots who accompanied him into the Promised Land. Among the latter was a handsome young man, James Hay, who, in addition to his looks, had the advantage of the breeding and manners (and the morals) of the French Court. He was soon made a gentleman of the bed-chamber, a convenient post for a young man on the way to becoming a prime favourite with the susceptible King, who had been starved of affection all the days of his youth. King James was not a bad man, in fact he was rather a good one — too good-natured to these predatory young men, who took advantage of him. He was also no fool, but an intelligent man of a pedantic donnish sort, whose ideas of universal peace and religious toleration were much above the barbarism of the age, or indeed of almost any age. He was very well-educated, a good Latin scholar, extremely well-read in theology in which (unlike Queen Elizabeth) he took too much interest for a sensible man : brought up a Calvinist, he always remained one. Perhaps this may be regarded as his chief intellectual diversion, for he was an intellectual. He spoke Latin and French fluently, he read but did not speak Italian. English he spoke with a broad Scots accent, which must have added to the humorous effect of what he said ; for he was witty, in a pawky way, and would frequently come out with some jest, keeping a solemn face the while. It is to be feared that the supercilious English laughed at him rather than with him ; for the *naïveté* of his vanity was unbelievable. Elizabeth's vanity had been immense, but it was perfectly self-conscious, even under control and used for her own purposes, to keep other people in their place. And she had been, above all, dignified. The English found their new king without dignity.

Even so, their curiosity led them to crowd round him wherever he appeared, and James soon tired of it — apart from his fear of assassination, for he had had many frights at the hands of his unruly Scots subjects. We learn that he 'naturally did not love to be looked on, and the formalities of state were but so many burdens to him'.[6] When assured that it was out of love that the people crowded to see his face, he said in his broad Scots, 'God's wounds! I will pull down my breeches and they shall also see my arse'. In the play that Shakespeare was writing that year, *Measure for Measure*, we have references to this, though with Elizabethan dignity and decorum :

> I love the people,

says the Duke,

> But do not like to stage me to their eyes ;
> Though it do well, I do not relish well
> Their loud applause and Aves vehement.

And again :

> The general subject to a well-wished king
> Quit their own part, and in obsequious fondness
> Crowd to his presence, where their untaught love
> Must needs appear offence.

Thus it was that the King kept away as much as possible from the capital and roamed round the country giving himself up to his passion for hunting. This added to the difficulties of government and made much more work for Cecil, who often regretted the easy despatch of business by simply going in to the old Queen. 'I wish I waited now in her Presence Chamber', he wrote, 'with ease at my food and rest in my bed. I am pushed from the shore of comfort and know not where the winds and waves of a Court will bear me. . . . In trouble, hurrying, feigning, suing and such-like matters, I now rest,

your true friend, R. Cecil.' [7] However, it had the advantage
of keeping James out of the way, while Cecil got on with the
business of governing the country. From James's point of
view, too, this had some advantages, for remaining so much at
Newmarket or Royston 'he might enjoy his favourite with
more privacy' ; Weldon adds that he was always best away
from Queen Anne, a kind-hearted, but silly and meddling
creature.[8] The truth was that James did not like women and
did not enjoy their company. The son of Mary Stuart and
poor Darnley, he had had a miserable childhood and youth ;
now, having come into his inheritance, he was out to enjoy
himself. It is difficult for politicians to enjoy themselves : he
ended up a sad, broken, and pathetic man.

In these earlier years of general euphoria what did the
English courtiers who were near him see ?

A man of middle height with his clothes quilted and stuffed
out, his doublets for proof against stiletto blows. He had large
sad intelligent eyes, for ever roving after any stranger who
came into his presence — some were put out of countenance
by this. His beard was thin and straggly, 'his tongue too large
for his mouth, which ever made him drink very uncomely, as
if eating his drink. . . . His skin was as soft as taffeta sarsenet,
which felt so because he never washed his hands, only washed
his fingers' ends slightly with the wet end of a napkin. His
legs were very weak . . . he was not able to stand at seven years
of age ; that weakness made him ever leaning on other men's
shoulders.' [9] He shambled about the room, 'his fingers ever
in that walk fiddling about his cod-piece'. He was very careless about his dress, hating to change his suits. What a contrast
all this was with the pomp, the panache and panoply of the late
Queen! One can imagine what the English thought. This
was the Jacobean age.

The new age brought its rewards for those who had been
out of favour in the old, and they responded in kind. Lord
Henry Howard, who had been Mary Stuart's man when

young, and had wormed his way into James's confidence in these last years — they had several things in common — saw the sun at last rise in his favour. Nothing but this would have made him conform even outwardly to the established Church. It was noticed that in the last illness of his cousin the Queen, he would rush from the room when her chaplain began to read the prayers, as if it were a conjuration of a spirit.[10] Now he went to church with the King and received the rewards of conformity : he shortly was made a Privy Councillor, became one of the inner governing circle and was created Earl of Northampton.[11] Southampton, too, conformed — it is obvious that his Catholicism had never meant as much to him as to his stupid father. He, too, began to taste the rewards of sense. He received a special pardon, with restoration of all his lands in May, 1603 ; in June he was nominated a Knight of the Garter, and next month installed at Windsor.[12] In July he was made Keeper of the Isle of Wight for life, a very pleasant domain with its castle at Carisbrooke to inhabit and a generous provision to maintain state in the island. In August he got the splendid grant of the lucrative farm of sweet wines — the monopoly of their importation, which brought in a large surplus of some £2,000 a year over the rent he paid for it. This generous grant had been held before by Essex and was his chief source of income ; it was its ending that had precipitated his affairs into chaos and himself into making a desperate bid to reverse his fortune. Now Southampton got it : it was a handsome mark of favour and provided him with the means to maintain some state in his turn.

Nor was Southampton's mother forgotten. As Sir Thomas Heneage's executor she had paid off his large arrears, some £13,000, to the Crown ; in return for which she was assured £600 a year from Heneage's daughter and heir, and now was granted a free gift of £600 from the Exchequer. The Countess's husband, Sir William Harvey, already one of the Gentleman Pensioners attending on the sovereign, got the profitable office of Remembrancer of the First Fruits, i.e. of the first year's value of benefices in the appointment of the Crown, and so could relinquish his keepership of Calshot castle.[13] That July there was a creation of peers in the great hall at Hampton Court ; among Essex's old following Mountjoy — who had now completed the subjugation of Ulster — was made Earl of Devonshire and Sir Henry Danvers created a peer. Southampton was created anew as Earl, since his title had been extinguished by his attainder.

At the same time he got the privilege of the entrée to the Privy Chamber, which might portend even better things, perhaps even the status of a favourite. However, one of the Herbert brothers was ahead of him in the King's affections : James was always fond of Philip, Earl of Montgomery, not only on account of his handsome looks but because he shared the King's mania for hunting. In December Southampton got a warrant as keeper of the king's game in the northern parts of Hampshire. All these things were adding up. With so many good things going the frustrated Count of the Holy Roman Empire bethought him of buying a barony. Thomas Arundell wrote to cousin Cecil that 'the fear which he had to be thought to buy a barony has been the special cause why he has this long absented himself from Court ; but the report of such traffic was never more bruited, and never more sought for, than at present'. He understood from Southampton Cecil's willingness to favour him in this kind, which he 'nothing doubted, considering his father's legacy in bequeathing him to Cecil'.[14] But he wanted 'a fit place in this creation. Though he knows that to strive for precedency has ever been thought a womanish ambition, yet doubting lest the ghosts of the Dukes of Norfolk, from whom he is descended, and of King Edward IV's Queen, his great-grandmother (whom he knows the King himself would somewhat respect) might chide him for giving place to such as can hardly prove themselves gentlemen, he thought fit so far to urge their right as to crave either a convenient place, or no barony.' Thomas Arundell never fails to come up, or down, to one's expectation of him.

This missive was addressed, appropriately, from Moreclack — probably Mortlake. He did not get his barony this year, but he had not long to wait. Where the Queen had been very sparing of titles and honours, and thus kept up the estimation of such things, there now set in an inflation of them : everything becoming more common and cheap, more ostentatious and opulent. There was a real vulgarity in the Jacobean age.

These grants were in return for service in attendance upon the King — being a prominent courtier was a very expensive business : no more conspicuous case of conspicuous consumption. There were social duties to perform, such as receiving the French envoy, Rosny, in September and escorting him to Court, and next year accompanying the Constable of Castile, plenipotentiary for the peace-negotiations.[15] We find Southampton frequently called upon as intermediary for people's requests from the King — the small change of his attendance upon him, though it would bring its profits, presents, and gifts. In March 1604 we hear of him being commended, along with the spirited and privateering Earl of Cumberland, for tilting at Court. In the same month Southampton and Devonshire were made joint Lord Lieutenants of Hampshire, with the local duties that office involved.[16] In April a second daughter was baptised grandly in the royal chapel at Whitehall, with the Queen as godmother, and named after her Anne. In May we find warrants to deliver their scarlet robes to Southampton and Pembroke as Knights of the Garter ; while Southampton's attainder was reversed and he fully restored in blood by Parliament.

In July there befel a curious episode, which illuminates the character of the times. Suddenly one night the Council arrested Southampton, Danvers, and five others — it appeared on a slanderous charge that they were plotting to kill some of the Scots about the King.[17] Southampton appealed to James — since the author of the calumny was not to be discovered — and established his innocence. One does not know whether to connect this with what Weldon tells us, that 'there was an apparition of Southampton's being a favourite to his Majesty, by that privacy and dearness presented to the Court view. But Salisbury [i.e. Cecil], liking not that any of Essex's faction should come into play, made that apparition appear as it were *in transitu*, and so vanished, by putting some jealousy that he did not much desire to be in his Queen's company.' [18]   This is so ill-expressed that it is difficult to be sure what it means.   Actually we find Southampton a member of the Queen's Council and Master of her game.   On the other hand, Salisbury would not wish an English peer to be entrenched in the royal bedchamber as favourite, though Southampton, now 30, would be old for the post.   An upstart Scot was supportable in the position, and James Hay, who studied the King's moods and wishes, made himself agreeable to everyone.   Moreover, he was so extravagant and generous that, Clarendon tells us, 'he left behind him the reputation of a very fine gentleman and a most accomplished courtier ; and after having spent, in a very jovial life, above £400,000 which, upon a strict computation, he received from the Crown, he left not a house or acre of land to be remembered by'.[19]

The cloud blew over, and perhaps in recompense Southampton got the lease of two fat manors in fee-farm, Romsey in Hampshire and Compton magna in Somerset ; but, generous as always, he seems to have made these leases over to servants.[20]   Later we find a similar grant of Duchy of Lancaster lands to the value of £40 a year.   Lastly, it is rather amusing to find this ex-Catholic sharing with undoubted Protestants, like Lady Walsingham, in the fines exacted from a number of recusants.

The one drawback to the general happiness was that 1603 had been a bad plague-year, and this curtailed festivities in London.   The Court took to the country and at the end of the year was down at Wilton, Pembroke's house, where Southampton was in attendance and Shakespeare's company came down to perform before the King.   James's accession had improved their status too : he took them under his patronage and the former Chamberlain's men became the King's men. As such they were recognised as liveried royal servants : Shakespeare and his fellows walked in their scarlet liveries in procession on the King's reception by the City in 1603. Again, in the summer of 1604 when the Spanish peace-plenipotentiaries came to London, Shakespeare and his eleven fellows in scarlet were in waiting during the negotiations. At the grand entertainment given at Whitehall to celebrate the peace, Southampton and Pembroke officiated as masters of ceremonies.

James and his Queen (a secret Catholic) could not have enough of English plays and masques, after the Presbyterian delights of Edinburgh. And it is from this time that we have a letter from Sir Walter Cope to Cecil, now Lord Cranborne : 'I have sent and been all this morning hunting for players, jugglers and such kinds of creatures, but find them hard to find. Wherefore leaving notes for them to seek me, Burbage is come and says there is no new play that the Queen has not seen. But they have revived one called *Love's Labour's Lost*, which for wit and mirth, he says, will please her exceedingly. And this is appointed to be played tomorrow night at my lord of Southampton's, unless you send a writ to remove the *corpus cum causa* to your house in the Strand. Burbage is my messenger, ready attending your pleasure.' [21] It is more than pleasant to think of *Love's Labour's Lost*, after all that had happened in the intervening ten years, being performed at Southampton House ; for the play had personal associations for the Earl and his poet, and it is more than likely that it had received its first production there.[22]

Once more Southampton was in a position to receive the tributes of authors aspiring to his notice. John Davies of Hereford coupled his name with James in his verses on the new joyfulness, and dedicated a sonnet to him :

> Welcome to shore, unhappy-happy lord,
> From the deep seas of danger and distress . . .

A better poet, Samuel Daniel, wrote him a better poem :

The world had never taken so full note
Of what thou art, hadst thou not been undone ;
And only thy affliction hath begot
More fame than thy best fortunes could have done . . .

There is something in this. We have already seen that Southampton's narrow escape from the scaffold and his bearing in
adversity had won him sympathy ; henceforward he enjoys
general popularity, and later on we shall find him looked up
to as the head of the popular party, as against the corruption of
the Court. Time has indeed its revenges. Daniel proceeds to
moralise upon the theme :

Not to be unhappy is unhappiness,
And misery not to have known misery ;
For the best way unto discretion is
The way that leads us by adversity.
And men are better showed what is amiss,
By the expert finger of calamity,
Than they can be with all that fortune brings,
Who never shows them the true face of things.

Evidently, from his conduct henceforward, Southampton had
learned from adversity, and to recognise things for what they
truly are.

On 19 March 1604 James met his first Parliament, and at
once got off on the wrong footing with the House of Commons
on the question of their election returns. There was a disputed
return for a Buckinghamshire seat, and the Commons claimed
that it was their privilege to decide it. James as an incoming
Scottish king can hardly have been expected to appreciate
their privileges, but he had high doctrinaire notions of his
prerogative and informed them that 'they derived all matters
of privilege from him and by his grant'.[23] When the Commons informed him, reasonably enough, that the privileges of
the House were their own right and inheritance James was
angry and commanded that there should be a conference with
the judges on the matter in the presence of the Privy Council

— and this he commanded as 'an absolute king'. He was an ass to say so, for the conference never took place, and on the substance of the matter he ultimately yielded : the House remained master on the issue of its own membership. This prefigured the pattern of much in the relations between the Scottish King and the House of Commons, which after all represented the English nation — the King asserting the highest doctrine of prerogative, and then having to give way on the substance, or not getting his own way.

There remained over from Elizabeth's reign the very real grievances people suffered in the antiquated Crown rights pertaining to purveyance — provision for the royal household — and wardship. The Commons offered to raise the Crown a larger revenue in lieu of these, and suggested a commission to make a reasonable survey of the incidence of these burdens, the proportions borne by the different counties, a possible composition. The Court was unwilling to proceed with it and it was dropped. James's heart was really in his somewhat doctrinaire desire for a complete Union between England and Scotland and the merging of their identity into a greater Britain — doctrinaire, not only because it was far too much in advance of public opinion in both countries, but because it took no account of the complex practical difficulties in bringing it about. The House of Commons was very well aware of these, even apart from its ardent English nationalism, which made it reject outright the proposal of free trade between the two countries. The island exemplified simply a union of the two kingdoms in the person of the King — even the naturalisation of Scottish subjects in England born after the King's accession, the *post-nati*, had to be brought in through the backdoor by judicial decision, not through Parliament.

Southampton was present at the opening of Parliament ; a week later, immediately after the bill of 'most joyful and just recognition of the succession and descent of the Crown' the bill for the restitution of Southampton's earldom, after the attainder, was given its first reading.[24] Southampton and

Pembroke were excused from absence, being in attendance upon the King to Royston. Southampton was not present again until 5 April, and on 11 April when the Lords had the pleasure of considering the bill concerning witchcraft and the conjuration of evil spirits — a subject very close to the Scottish Calvinist's heart. (*Macbeth* was only a year away in incubation.) From this time onwards we find Southampton taking a very full part in all the business of the Lords, placed on numerous committees, including all the important ones and a number dealing with private matters, often named among those to confer on leading issues with the representatives of the Commons. These last included such prominent members as Sir Edwin Sandys, with whom Southampton later became closely associated in the Virginia Company. These frequent conferences must have given him a considerable acquaintance with members of Parliament; later we find him popular in the City, and he ends up as a Parliament man in touch with House of Commons men in opposition to the Court.

In April Southampton was placed on the committee considering the Union, and shortly was named one of the forty-two peers to confer with the Commons on this leading issue. Meetings of these committees went on through May. Similarly he was selected one of those to confer with the Commons on another foremost subject at issue, purveyance and the reform of its abuses; later in May, when the question of wardships came up, he was one of those to represent the Lords in conference with the Commons. The report from the committee of the Lords proposed a revenue of £50,000 a year to the Crown in lieu of all purveyance. At the end of the month he was conferring with a committee of the Commons about the Bishop of Bristol's book on the Union, which caused a great deal of fuss because it reflected on the Lower House. The tactless Bishop was made to make formal acknowledgment of his error.

In June Southampton was on the leading committees dealing with the subsidy on tonnage and poundage, and for the proper execution of the statutes against Jesuits, seminary priests and recusants. Instead of gratifying James's wish for a more tolerant attitude towards the Catholics, the Commons came up with a bill for increasing the penalties and rigour of the laws. Such was the horrid *stimmung* of the age — it proved impossible to resist the increasingly aggressive Protestantism of the country. It is interesting that Southampton, an ex-Catholic, was always placed on these committees — and in fact he was carried forward by the movement of the time to align himself with the demand for an aggressively Protestant foreign policy, against James's leanings towards Spain. Towards the end of June he was absent, in attendance upon the King, but was present on 7 July when the King prorogued Parliament and did himself no good with a scolding speech without dignity, inconceivable in his predecessor : 'I wish you had kept a better form. I like form as much as matter. It shows respect and I expect it, being a king as well born (suppose I say it) as any of my progenitors. I wish you would use your liberty with more modesty in time to come.'

The resentment of the Catholics at their disappointment over toleration produced its reaction among a group of irresponsible young desperados in Gunpowder Plot. Four days after its discovery, on 9 November 1605, James opened the new session with a lyrical speech on his deliverance, as undignified and self-congratulatory as ever, thanking God that if he had died it would have been 'not ingloriously in an alehouse, a stew or such vile place' but in the best and most honourable company of Parliament. After various prorogations Parliament met for business on 21 January 1606. The Gunpowder scare naturally produced its reaction in the demand for still stricter laws against the Catholics. We find Southampton regularly on the Lords' committees on these matters, and to confer with the Commons in the Painted Chamber on the bill for the preservation of religion, his Majesty and the state. He was also on the large committee, headed by Archbishop Bancroft, to deal with 'the bringing in, printing or selling seditious, Popish and lascivious books'; and on others for 'the better keeping holy the sabbath day', and for the letters patents to maintain two divinity Readers at Cambridge. We shall find that he kept up his associations with Cambridge, and particularly with St. John's; but perhaps we may conclude from his always being placed on these committees dealing with religious and moral questions that his colleagues in the Lords thought of him as a rectitudinous man, and this the evidence bears out.

Through February and March we find him working on committees dealing with bills on various subjects, for restraining swearing and blasphemy, regarding seditious words against his Majesty, for clarifying Henry VIII's Act of Union with Wales, for freeing trade with Spain and Portugal, to confirm the attainders of Lord Cobham and his brother, for assuring the jointure of his old friend Essex's widow. All through April the main issues were being considered — Purveyance, the Union with Scotland and free trade between the kingdoms — and in conference with the Commons. Nothing emerged, and Parliament was prorogued at the end of May. It met again in November, went on through the early months of 1607 to June, to be finally prorogued that November. The committees were thrashing about as usual, but nothing was settled on the big issues, for there was increasing disaccord between the Court and Parliament. At the end of May Southampton's servant, John Foster, was arrested and imprisoned at the suit of Robert Dyer; this was contrary to the privilege of Parliament when it was in session. A writ of *habeas corpus* was issued, and Foster and Dyer were brought before the Lords. Southampton behaved nobly, as we should expect, by proposing a motion to forbear Dyer's imprisonment for his breach of privilege, and after some further fuss all ended happily. In June the Earl was naturally placed on the committee for confirming its charter to the town of Southampton. The King's affairs, as we have seen, ended less happily: the hostile laws against Scotland and the Scots were abolished, but apart from that there was no commercial union, no naturalisation, merely the personal union in the king of two separate kingdoms. This failure, for all that it was too difficult to surmount at the time, bore its ill fruits later.

Meanwhile, in March 1605, at last a son and heir to Southampton's peerage was born — many years after people had begun to interest themselves in the matter. We hear, 'my Lady Southampton was brought to bed of a young lord upon St. David's day in the morning, a saint to be much honoured by that house for so great a blessing by wearing a leek for ever upon that day'.[25] (Did anyone remember the scene, not so long ago in *Henry V*, when Fluellen wore his leek when it was past St. David's day and forced Pistol to eat it ?) Southampton determined to signalise the event by asking the King and Cecil, now Lord Cranborne, to be sponsors. The latter was taking a spell away from duty hawking with Southampton and Mountjoy, now Earl of Devonshire, 'but tomorrow all go back to school'. When Southampton invited the King, there followed a characteristic passage of James's pawky humour : he could not stop teasing Cecil with the nickname his 'little beagle'— which naturally the great man did not much appreciate. James said that if Southampton 'had matched him with a Christian [i.e. a human being], he could have believed my lord had good meaning in it; but having coupled him with a hound, he thinketh my lord did it only to flatter him, because he knoweth his Majesty loveth hunting and the beagle as well as any of the company at least'.[26] So much for Jacobean humour. The child was grandly christened in the royal chapel at Greenwich, and given the name of James. At the end of the month we learn that the office of Keeper of the New Forest 'stands between the Earl of Pembroke and the Earl of Southampton'.[27] Two years later Southampton got the grant of it for life.

In June he was down at Titchfield when he received an inquiry from Cecil, now Earl of Salisbury, about Captain Throckmorton drumming up recruits for the Archduke's service in the Netherlands. Peace with Spain had been made in 1604, but the war in the Netherlands still continued and provided an awkward issue in internal politics — it was particularly awkward to have recruits drummed up from the English countryside on behalf of the Catholic Archduke. There was in addition the sensitive question of sovereignty. The incident had taken place before Southampton's arrival in his little domain, and a message from Salisbury instructed him to inquire into the matter. Southampton duly reported, conceiving 'it is not the King's pleasure that his subjects should be levied by sound of drum for the service of any but himself, unless leave be specially granted'.[28]

Having made his inquiries Southampton replied to Salisbury, 'I am bound unto you for your care to hold me in a right way, which, God willing, I will not stray from, but follow the course your lordship has directed'. From the letter we hear of Captain Edmonds as keeper of Cowes Castle — can this be the Piers Edmonds we have already heard of in Southampton's company in Ireland? Southampton reported that the offender in drumming up recruits had excused himself on the ground that he was following the example of one Cheney, who had done 'the like in Winchester and passed without controlment'. Southampton had learned from the Bishop that Cheney was a known recusant, 'and therefore, as I take it, his act the more scandalous'. It certainly was more likely to give trouble, beating up recruits for the Catholic cause in Protestant England — but it is amusing to find Southampton, so lately a Catholic himself, being so virtuous. 'If I shall hear of any fleet out of Spain I will advertise you. In the meantime wishing myself with you, when you shall be together at Theobalds.'

In July Southampton was back in his small island kingdom, in residence at Carisbrooke castle — which in time to come would have fatal associations for James's son, Charles I. Salisbury had promised his friend to visit him here; Southampton asked for a few days' warning, 'only that I may meet you at Titchfield . . . from whence I will convey you (God willing) safely over the water — there being your best passage — and see you well on shore again at your return'.²⁹ In August Southampton was at Oxford once more for a royal visit, as in 1592 when his youthful beauty had been commented on, along with Essex in the suite of the Queen.³⁰ Now in his thirty-second year, he bore the sword of state before King James, who took a pedagogue's interest in the academic disputations. Outside St. John's College there was an apparition of three Sibyls saluting Banquo, supposed ancestor of the Stuarts, 'no king, but to be the father of many kings'. Was it this that inspired Shakespeare's

> Thou shalt get kings, though thou be none,

in his next play *Macbeth*, which did more for Scottish James than ever he had done for English Elizabeth ? Was he in the throng that August day, passing through Oxford for the summer at Stratford ? We have no more evidence of any close connection with his former patron — though we do have later of an association with Southampton's friend, Rutland. Both men were growing older, with their interests diverging, each under the pressure of business, life carrying them apart. It was probably on the occasion of his visit to Oxford that Southampton made his handsome donation of £100 this year to the Bodleian Library — so like his generosity, for we must multiply by 30 or 40 for a contemporary valuation.

Arrived back in his island charge in September, he regretted the amenities of the Court : 'the barrenness of this place affords nothing to discourse of but heat in summer and storms in winter, which is now with us begun'.³¹ Mountjoy had returned from 'the desolate parts of the New Forest' to 'his pleasures at Wanstead', i.e. Leicester's princely palace in Essex. 'I wish myself also often at the Court to enjoy the presence of your lordship and the rest of my friends, though otherwise I am enough pleased with the quiet life I lead here. Yet do I intend ere long to be with you.' We find him strongly recommending Captain Dale, one of the captains he had known in Ireland, for service in the Netherlands.³² As Sir Thomas

Dale this protégé later on became governor of Virginia, the colonisation of which became a prime interest of Southampton's later career.

Both King and country had had a great shock with the discovery of the Gunpowder Treason. The feeling of relief after this shocking exposure and the sensational events that attended it brought about a surge of good will towards the new dynasty. These events entered largely into the play that Shakespeare — always keen to catch the mood of the moment — wrote in the spring of 1606 : *Macbeth*, with its Scottish story, background, and atmosphere. He read up King James's book on demonology for the purpose, along with other Scottish lore — the Calvinist King was strongly convinced of the existence of witches. (A little knowledge of Freudian psychology illuminates here: James had a dislike of, and contempt for, women.) The play has further contemporary references — to James's powers, as an anointed king, of healing the King's Evil. In March 1606 Father Garnet, the Jesuit Provincial, was brought to trial : he had known that something dastardly was afoot, but had not divulged it. He stood by the doctrine of equivocation when faced with the dilemma of divulging truth that might be damaging to his cause. There is a direct reference to him in *Macbeth* as an 'equivocator that could swear in both scales against either scale, who committed treason enough for God's sake, yet could not equivocate to heaven'. Again, 'what is a traitor ?' asks young Macduff. He gets the answer, 'why, one that swears and lies. . . . Everyone that does so is a traitor, and must be hanged.' All this is completely consistent with Shakespeare's attitude a decade earlier, with the government's compaign in 1594 against the Jesuits operating as a Fifth Column in time of war ; he aligned himself with the view of the country in general, in regarding them as

> the fools of time
> Which die for goodness [i.e. as martyrs]
> who have lived for crime.[33]

Always a conformist, Shakespeare was neither a Catholic nor a Puritan, but a sensible middle-of-the-road man.

Southampton was not affected by this dastardly affair or its outcome, for he had never been but a luke-warm Catholic — unlike his father — and now, with the new régime, he had conformed. But some of his mother's family, the more *dévot* Montagus, were touched ; we find Sir Maurice Berkeley, one of the Catholics examined, confessing that 'the Countess of Southampton [i.e. the dowager] told me that there was a very severe and terrible bill coming from the higher House against Catholic recusants, but that I promised her to speak against it when it came amongst us [i.e. in the Commons], or not to speak for it, that I utterly deny'. Berkeley suggested, ungallantly, that if he had expressed a wish that the Catholics would rise, in the Countess's presence, 'it might have proceeded from some humour to make her discover in what perplexity she was, being a Catholic, or to make her discover as much as she knew of the humour of the Catholic party'.[34] One sees what quicksands there were in deviating from sense in such dangerous times.

Later that year Southampton had to write to Salisbury on behalf of an old lady of his family, from whom he had expectations. He was under the necessity of renewing 'an old suit in the behalf of my poor aunt Catherine Cornwallis, who by your favour has hitherto lived free from trouble for her recusancy, but is now by malice likely to be indicted if you interpose not to help her. She is an old woman that lives without scandal, and I am in expectation of some good from her . . . If therefore your lordship hold it fit and will help her, it will be to me, I think, a very good turn.'[35] It was usually the women of the house who were more troublesome and obstinate in regard to recusancy — understandably perhaps : more credulous.

As a leading courtier Southampton was in line to receive and give New Year presents from and to the King. This year 1606, for instance, he received gilt plate of 32 oz., presumably in the form of a cup ; his gift to the King was £20 in gold.

And this was the standard form for earls.[36] In the same month of January the Council of the North at York imprisoned a minister called Nalton for his 'unfitting' speeches about Southampton.[37] One may guess from the context what he had said — probably something about Southampton being a crypto-Papist ; but this would have been more true of Northampton. In April his friend Mountjoy, still young and full of ability, died. Mountjoy, who had lived happily with Lady Rich for years and had a family by her — the situation was recognised by everyone — made the mistake of marrying the lady after her divorce. At once a howl of humbug went up from Church and Court alike, and Mountjoy did not long survive it. At his funeral Southampton was chief mourner, but Lady Rich's arms were not allowed to be empaled with Mountjoy's.

In the summer, July and August, took place the celebrated (and inebriated) visit of Queen Anne's brother, Christian IV of Denmark, to the English Court. Southampton and his wife were present at the state reception and many in the round of entertainments. Of one such at Theobalds we have an account by Harington of the effect of Danish drinking habits on the English Court. 'The ladies abandon their sobriety and roll about in intoxication.' [38] At a representation of Solomon and the Queen of Sheba, the lady playing the part 'overset her caskets into his Danish Majesty's lap and fell at his feet. . . . His Majesty then got up and would dance with the Queen of Sheba ; but he fell down and humbled himself before her and was carried to an inner chamber and laid on a bed of state, which was not a little defiled with the presents of the Queen which had been bestowed on his garments, such as wine, cream, jelly, beverage, cakes, spices and other good matters. . . . Now did appear Hope, Faith and Charity. Hope did essay to speak, but wine rendered her endeavours so feeble that she withdrew. Faith was then all alone, for I am certain she was not joined with good works, but left the Court in a staggering condition.' And so on — all more and more unlike the decorum observed under the Virgin Queen.

After these strenuous entertainments the Court was glad to adjourn to the country and the King to resume his hunting. At the end of August James was at Beaulieu with Southampton, and 'is so well pleased with his hunting here as he seems to have a purpose to visit it often'.[39] The Earl entertained him well, and combined pleasure with business by having the trained bands of the Isle of Wight exercise before the King. Southampton's long friendship with Salisbury, dating back to his boyhood as a ward of Lord Burghley's, held good. King James had long cast envious eyes on Theobalds, the country palace Burghley had built conveniently to the north of London, with its exquisite walks and waters, which Salisbury had inherited. At last the minister could resist the King's envious desire no longer, and prepared to cede Theobalds to him in exchange for the manor of Hatfield. There Salisbury designed to build a new palace, in lieu of the old red-brick manor-house that had housed the Princess Elizabeth in her younger years — something that would exemplify his own magnificent Renaissance tastes and be a monument to posterity of his historic position in the state. In April 1607 Salisbury went to take a last look at Theobalds before it passed into the King's hands, and took Southampton, Worcester and Suffolk with him to advise on the site of his new house at Hatfield, a little way off from the old.[40]

In April Southampton's mother died. It was reported that she 'hath left the best part of her stuff to her son, and the most part to her husband', Sir William Harvey. She was indeed generous to both. We have already seen how much she had profited by her brief marriage to Sir Thomas Heneage, the 'Master Heneage' of her letters. She left to her son ten pieces of hangings, presumably tapestries, with the story of Cyrus depicted, six pieces of the Months, two with wrought gold and Heneage's arms in them. There followed a bequest of the grandest beds to her son with all their rich equipment, the furniture that went with them, four of the best Turkey carpets, two of the best silver ewers and basins, six great silver candlesticks and 'a ring of gold with a fair table diamond in it, which Sir Thomas Heneage had of Sir Walter Ralegh, sixteen loose diamonds which my desire is that my said dear son should set in a George of gold and wear in memory of me, his loving mother'.[41] To her daughter-in-law she left the double rope of pearls which she usually had worn, with six pairs of her finest sheets. To 'my good daughter the Lady Arundell ... my jewel of gold set with diamonds, called a Jesus, if she happen to be living at the time of my decease' — so evidently she was already ill, and in fact she died in June. The Countess left money and all her clothes to her two waiting gentlewomen, more money to her other servants. She made Shakespeare's neighbour, George, Lord Carew, Baron of Clopton — whom we now see extended in armour upon his tomb in Stratford church — overseer of her will. And then, 'all the rest of my goods and chattels, household stuff and estate, to my dear and well-beloved husband Sir William Harvey, whom I make sole executor of this my last will and testament, praying him as an argument of his love to me, that he will be careful of my page Robert Jones, his sister's son, and in his discretion, at my request, to provide for him that he may be enabled to live, and to know that I had a care for him'. We see the nature of Southampton's mother, at the last as all through her life, considerate and kind, affectionate and thoughtful for others. For herself she wished to be buried 'as near as may be to the body of my dearly loved husband, Henry, late Earl of Southampton, in the church at Titchfield : my executors to see to this, inhibiting them to use any pomp, vain ostentation or idle ceremony, or any superfluous charge at or about my funeral'. This was in marked contrast to the extravagance the Earl had ordained about his funeral and the monument there ; no doubt she had loved him in her time and forgiven the ill-usage she had received from him.

In March 1608 Southampton's second son was born and called Thomas after the founder of the family's greatness.

Since the elder son died of the plague in Holland, it was this second son who succeeded to the earldom. The child was baptised 2 April 1608 in the church of Little Shelford in Cambridgeshire, where Southampton had a country villa in the Italian style with a noble portico, built by a Pallavicino — one more evidence of his cultivated tastes.[42]

That April Salisbury became Lord Treasurer and had to face, in addition to his other burdens, the chief problem of the state, which was a financial one. The whole financial system was out of date ; there was a large and growing gap between the Crown's revenues and its expenditure. Prices were rising, and the Crown's resources diminishing through the constant sales of Crown lands — disposing of capital to meet current expenditure. King and Court were immensely extravagant ; James had no idea of money, and in his weak generosity gave away right and left. 'Of Elizabeth's constant scrutiny of the whole fabric of public finance he was utterly incapable.'[43]

Salisbury at once set about tackling this problem with his usual courage and statesmanship. Since the country's economy was prosperous and trade was increasing, he realised that both could support an increase of revenue derived from duties on imports. A decision handed down in the Court of Exchequer — the celebrated Bate's case — had ruled that these duties could be imposed conveniently by prerogative, without recourse to Parliament. At once everybody was up in arms, including Southampton, who feared that it would affect his revenue from the monopoly of the import of sweet wines. The merchants were protesting to Salisbury, 'which news makes me fear the burden will fall as well upon me as upon the merchants ; for if there shall be a new imposition raised upon the sweet wines, whereof I am farmer, I have great reason to fear that it will impair that kind of trade, and so consequently much prejudice me'. Southampton protested that 'the best means I have to subsist is by this farm, which, if it should be overthrown, I should be enforced to live in a very mean fashion'.[44] In return Salisbury assured Southampton that he should receive no prejudice. Later, however, when the new scale of customs duties got into full operation, he may have received some prejudice ; for we find a grant of an annuity of £2,000 to him out of the customs on sweet wines. That probably represents the full value of the farm to him ; we observe that it is rather more than the annual value of his inherited lands.

Earlier in 1608 he had received the small *douceur* of the grant of free warren — the right to keep and hunt all beasts — on all his lands, without infringement from royal rights and claims.[45] In May his name was rumoured for Lord Deputy of Ireland, but he did not get the appointment.[46] In August he was claiming one-half of a forfeit ship as his perquisite as Vice-Admiral of Hampshire. In September he had to report a severe scarcity of grain in his county ; supplies had to be brought in from outside, and he requested a warrant for a hundred quarters to be brought from Sandwich. In December there was an awkward passage with the young and assertive Prince Henry, who did not like his father's favourites and was a convinced admirer of James's prisoner, Sir Walter Ralegh. The Prince, wanting to exert more influence on his father, complained of the distance at which he was kept from him. The Venetian ambassador reports that Henry 'sent to tell the Earls of Southampton and Pembroke to move their households and their horses, as he desired to occupy their lodging. They refused, and the Prince had them removed by his people, to the indignation of those gentlemen, who are of very high rank. This is a great proof of spirit on the part of the Prince, who, though only fifteen years of age, gives the highest promise in all he does.'

The episode seems to have left no ill will — just one of those things one had to put up with in the life of a courtier. In the summer of 1609 the Prince paid a visit to Southampton's little kingdom, stopping at Carisbrooke at the end of July, thence to Titchfield and Beaulieu, where he joined his father in hunting in the New Forest. Southampton won a good name for himself for the way he kept up hospitality in the island. A diarist recorded later, 'when this island was fortunate and enjoyed the company of Sir Edward Horsey, my lord Hunsdon, or my lord of Southampton, then it flourished with gentlemen. I have seen with my lord of Southampton on St. George's Down at bowls from thirty to forty knights and gentlemen, where our meetings were then twice every week, Tuesdays and Thursdays, and we had an ordinary there, and cards and tables. *Mutamur.* The gentlemen which lived in the island in the seventh year of King James's reign all lived well, and were most commonly at our ordinary [i.e. public table]. His [Southampton's] just, affable and obliging deportment gained him the love of all ranks of people, and raised the island to a most flourishing state.' [47] Here was that gift for popularity — tribute to his nature, his generosity and charm — that Southampton by general consent could always command.

He was no less conscientious in the proper upkeep of the defences of the island. In July 1609 he reported that Sandown Castle needed £1,000 spending upon it, but that it could be materially repaired for £300.[48] Yarmouth Castle also was in want of some repairs. When the money was not forthcoming from the Treasury, he advanced it himself, and was paid back his £300 later.

It was in the spring and summer of this year that the interest of the whole nation in the colonisation of North America reached its height. The concern of the seamen, the maritime interests, merchants, forward-looking imperialists — men like Hawkins, Drake, the Gilberts, Ralegh, Grenville, Dr. Dee, the Hakluyts — went back to the early decades of Elizabeth's reign. It was now that the harvest of their efforts was to be reaped. The English had fought the long war with Spain, in part, for the open door in North America. The conclusion of the peace in 1604 had left the matter open ; the English were now determined to go ahead. Jamestown, first of the permanent settlements, was founded in 1607. Now the idea caught on and all the leading elements in the country felt that the nation's interests were involved. The Company of Adventurers and Planters of the City of London for the first colony of Virginia — the English name for North America — was incorporated in May with Salisbury, Suffolk, Southampton, Pembroke at the head of its members. The list of its subscribers occupies some twenty-eight pages in the charter of incorporation.[49] Everybody who was anybody in Jacobean society was in it, from the Archbishop of Canterbury down to a small Cornish squire like William Roscarrock living hard by Padstow haven on the north coast of Cornwall.

Southampton, as we shall see, had long taken an active interest in American discovery and plantation, and had put money into promoting a voyage. Now he was named one of the members of the Council of the Virginia Company, and henceforth this would be a leading interest in his life.

Everyone was touched by the excitement of this year and filled with hopes of the big expedition going out to Virginia, for which the laureate Drayton wrote his famous ode. There is a reflection of it in the dedication of a still more famous little volume that came out this year, Shakespeare's *Sonnets*.

Southampton's mother had died in 1607, and next year her much younger husband, Sir William Harvey, married a young wife, Cordell or Cordelia Annesley, like himself, of a Kentish family. This kind Cordelia had, only a few years before, in 1603 tried to keep her poor old father, Sir Brian Annesley, from being designated a lunatic and handed over to the disposition of others. Sir Brian had been a Gentleman Pensioner to the Queen, 'whose many years' service to our late dread sovereign Mistress and native country deserved a better agnomination than at his last gasp to be recorded and registered a lunatic'.[50] Shakespeare's *King Lear*, with its marked Kentish associations and references, was written the very next year, in 1604–5.

We find the circumstances of 1609 reflected simply and

clearly in the dedication of the *Sonnets*, which has given needless difficulty to people over the generations. But one must remember that it was not written to create a puzzle, any more than the sonnets were. It is really quite clear, and the circumstances behind it are perfectly recognisable in the phrasing of it.

> To the only begetter of these ensuing sonnets Mr. W. H. all happiness and that eternity promised by our ever-living poet wisheth the well-wishing adventurer in setting forth, T.T.

This is the publisher Thomas Thorpe's dedication, not Shakespeare's. Thomas Thorpe was a well-known publisher, a friend of Marlowe's friend, Edward Blount, and had already published Marlowe's translation of Lucan. Thorpe dedicates the little book, rather effusively and gratefully, to the one person who had obtained the manuscript for him. The word 'beget' in Elizabethan usage is also used for 'get' or 'obtain'; and 'begetter' here cannot possibly mean 'inspirer' for there are two inspirers of the Sonnets, the Dark Lady, Shakespeare's mistress, being hardly less important than the young man, his patron. Those who are familiar with Elizabethan usage also know that it was quite regular to refer to a knight as Master (Mr. is short for Master); it was more familiar, though still respectful, to do so — the Countess usually referred to Sir Thomas Heneage as Master Heneage. A peer could not possibly be referred to as Mr. W.H. She left Sir William Harvey all her household goods and chattels in 1607. In 1608 he married a young wife : this is what Thorpe is referring to in wishing Harvey 'all happiness and that eternity promised by our ever-living poet'. What he means is the eternity Shakespeare had promised Southampton in the Sonnets by marrying and having progeny, carrying on the line. Harvey now precisely had a chance of it. 'The well-wishing adventurer in setting forth' reflects the current excitement in London over the Virginia colony and the adventurers in the enterprise.

We see how consistent these circumstances are and how they corroborate each other. There really is no problem.

CHAPTER XI

Court and Country

WE have to imagine for ourselves, if we are to grasp it at all fully, the rhythm of life of a Jacobean nobleman who was also a leading courtier, if never quite a member of the inner governing circle — the alternation of duties and activities at the centre and in the country, both public and private. It is in regard to this last, Southampton's family and private affairs, that the evidence is sadly incomplete, owing to the failure of the male line after his son, the fourth Earl, the division of the estates among coheiresses, the dispersal of possessions, the destruction of papers.

At the centre there were the duties of attendance on the King, the work as well as the play — or rather, display — of the Court ; of regular attendance in the House of Lords during sessions of Parliament (infrequent during James's reign) and at the Privy Council, when Southampton at last became a member in 1619 ; the business activities of public corporations such as the Virginia Company, of which he became the head. In the country such a personage represented the government, was at the apex of government so far as his own county was concerned, as Lord Lieutenant of Hampshire and with his own little kingdom as Governor of the Isle of Wight. In addition there were the concerns of the man : the continuing interest in culture, particularly literary culture, the kindness to writers, the recurrent reception of dedications, the generous donation of a notable collection of manuscripts and books to his old college at Cambridge. There were the concerns of the family, about which we know least, of his life with his wife, which seems to have been happy and contented, of the education of and provision for his children. We know something more of the relaxations of such a life both at Court and in the country, the banqueting, the ceremonies, the masques and dances on one side, the country sports on the other, bowls on St. George's down in the Isle, above all the aristocratic delights of the chase, which were particularly to the fore in the New Forest, that favoured haunt of King James, who came again and again to Beaulieu as Southampton's guest. With the King's passion for hunting and his distaste for women, the tone was that of a stag-party, in both senses of the word, life in summer a succession of picnics *al fresco*, with state business and couriers coming and going wherever he happened to be. One sees the New Forest in all its virgin beauty, the fresh green coverts and the young fawns in the glades in early summer, those healthy, wide-spreading heaths for fowling and coursing, the golden stubbles after harvest, the rich panoply of colour, red and ochre and brackeny russet in autumn. With winter they all went back to Whitehall. Such was Southampton's country background, this was his domain.

For the completeness of art we have to imagine his private life, though in a sense it was less important, for his was essentially the life of a public man and a very busy one.

However, we have the country poets of the time to help us — that time, of which Clarendon wrote so sadly later, of the long peace when the country did not know its own good fortune or the ruin to come. It is the time of William Browne's *Britannia's Pastorals*, or 'It happened lately at a fair', of the old Drayton and Ben Jonson's masques, of the young Herbert and Herrick. The poems of this blissful time are full of country delights :

> There's not a budding boy or girl this day
> But is got up and gone to bring in May.
> A deal of youth, ere this, is come
> Back and with whitethorn laden home.

> Some have dispatched their cakes and cream
> Before that we have left to dream ;
> And some have wept and wooed and plighted troth
> And chose their priest ere we can cast off sloth.

Or there are the charms and superstititions that accompany rustic life, the country lore :

> Bring the holy crust of bread,
> Lay it underneath the head :
> 'Tis a certain charm to keep
> Hags away while children sleep.

Or one for the stables, so important in that riding age, when people depended on horses for transport :

> Hang up hooks and shears to scare
> Hence the hag that rides the mare
> Till they be all over wet
> With the mire and the sweat.
> This observed, the manes shall be
> Of your horses all knot-free.

The end of the year came with Christmas and there followed the ceremonies for Candlemas day :

> Kindle the Christmas brand and then
>   Till sunset let it burn,
> Which quenched then lay it up again
>   Till Christmas next return.
> Part must be kept wherewith to tend
>   The Christmas log next year,
> And where 'tis safely kept the Fiend
>   Can do no mischief there.

There they all are brought together in these elegies and dedications — Prince Henry and Prince Charles, their sister the Winter Queen ('You meaner beauties of the night'), the Countess of Pembroke ('the subject of all verse'), Sir Thomas Overbury and the wicked Countess of Essex, Henry and William Lawes the musicians, young Mr. Endymion Porter and old Sir Henry Wotton, Dr. Williams and Dr. Donne, the

beautiful Buckingham and Henry Wriothesley, Earl of Southampton : the society of their time. There in our literature
they all once more live.

The years 1610–11 were dominated by Salisbury's last great
political struggle, to place the finances of the Crown on a firm
and satisfactory basis by the Great Contract with Parliament.
Impossible to go into it all in detail here, the clue to the situation is that the revenues of the Crown had become sadly
depleted — by the necessities of Elizabeth I's war-expenditure
over years, among other things. On the other hand, James
was incurably extravagant and could not resist handing out
gifts, grants, estates to family, favourites, courtiers. On suc-
ceeding to the key position in the state as Lord Treasurer in
1608, Salisbury made an heroic effort to increase the revenues
of the Crown and reduce the large debt James's administration
had accumulated. At the end of all his efforts there was still
a deficit of some £130,000 a year running and no means of
closing the gap. Salisbury advised the summoning of a Parliament, which met in April 1610, and by July he reached a
tentative agreement with the Commons by which, in return
for a fixed revenue of £200,000 a year, the Crown would give
up its antiquated and vexatious feudal rights of purveyance,
wardship, and other dues.[1] Salisbury worked indefatigably
towards this great reform, which, if carried through, would
have completed his life's work for the English state and have
spared the Crown something of the increasing irritations and
complaints, the festering unpopularity that led to the Civil
War.

Others were less interested in a settlement, notably the
favourite Carr, engaged in poisoning James's mind against
Salisbury, and Northampton who hated the great little
Treasurer, envious of anyone with superior abilities. Southampton was not directly concerned in this prime struggle, and
in any case it was observed that Salisbury, so long as he held
power, kept Essex's old adherents out of it. Southampton was

present at the opening of Parliament on 5 April, was regular in attendance in his place and served on a number of committees.[2] The Commons asked for a conference with the Lords to resolve some doubts they had regarding the bill for assuring the title of the Elector Palatine, and no doubt provision for his wife, Princess Elizabeth. Southampton was on the high-powered committee to confer on this, as on others for avoiding lawsuits concerning bequests of land, and that favourite Jacobean pursuit of punishing abuses of the sabbath. On 4 June there was a full house for Prince Henry's investiture as Prince of Wales, with the King present in the Lords. At the banquet afterwards in the great hall at Whitehall Southampton served as carver, Pembroke as sewer, Montgomery as cup-bearer to the Prince.[3] Next day Queen Anne provided a masque devised by Samuel Daniel, poet-in-chief to the Herberts.

At the end of April there had befallen a passing quarrel between Southampton and the younger Herbert, Philip, Earl of Montgomery, which made news. Chamberlain tells us : 'in one week we had three or four great quarrels, the first twixt the Earls of Southampton and Montgomery that fell out at tennis, where the rackets flew about their ears. But the matter was taken up and compounded by the King without further bloodshed.'[4] Montgomery was ten years junior to Southampton and was known to be both choleric and foul-mouthed.

Southampton's relations with the Herberts are interesting to observe. On the whole they were friendly ; they were constantly together in close attendance on the King, and both Southampton and Pembroke enjoyed exceptional popularity and were much looked up to by the popular party as personally incorruptible and politically patriots, anti-Spanish, in favour of a pro-Protestant policy abroad. This did not endear them to James, and they never enjoyed his political confidence. Then, too, both were active supporters of the Virginia, Bermuda and East India companies, and of colonial and maritime expansion in general. They were often to be found working together in politics, as in the coalition that came to be formed against Carr. In the end, as men noted to be patriots, they were together in virtual opposition to James, leaders of the country party that forced him out of his subservience to Spain and into alliance with the Netherlands renewing the war against her. The Herberts were the chief power in Wiltshire and the Welsh Marches. They were richer and more broadly based in acres than Southampton. On the other hand, they were closer to the King and treated with more favour by him ; though junior to Southampton — Pembroke by six, Montgomery by ten, years — they got ahead of him in office and power. This was displeasing ; Southampton was frustrated again and again of employments for which he was mentioned. The temperature of his relations with the Herberts was in consequence somewhat cool ; though near neighbours in politics and in the country there were no marriage-alliances or kinship between the two families.

William and Philip Herbert were the sons of the second Earl of Pembroke and his famous third wife, Mary, Philip Sidney's sister. William was born at Wilton in 1580, was tutored by the family poet Daniel, and was a boy at New College, 1593-5, while Shakespeare was writing his sonnets to Southampton. Soon after his succession to the peerage, in 1601, Mary Fitton was found with child, but Pembroke 'renounced all marriage' with her. This left him free to marry the dwarfish and unattractive Lady Mary Talbot, co-heiress of the vast Shrewsbury estates. Clarendon says that 'he paid much too dear for his wife's fortune by taking her person into the bargain'.5 It is not merely beyond likelihood but beyond all possibility that the entirely hetero-sexual Pembroke could ever have been the ambivalent young man of the Sonnets.

On Ralegh's fall Pembroke succeeded him in 1604 as Lord Lieutenant of Cornwall and Lord Warden of the Stannaries. As early as 1611 he was made a Privy Councillor — while Southampton had to wait another eight years. In 1615, after

Carr's disgrace, James made Pembroke Lord Chamberlain, but this was a move to conciliate popular opinion. For, Clarendon says, 'he was the most universally loved and esteemed of any man of that age. . . . He was a man very well bred and of excellent parts, and a graceful speaker upon any subject, having a good proportion of learning and a ready wit to apply it and enlarge upon it ; of a pleasant and facetious humour and a disposition affable, generous and magnificent. . . . He was a great lover of his country and of the religion and justice which he believed could only support it ; and his friendships were only with men of those principles.'[6] On the other hand, like other men who set too much store by popularity, it appears that Pembroke 'never acted with much strength of will' ; and this was corroborated by Bacon : 'for his person, he was not effectual.'[7]

This stands in contrast to Southampton, who inherited Essex's forward, activist principles ; it is interesting that this ex-Catholic should have been foremost in pushing for an aggressively Protestant foreign policy. He was essentially serious-minded, virtuous, direct, straightforward : none of them qualities to recommend him at the Court of James I.

The character of the younger Herbert stands in some contrast to his elder brother, for he was fundamentally uneducated. Born in 1584 he was named after his uncle Philip Sidney ; matriculating from New College, he did not stay at Oxford. A handsome young man 'scarce of age at the entrance of King James, he had the good fortune, by the comeliness of his person, his skill and indefatigable industry in hunting, to be the first who drew the King's eyes towards him with affection, which was quickly so far improved that he had the reputation of a favourite. . . . He pretended to no other qualifications than to understand horses and dogs very well, which his master loved him the better for (being at his first coming into England very jealous of those who had the reputation of great parts), and to be believed honest and generous, which made him many friends and left him no enemy.'[8] In 1605 James made him a gentleman of the bedchamber, that convenient post for a rising young man, created him Earl of Montgomery and later added to it, in Aubrey's phrase, 'the romancy castle' of that name. But when young Carr appeared on the scene, Montgomery made way for him with all the more grace since his interests were entirely fixed on women (he was, moreover, already married ; Carr not, and he depended entirely on the King's favour).

Like his brother, too, he was a womaniser, and lived mostly with a mistress, who once ran away from him and had to be brought back. He had two wives, the first of whom died in 1629, when he married the strong-minded Lady Anne Clifford, who separated from him and left him to it. The fascinating thing is that this coarse and foul-mouthed hunting man should have developed a perfect passion for art and become the creator of Wilton, the most sumptuous and finished mirror of the Caroline age. For it he collected his Van Dycks : Aubrey tells us that 'he had the most of his paintings of anyone in the world'. In this unexpected combination he reminds us of Sir Robert Walpole : out of the coarsest soil the refinements of art. It was said that his fears for Wilton made him take a very uncourageous part in the Civil War. If so, we can but respect him the more : Wilton is better than any amount of conviction on either side.

On this Clarendon wrote of him later with more asperity than in an earlier 'better conjuncture of time, when his virtues were thought greater than they were, and his vices very little discerned. Yet, by what was then said, his nature and his parts might be well enough understood ; and as neither the one nor the other were improvable, so they were liable to be corrupted by any assaults ; his understanding being easy to be imposed upon, and his nature being made up of very strong passions.' 9 Fear, according to Clarendon, predominated over choler and rage, and this made him put himself in the hands of the Parliamentarian party — though he 'was so weak still as to believe they never meant to rebel against the king ; or that the king could long subsist without putting himself into their hands . . . and so got into actual rebellion, which he never intended to do'. We may well sympathise with him in the dilemma imposed upon the nation by a hopeless king.

Such were the Herberts, with whom Southampton's name has been, for the most part fortuitously and irrationally, mixed up. We shall see what their real associations in history were ; we can already appreciate the marked contrasts in character.

By the autumn session of Parliament the prospects of clinching the Great Contract were much diminished : demands were being raised on both sides, tempers frayed, and the King not wishing to see it succeed. Salisbury exerted his last strength — for he was an over-worked and over-taxed man — to bring about an accommodation between Crown and Parliament. Like his father before him no one was more representative of the nation as a whole — James was least of all representative of the English people — or cared more for the long-term interests of the state as such. In November Salisbury begged the King to come to London, so that both sides might be brought together. James saw no necessity : he had turned against his Parliament. To the minister he wrote censoriously, 'your greatest error hath been that ye ever expected to draw honey out of gall, being a little blinded with the self-love of your own counsel in the holding together of this Parliament, whereof all men were despaired, as I have oft told you, but yourself alone'.[10] The accent of personal jealousy is unmistakable ; hitherto Robert Cecil had ruled in the English state, but his rule was coming to an end. The man to whom, more than any other, James owed his crown replied with dignity and some pathos : 'you will please so to dispose of me or suffer me to be treated as you shall think may best agree with your service ; for when I resolved to serve your Majesty as I have done (in a time of want, of practice, and in a place of envy) I searched my heart and found it well resolved to suffer for such a master all the incidents to such a condition'.

The great servant of the state had failed in his greatest effort for it. In the middle of January James dissolved his first Parliament, the best disposed that ever he had. Good judges were later of the opinion that the hopeless Stuarts thereby lost their best chance with the English people, who looked more and more to Parliament to represent them, since the Crown did not.

At Court the Christmas festivities proceeded merrily. On New Year's night 1611 Prince Henry gave a grand masque, *Oberon or the Fairy Prince*, of which Ben Jonson wrote the text. It was produced in the new hall of the palace at Whitehall and mounted elaborate scenery : a large rock opened to discover the Prince and thirteen gentlemen 'chosen as famous dancers of the Court'.[11] Dancing in public was one of the necessary qualifications of public personages in those days, at least of Court persons — it was not expected of bishops, deans, and such. After the masque there were two ballets ; the Prince took the Queen out to dance, Southampton the Princess Elizabeth.

King James was hardly of a dancing disposition, and he disliked public appearances. He took more delight in the tame cheetah given him this year by the Savoy ambassador : the animal followed him round like a dog and would kill any deer it was sent after in the chase. A couple of years before Southampton had written to Salisbury : 'talking with the King by chance I told him of the Virginia squirrels which, they say, will fly, whereof there are divers brought into England. And he presently [i.e. immediately] and very earnestly asked me if none of them were provided for him, and whether your lordship had none for him, saying that he was sure you would get him one of them. I would not have troubled you with this, but that you know so well how he is affected to these toys.'[12] From which we see very well what these English grandees thought of James.

Meanwhile, we learn from Chamberlain, Southampton took very unkindly Pembroke's promotion to the Privy Council over his head.[13] Next there was a rumour that he would be despatched as ambassador to Spain, really to sound out a marriage for Prince Henry, and that this might be a step to the Privy Council, but that Southampton excused himself.[14] That autumn Salisbury, transacting some business for Queen Anne and always gallant towards the ladies, dropped a word that her Majesty loved nobody but dead pictures. The Queen replied with spirit that she was more contented with her pictures than he with all his great employments.[15]

Next year he was dying. In April he stopped working, for the first time in his life, and went down to Bath hoping to gain some relief from the waters. On the way back, at Marl-borough, he died. 'His making ready to die was the greatest blessing of his life unto him, for he never went to bed without cares till then, but had alarms everywhere to wake him, save in his conscience. When death came to be his business, he was in peace.'[16] No one mourned him, least of all James. Secre-tary Calvert wrote, 'our great strange little lord is gone and as soon forgotten'.[17] He had never been popular and few could understand so superior a political intelligence. So much abler than anyone around him and with constant care for the true well-being of his country, he could never command — what Essex had commanded so easily — popularity, the affection and following of the uncomprehending people. Now they felt free to malign him : 'I never knew so great a man so soon and so generally censured,' wrote Chamberlain.[18] The odious Northampton could not conceal his glee at 'the death of the little man, for which so many rejoice and so few do so much as seem to be sorry'.[19]

Salisbury had engrossed power to himself, combining the two chief offices of Lord Treasurer and Secretary of State, working himself to death. James now fancied that he would be his own Secretary, with the aid of Carr — whose qualifica-tions were physical rather than intellectual. This was where Carr's friend Overbury came in, whose ability supplied Carr with something of the wherewithal to keep his end up, or at least keep up appearances. This was enough for Northampton, whose chief weapon in this false world was flattery — it rarely failed. We shortly find him writing to Carr that many people, noting his skill in answering letters and his urbanity, wished to see him Secretary.[20] Characteristically he added a drop of poison for the Metropolitan Abbot — he would not call him Archbishop — for his severity towards recusants. At this time Southampton was the candidate generally favoured for Lord Treasurer : in June, a month after Salisbury's death, 'no man is spoken of but my lord of Southampton'.[21] Northampton, who wanted the office for himself, managed to stop this, for there ensued an open breach between the two men and they were not reconciled until the end of the year. Northampton took Salisbury's place as leading member of the government with himself as commissioner of the Treasury, in control of the most important matters of policy. Apropos of a missing letter on the negotiations with France, he takes a kick at the dead man in a letter to Carr, 'the little Lord having made his own cabinet the treasury of the state's whole evidences and intelligence'.[22] He adds a note that the King should be cautious in going to Wanstead, 'as many have died there'. The inwardness of this is that Wanstead had been Leicester's country palace, and was now lived in by his stepson Essex's nephew, Mountjoy Blount, son of Penelope Rich and Mountjoy, Southampton's friend. The intention, obvious enough, was to keep the King away from this circle ; the suggestion, that James might be poisoned there. The idea of poisoning was never very far from Northampton's mind.

In these next two years 1612–14, under Northampton's control, using Carr as his go-between with the King, James's government reached its nadir. It saw Carr's apogee as Earl of Somerset, his splendid marriage to Northampton's niece, the Countess of Essex, Sir Thomas Overbury's imprisonment in the Tower and his poisoning there — in all which we can recognise the contriving brain of Northampton. Policy was reversed : leniency towards recusants in place of Salisbury's pressure for the execution of the laws. More important, James's foreign policy took on the pro-Spanish inflexion, a kind of appeasement, which ultimately reduced the country to nullity in European affairs, produced confusion and then complete bankruptcy of policy at the end of the reign, alienated public opinion and contributed, through weakness and ambiguity, to the renewal of war that led to the Thirty Years War. It was observed that the Spanish ambassador arriving that year had a very different reception from what he would have had if Salisbury had been alive. It is not that Salisbury would have led the country into war, but that he would have preserved England's diplomatic weight to exert maximum power and ensure her interests and those of the Protestant powers on the continent. James, perfectly right in his ardent desire to maintain peace — as Victorian historians with their Protestant bias have inadequately appreciated — threw this away by the weakness of his handling, rather than of his hand. Peace through strength was Salisbury's idea : anyone who lived through the 1930's can well appreciate the situation, the dilemma it presented, and how such situations recur in history.

These years which were the turning point of the reign, when the Stuart monarchy lost much of the nation's respect so carefully built up (and deserved) by the Tudors, offered also a turning point for Southampton. His was a simple, straightforward nature, all of a piece ; he was an honest man, highly respected as such, uncorrupt and a patriot. No wonder he turned to opposition, became known as a Malcontent, concerned himself more with his own affairs and withdrew abroad for each of the summers of 1613 and 1614, while Northampton and Carr, now glorified as Somerset, ruled the roost.

Immediately after Salisbury's death Southampton combined with a number of House of Commons men to press for Sir Henry Neville as Secretary of State. An old friend and follower of Essex, an experienced diplomat, he would have been a reliable Protestant and patriot in this key-position. But James would not have a Secretary imposed upon him by Parliament and Southampton was made to pay for his importunity by going without the Privy Councillorship once more. This did not prevent him from pressing Neville's claims, who was really the obvious person for the post. Next January he was still at it, but it was said that 'the importunity of his [Neville's] great patron' was the chief obstacle with James, who pedalled along with Somerset until an almighty awakening shook them all up.

Whatever he felt Southampton continued to fulfil the duties of his position and offices. To offset the Spanish marriage James designed for his son and heir, and to maintain his fantasy of being the arbiter of peace in Europe, he had arranged a Protestant marriage for his daughter Elizabeth, to young Frederick, Elector Palatine of the Rhine. In October there was a state reception of him, coming up the river, at the great stairs at Whitehall by Prince Charles, attended by six of the greatest Earls, including Southampton and Pembroke. The young man made as favourable an impression as such persons do, 'a very fine prince, tall for his years', et cetera.[23] Unfortunately his intelligence was not up to his appearance : his personality, light-headed, restless and fanatical, provided the occasion that sparked off the Thirty Years War, with his unwarrantable acceptance of the Habsburg crown of Bohemia. Thus he lost his own Palatinate, and James's daughter spent a lifetime in exile as the Winter Queen. All this gave James infinite trouble in his last years : he came to fix his hopes on a Spanish marriage as a pacific way of getting back the Palatinate. But he had already thrown his hand away : negotiating from a position of weakness, instead of strength, achieved the nugatory results that might have been expected.

Prince Henry had not received the Elector Palatine, for at the time he was lying ill of typhoid and in November he died. A few days after his death there was an extraordinary scene at St. James's, when a stark naked youth presented himself and marched boldly up to the Privy Chamber, announcing to all the company watching there that he was the Prince's soul come from heaven.[24] Such was the Jacobean age. At his state funeral in December Southampton was one of the twelve Earls in attendance on Prince Charles as chief mourner, Southampton bearing the dead Prince's helmet, Pembroke his crest.[25] Thus passed the one popular member of the dynasty, the rising hope of the stern, unbending Protestants, the admirer of Ralegh who could not think how his father could keep such a bird caged, the encourager of ship-building and colonial expansion, no friend of Spain or of a pro-Spanish policy : a reversion to Tudor type, like his name. He had been no friend to Carr or Northampton either : now these creatures held unchallenged sway. Just as Southampton had had to accept defeat from the new master, Northampton, so Pembroke made it up with Carr.

In return Southampton received assurance of his pension of £2,000 a year on the customs on sweet wines.[26] We find him engaged as usual in the military business of his Lieutenancy, helping to recruit volunteers for the force Lord Willoughby was raising to aid the king of Denmark,[27] inspecting the musters, stocks of ammunition and the beacons each year in Hampshire as well as attending to his charge of the Isle of Wight. Sometimes something out of the past Catholic associations of Southampton House grazed him, as in the comic case of John Cotton, suspected to be the author of *Balaam's Ass*, a rude reply to King James's book.[28] (It was rather *infra dig.* for the King to write a book at all — it was bound to call out some ass in reply.) The reply offered an interpretation of the Apocalypse, with Britain as the seat of Anti-Christ, Queen Elizabeth as the Whore of Babylon, and King James as Anti-Christ in person. This Catholic trash might be regarded as treasonable, when such things were taken seriously. It fell to Southampton to investigate Cotton's books and papers at his house in Hampshire — he came of an obstinate recusant family. Curiously enough, when Cotton absconded from Hampshire he made for Chancery Lane and Southampton House, a favourite haunt of recusants. No doubt there were sympathisers in the Earl's large household, though he himself had not only conformed but was a convinced proponent of a Protestant foreign policy.

In the summer of 1613 he betook himself abroad ; we find him writing to Sir Ralph Winwood, a strong Protestant ally, in terms of bitter opposition to the group in power, concerning some concerted political action we cannot fully interpret now. There seems to have been an understanding with Sir Thomas Overbury, who had been trapped by Northampton into refusing the King's offer of an embassy to get him abroad and in consequence was sent to the Tower. (Here all the measures were contrived by Northampton's niece to remove this dangerous opponent by poisoning him at leisure.) Southampton apparently hoped that upon Overbury's submission he would have leave to travel, and that would leave the coast clear for Neville's promotion as Secretary of State. From this we may infer that Overbury had been putting pressure on Carr — he had the means and the ability — to have himself made Secretary. He was ambitious enough, but James hated him, and his friends had had much ado to ward off a public sentence of banishment, in return for his rude rejection of the royal promotion of him out of the way. The fact was that Overbury was (politically) blackmailing Carr and holding up his marriage with Northampton's niece, about whom he knew, and said, too much.

Before this brilliant match could take place there had to be a nullity suit to declare the dreadful niece's marriage to the young Essex null and void, on the ground of the husband's incapacity. The young man denied this imputation on his virility, and children by a second marriage proved it. But the beautiful Countess submitted herself, under a thick veil for modesty's sake, to a jury of experienced matrons, who were enabled to declare her — though she had already been had by Carr — a virgin. However, where the marriage of a king's favourite was concerned, everybody, judges, bishops — except the unaccommodating Archbishop Abbot — was ready to oblige, the more especially since in the end the King himself intervened to advance the good cause. This is the background of Southampton's confidential letter to Winwood from abroad, in opposition. 'Of the Nullity I see you have heard as much as I can write ; by which you may discern the power of a king with judges, for of those which are now for it, I knew some of them when I was in England were vehemently against it — as the Bishops of Ely and Coventry. For the business itself, I protest I shall be glad, if it may lawfully, that it may go forward ; though of late I have been fearful of the consequence and have had my fears increased by the last letters which came to me. But, howsoever, the manner of interposing gives me no cause of contentment.' [29]

Southampton was waiting for a wind to take him to England, where he had to entertain the King at Beaulieu ; for James had announced his intention of a visit, and not only, we may be sure with these political personages, for the hunting but to keep his eye on a malcontent. In November Carr was created an earl so that his Howard bride should not lose her rank as a countess by marrying him. At the creation ceremony Southampton had to take his place along with the other Earls, Pembroke, Montgomery, and wicked old Northampton : Southampton had the honour of bearing the new Somerset's cap of estate.[30] But he does not seem to have been present at the infamous marriage during the Christmas, the bride wearing her hair long on her shoulders in brazen token of her virginity, given away at the altar by Northampton, who had no belief in Anglican ceremonies anyway. Though the state was in great straits for money, the King paid for it all, showered jewels and gifts upon bride and bridegroom, and purchased the Queen's agreement by adding Greenwich to her jointure. A rich and costly masque was given that marriage-night, in which Pembroke and Montgomery were among the masquers, Southampton not, though by a nice gesture he allowed his servants to serve. Sir Francis Bacon surpassed himself in servility, giving a grand masque all on his own, which cost him £2,000 ; but then he was under great obligations to Carr and the

Howards, who had got him the Attorney-Generalship at last, where Queen Elizabeth and his cousin Cecil would give him nothing. Altogether it was said that presents from the quality amounted to £30,000 in plate and jewels, sucking up to the triumphant favourite. His former friend, Overbury, was already dead in the Tower, poisoned not by him but by his virginal bride : Overbury had died on 15 September 1613, some ten days before the Countess had secured the judgment from the commissioners that freed her for another experiment in married bliss.

The government was at its wits' end for money. It is true that the country was rich and prosperous, but the Crown's revenues were much diminished and could not possibly meet the expenses of government, even apart from James's extravagance and lack of money-sense. That in itself was not the main issue ; it merely added an irritant, constituted a provocation, supplied an argument to enemies. Abroad, the movement of the time was all towards the increase of monarchical power, and Continental monarchs taxed their subjects and raised supplies by prerogative. But England was heading on a different tack ; her constitutional difference from Continental monarchies was becoming more and more apparent with the increasing representativeness, the sense of continuity, the clamant demands, of the Commons. The Commons on their side felt, with justice, that they were more representative of the English nation than ever the Stuart monarchy was. This was highly uncongenial to James with his loftily held, though less loftily exemplified, notions of royal prerogative — kings as the representatives of God, and the rest of the rubbish, while all too visible on earth with companions like Carr! The humorous King had no sense of humour where himself was concerned.

Northampton had long resisted a resort to Parliament, but, with the deficit mounting again, the majority in Council moved against him and in 1614 a new Parliament was summoned. The Court attempted to influence the elections, naturally enough, by promoting where possible the return of members favourable to it. This created an atmosphere of distrust from the beginning. But who was to lead the Commons ? There was only one candidate who commanded the necessary experience and ability to do so as Secretary of State, and who moreover had the confidence of the Commons. This was Sir Henry Neville, whom Southampton had backed all along and whom everybody expected, himself included, to see in office to handle the new Parliament. But his nomination would have meant James's capitulation to his demands and those of the Commons.

In March Sir Ralph Winwood was made Secretary of State instead, a step to placate the Commons, for he was wholeheartedly Protestant and anti-Spanish in his sympathies and moreover had negotiated the treaties that bound England to the Netherlands. He was, as we have seen, a friend and confidant of Southampton and was of his way of thinking. Honest man as he was, he was no leader for the Commons, which at once took up their demands for redress of grievances, a declaration against impositions and monopolies, where they had been left by the dissolution of 1610. As against the King's renewed appeals and defence of his policy, the Commons appealed to the Lords for common action on their lines. In a very significant division nearly one half of the peers voted to line up with the Commons against the government and the Court — in fact only some dozen independent lay peers supported the latter at all. Here was an indication how much out of touch with the sentiment of the country James's rule was. Himself seemed sublimely unaware of it, and put it all down to factious opposition.

The discussion grew more acrimonious, as was only to be expected, as each side appealed to rights and principles. In the Commons Sir Edwin Sandys — an archbishop's son, too ! — made an historic speech traversing James's oft-repeated conception of government, the divine legation of kings, et cetera.[31]

As against this Sandys appealed to the rights of the people by whose consent, if only tacit, rulers ruled ; the origin of every hereditary monarchy, unless by conquest, lay in election, with reciprocal conditions between king and people. A king by conquest might with as much right be expelled. Sandys was never forgiven for this speech. But James had only himself to thank for bringing such matters into discussion : like the don he was, he had unwisely kept insisting upon the fundamental rights of his prerogative — and laid himself open to an answer in similar abstract terms. Elizabeth had had the sense never to raise or discuss such matters. It is always a mistake to seek to lay bare the grounds of human action, to discuss ultimate issues of political principle : it never settles anything, but leads straight to Declarations of Right, Declarations of Independence or what not.

We shall later find Southampton working more closely with Sandys than with anyone else, particularly, though not only, in running the Virginia Company. It seems that Sandys claimed credit for Southampton's conversion to Protestantism ; but it is fairly clear that Southampton's earlier Catholicism, though it stood in his light, never meant much to him.

To one person these exchanges gave nothing but pleasure : under the surface Northampton (like Marie Antoinette encouraging the Jacobins) exacerbated them. It was said that he put Hoskins up to his attack on the Scottish favourites, with its unforgivable threat of a Sicilian Vespers for them. He succeeded all too well : the Commons now went too far and put themselves in the wrong ; exasperated beyond endurance, James dissolved Parliament in June. Not a single bill had been passed ; James did not call another Parliament until the last years of his reign, the scission between the new dynasty and the English nation grew more marked. James was henceforth bent on an alternative policy : understanding with Spain — for which in itself there was much to be said, if peace were to be kept in Europe — a Spanish marriage for his heir, with a dowry large enough to pay the Crown's debts and be independent of Parliament. (We can follow this unpatriotic line again with James's grandson, Charles II.) James had no real grasp of the country whose affairs he was conducting. He confided to the Spanish ambassador, Gondómar — who became more and more his confidant — what he thought of the English Parliament: 'I am surprised that my ancestors should ever have permitted such an institution to come into existence. I am a stranger, and found it here when I arrived, so that I am obliged to put up with what I cannot get rid of.'[32] On their side the stupid Spaniards hopelessly misread the situation in England : with an overwhelmingly Protestant country, becoming ever more fanatically so — of five hundred members of Parliament not one had dared not to communicate at St. Margaret's, Westminster (they would not go to the Abbey for fear of copes and wafers) — the Spaniards really thought there was a chance of the Stuart kings turning England Catholic ! This was the kind of thing that led to the Civil War and Oliver Cromwell, the Exclusion Bill and the Revolution of 1688.

The dissolution was a triumph for Northampton with his pro-Catholic policy at home and abroad. He had long been looking forward to taking Salisbury's place as Lord Treasurer — and if he were in receipt of a Spanish pension, so too Salisbury had been. But now Providence took a hand : Northampton had a growth, which he had operated and died from the effects in June. Though the state was bankrupt, he left thousands of pounds in ready money in his study.[33] He made his nephew, the Earl of Arundel, his chief heir, with lands worth £3,000 a year ; another nephew, Henry Howard, got lands of £1,000 a year ; Northampton's London palace (later Northumberland House) at Charing Cross, went to his brother Suffolk, who now got the Lord Treasurership and proceeded handsomely to embezzle the funds under his rule. After a lifetime of frustration under the old Protestant Queen, Northampton had at last made good — or at least had done exceedingly well for the Howards.

With England increasingly counted out, as it could never be under Henry VIII or Elizabeth, we watch the preliminary manoeuvres for what became the Thirty Years War take shape. The absurd young Palatine of Neuburg — a fit companion for James's Palatine son-in-law, Frederick — went over to Catholicism and threatened to carry the strategic Duchy of Cleves, with Düsseldorf, with him. The Dutch, feeling the approaches to their country threatened, occupied Jülich. Spinola, at the head of the army of the Catholic League, now invaded the Duchies and mastered the towns on the left bank of the Rhine. General war threatened. England had treaties with the Dutch, and English contingents served under the States General. Prince Maurice advanced to take possession of Emmerich.

Southampton, disgusted with the course of affairs at home and always anxious to take the opportunity of action, went abroad to the Low Countries after the end of Parliament in the summer of 1614, as he had done the summer before. He took the no less discontented young Essex (and with what reason!) abroad with him, hoping to take part in the Jülich campaign.[34] Southampton landed at Flushing with his own private recruits ; towards the end of July he was at Antwerp with Lord Chandos, setting forth towards Spa. In August Spinola captured Wesel. Prince Maurice had no authority to make war, but, with Southampton now with him, occupied Emmerich and put in a garrison. In England Southampton's absence from the ceremonies of a state visit by the King of Denmark was commented on ; it was considered 'not accidental or for Spa water, so much as for other politic consideration'.[35] However, when he returned to his duties at Court at the end of the year, he received a good welcome from the King.

Meanwhile, it was in this year that James first met young George Villiers and his fate was sealed : this was love at first sight. The young Villiers not only possessed indescribable good looks, but was intelligent and teachable, of a good nature and disposition, whose manners were, as Clarendon tells us, 'of an elaborate and overflowing courtesy'. His ambitious mother had had him carefully educated at the French Court for the post of king's favourite. At the English Court a cabal of respectables, sick of Carr and the Howards, a Protestant combination headed by Archbishop Abbot came together to recommend this promising youth to the attention of the disillusioned King, in whose breast hope yet sprang vernal and eternal. With a nice respect for the proprieties, James would not make him a gentleman of the bed-chamber, that operative post, until the Queen herself pressed this kindness upon him. Somerset at once appreciated the threat to his position. Poor James, who wanted to keep everyone happy around him, urged the newcomer to offer his service to Somerset, who is said to have replied, 'I will none of your service, and you shall none of my favour. I will, if I can, break your neck, and of that be confident.' [36]

It was Somerset's neck that was broken. Secretary Winwood had at last got the clue to the secret of Overbury's death in the Tower, and it was at Beaulieu, while staying with Southampton in the summer of 1615, that this was communicated to the horrified James, who at last saw how he had been taken advantage of and was willing to have the matter probed to its depths. The investigations took a long time, but in May 1616 the Somersets were brought to trial in Westminster Hall and both found guilty. It is not likely that Somerset was guilty of poisoning his friend : he, too, had been taken advantage of by the unspeakable girl-Countess. So the King commuted their joint sentence to one of life-imprisonment. It is not known whether clever Northampton connived at Overbury's poisoning : he merely got him incarcerated, took the measures to insulate him so that he could be got at, and then took steps to dispose of the body as quickly as possible. It is a pity that so religious a protagonist of conservative causes should not have been more respectable.

With the Somersets disposed of and the King happy with his Steenie — James fancied a resemblance between young Villiers and a stained glass window of St. Stephen at Whitehall — a feeling of euphoria returned to Court. Court life continued with its ritual, its ceremonies, its duties and rewards. In July 1616 Southampton received a mark of favour : pardon of a bond of 1,000 marks which he had forfeited for neglecting to have a survey made of the woods belonging to a number of manors, along with permission to dispose of them as he pleased.[37] In November Charles was created Prince of Wales; at the banquet Pembroke officiated as Lord Chamberlain, Southampton served as cup-bearer.[38] His son, James, Lord Wriothesley, was made a Knight of the Bath on the occasion. Still he was not given employment of any significance — the piping times of peace were not propitious to a man of would-be action. Again and again, all through his life he was frustrated of the hope of command. With the decline of England's naval power the seas and even the coasts were infested with Algerine pirates. The London merchants offered 40,000 crowns to equip a fleet, if Southampton would undertake the command, to raid the pirates in their lair.[39] If a fleet were to be sent James designated Southampton for the command, in view of the age and illness of Lord Admiral Nottingham.[40] But this project came up against a Spanish veto : it would be humiliating to Spain's dignity to have an English fleet clear up the nuisance on her doorstep.

More to James's mind was his return-journey to Scotland, on which he determined in 1617. This appealed both to vanity and sentiment, both strongly marked in him. But the Venetian envoys enlighten us as to the political objectives : to introduce Anglicanism, with bishops and 'other ceremonies of the Catholic church which were not abandoned in England' ; to introduce the English model of justice, instead of that of sheriffs with perpetual tenure ; to increase the king's revenue, for he had received only the scantiest from his beloved Scots — the expenses of administration almost equalled the income.[41] No doubt. Preparations lagged so much that people wondered whether it would take place. Southampton, Pembroke, and

Montgomery were to accompany the King, but they were making slow and slender provision.[42] In the end the retinue was much cut down for reasons of expense, and in the ill July weather they all set out for Berwick.

Arrived there, 'quilk is the martche betwixt England and Scotland', a scene characteristic of James's odd naïvety took place.[43] 'The King he stood with one foot in England, the other in Scotland, and said, "Now, my lords, I am both in Scotland and England", and was so glaid as could be.' The royal party stayed a couple of nights at Dunglas, a place of Lord Home's. Here something of the familiar Scottish inferiority-complex peeped out. James was so pleased that he said, 'Now, my lords, you know since I came from London I have had naughty weather all the way, and now since I came to Scotland the heaven smileth upon me. Tell me, my lords, did you feid so well sence you cam from London ?' We can well imagine what the supercilious reactions of polite English lords would be. Thence to Seton, and via Leith, where the two supply-ships were lying off in the roads, to Edinburgh, 'the north loch lying betwixt the city and it'. It must have been a still more beautiful spectacle in those days. James had travelled 'always in his cotche until the time he had allmost cum' to his state entry into his old capital and its familiar scenes, of humiliation and danger, of expectation and (occasional) rejoicing.

However, to James it was home, and he took an innocent pleasure in showing off its sights to his English entourage. Not all of them behaved exemplarily : the rude Montgomery had a quarrel with Lord Howard de Walden on the exotic subject of whether apes had tails, and on this there might have been a fight if the learned King had not composed the quarrel.[44] When James got down to his own business, trying to winkle money out of a Scots Parliament, the English lords left him to it, some of them awaiting him at Carlisle, while Southampton and Montgomery returned before him to London. In reward for service Southampton received a useful grant — in the shortage of cash this was the kind of way in which servants of the Crown received their reward : a confirmation of privileges in regard to his lands in various counties, with an extension of the liberties of Southampton House from Holborn Bars to the Rolls Chapel in Chancery Lane (site of the present Public Record Office).[45] Earlier that year, on James's Accession day, 24 March, Southampton had attended the sermon at Paul's Cross to celebrate it, with a grand company — Archbishop Abbot, Bacon newly elevated as Lord Keeper, the Earl of Arundel, and Secretary Winwood. The preacher was Dr. Donne, 'who made there a dainty sermon . . . and was exceedingly well liked generally, the rather for that he did Queen Elizabeth great right and held himself to the text without flattering the time too much'.[46] Now, at the end of the year, we find Southampton visiting his friend Winwood dying.[47]

In the early summer of 1618 Southampton was, as usual, in Hampshire for a spell overseeing the musters. This year he had a discouraging report to make : many were backward in making their appearance, many obstinately refused to do their share, some refused to pay their tax for the support of a Mustermaster.[48] It was like the humiliating response of the country to the Council's request for a benevolence, since Parliament had voted no supplies. In August James was down at Beaulieu once more hunting, while in November he made a great picnic at a farmhouse near Newmarket, 'whither every man should bring his dish. The King brought a great chine of beef, the marquis of Hamilton four pigs encircled with sausages, the earl of Southampton two turkeys, another six partridges, and one a whole tray full of buttered eggs, and so all passed very pleasantly.' [49] This was what James much preferred to the vexations of politics : who can blame him ? — except that he happened to be king.

He particularly needed consolation and withdrawal from the public eye at this time, for the previous month had witnessed Ralegh's execution, at the behest of the Spanish ambassador, and Ralegh had turned the last scene of his life, outside the Gatehouse at Westminster, into an unforgettable demonstration against the Stuart monarchy. Archbishop Abbot was able to draw the conclusion, however, that Ralegh's death was really a judgment on him for his scepticism.[50] Shortly after, the Archbishop had the misfortune to kill his keeper while hunting and had to suspend his sacred functions — perhaps this was a judgment on him ? In February 1619 the King made Southampton a handsome grant of £1,200 a year, in lieu of his arable land in the New Forest that had gone out of cultivation on account of the multitude of deer.[51] In March Queen Anne died, 'having benefited many and injured none ; she died most willingly and was more comely in death than ever in life'.[52] At her funeral in Henry VII's chapel Southampton was in attendance on Prince Charles as chief mourner ; James, himself ill, remained in seclusion at Theobalds with Villiers, now Marquis of Buckingham, to console him.

In April Southampton was at last promoted to the Privy Council — unexpectedly, and apparently by Buckingham's influence. Various people were in hope of achieving it, in particular the able financier, Lionel Cranfield, on his way up to becoming Lord Treasurer. 'But they came home all as they went, and the lot fell the Friday after on the Earl of Southampton, who was sworn at the Star Chamber, when he seemed least to look for it.'[53] What he thought on his belated elevation to the centre of power, after years of disappointment and frustration, we know from a letter of his to Sir Dudley Carleton, ambassador in the Netherlands. 'It is true his Majesty hath given me a place on his Council board, which preferment — I protest by the faith of an honest man — I expected not, neither sought directly nor indirectly, by myself or any of my friends, yea, I may say truly, nor wished in my heart. His favour I confess to be the greater, and I the more bound to serve him honestly . . . if I may attain that end I shall account my poor endeavours well employed. Otherwise, I had much rather have continued a spectator than become an actor. And I shall rather perform the office of a Councillor in keeping than giving counsel. . . . But I will make the same request to you that I have to some other of my good friends — not to expect too much from me. You know well how things stand and pass with us, and how little one vulgar [i.e. popular] Councillor is able to effect.' [54]

Not a very promising mood in which to arrive at office at last : evidently Southampton had no expectations and no illusions. He clearly set more store now on his reputation as an honest man than on being a member of King James's Privy Council. It had come too late, and in fact it was the prelude to a period of open opposition, royal disfavour, and another spell, if a brief one, of imprisonment.

So much for Southampton's public career through the main course of James's reign. It remains to pick up the few threads of his private life and concerns that are left to us.

And first for his family. His elder son, James, Lord Wrio-thesley was at Eton during these years, from 1613 to 1619 : he did not mess in Hall with the other boys, but drew commons for himself and a page in his own chamber.[55] In 1619 he matriculated from his father's old college at Cambridge, St. John's, though he did not stay long. Later we find him a member of Parliament, elected for Callington in Cornwall in 1620, at the age of 15, and for Winchester in 1624. Meanwhile, he was admitted a student at Lincoln's Inn in 1621. The second son, Thomas, born in 1608, put in a rather longer appearance at St. John's, 1625-6, in the two years after his father's death. Two more sons died in infancy. So also a little girl Mary, who was buried at Titchfield 10 January 1616. There she is on her little monument on the south wall of the chapel in the parish church, looking across to the marble splendours, the pyramids, of the great monument to her ancestors, shortly to receive her father and elder brother.

The eldest child, Penelope — called after Essex's sister, Lady Rich, we remember — was married to the second Lord Spencer of Wormleighton. In July 1617 we hear of Southampton arriving, with Montgomery and the celebrated Lucy, Countess of Bedford — patroness of the poets — at the Court at Nonsuch, on his way to spend some summer days with the Spencers in Warwickshire.[56] Penelope lived out her days there, the long days of the Civil War, the Protectorate and Restoration, dying in the same year as her brother, the fourth and last earl, in 1667. 'Leaving a character for all female virtues', she is buried in the splendid chapel, packed with glowing Spencer tombs, at Brington.

Southampton's circle of acquaintance was a wide one, necessarily as a Court grandee, but from earliest years he had the generous gift of friendship. It is sad that the loss of his correspondence restricts our knowledge of all this side to his life. We know how passionately devoted a member of the Essex circle he was earlier, and he remained faithful and helpful to the young sprigs of the next generation. We have seen him taking Essex's son abroad with him to pick up military experience in the Netherlands. In May 1615 he procured a licence for Mountjoy Blount — eldest son of his friend Mountjoy by his liaison with Penelope Rich — to travel overseas for three years to attain the languages, with one man and two pages, provided that he did not go to Rome.[57] This young man also had his military apprenticeship in the Low Countries, and went on to have an exciting career with various escapades, as Earl of Newport, in the Civil War. At Court Southampton was most constantly in the company of the Herberts, Pembroke and Montgomery, and was friendly with them — but, alas, their private correspondence has perished too. In the latter part of his life we find Southampton in closest touch with two circles that represented his interests : the Netherlands group of military men, Philip Sidney's brother, Lord Lisle, and Sir John Throckmorton, and the diplomats, Neville, Winwood and Carleton ; and the people interested in colonial and maritime expansion, like Sir Thomas Roe and Sir Edwin Sandys. Some men, who combined these two fields of experience, graduating from the Netherlands to Virginia — such soldiers as Sir Thomas

Gates and Sir Thomas Dale — belonged to his following rather than his friends. For Southampton, however friendly and popular, remained very much of a grandee, on a pinnacle of general deference and respect.

As such he continued to be the target for literary men's hopes of patronage. Chapman, in dedicating his Homer, includes a sonnet to Southampton, addressed not only as 'right valorous and virtuous' but also as 'learned'. These epithets give us a just picture of a much respected peer, whose private life was unspotted by the scandals of James's Court, of soldierly bearing and martial inclinations, but who was well educated, interested in books and learning. It was natural that George Wither, a Hampshire man, should devote a hopeful epigram to him :

> Southampton, since thy province gave me birth,
> And on these pleasant mountains I yet keep,
> I ought to be no stranger to thy worth . . .

In 1614 Richard Brathwaite, a journeyman of letters, dedicated *The Scholar's Medley* to Southampton as 'generally reputed learned, so a professed friend to such as be studious of learning'. In 1618 two books were offered to him, H.G.'s *The Mirror of Majesty*, and Henry Peacham's *Minerva Britannica*, which rings the changes once more on the combination of martial with scholarly qualities. The later editions of a more remarkable book were offered him — Thomas Wright's *The Passions of the Mind*, an original, perhaps the first, of Elizabethan treatises on psychology, a work drawn upon by Shakespeare for his depiction of Hamlet's melancholy.

On his side Southampton continued to be a generous patron to institutions of learning. We have noted his munificent gift of £100 to the Bodleian Library at Oxford. But naturally his interests and associations were all with his own university. In 1620 we find him intervening with 'my very loving friends, the Provost and Seniors of King's College in Cambridge' to grant leave of absence for three years to one of the Fellows to attend the ambassador appointed to Venice.[58] He kept his associations with his old college green, and after all Little Shelford was close to Cambridge. In 1613 he accompanied Prince Charles and the Elector Palatine there.[59] Some years later he arranged to take over the fine library collected — rather beyond his means — by William Crashaw, one of the Fellows, for ultimate presentation to St. John's. Crashaw, like that other Cambridge man, William Strachey, was a member of the Virginia Company, where Southampton would have come in contact with him. In 1618 negotiations to take over the library came to a point : the books were to be deposited at Southampton House, where the Earl had the use of them during his lifetime. After his death his widow sent them down to Cambridge, a collection of some hundreds of manuscripts and rare volumes, a munificent bequest to the new library lately built at St. John's. Hence it is that his portrait, painted at this time, in 1618, hangs in his old college among its benefactors.

Letters and friendly exchanges show the terms of affectionate respect he was on with the family college. The Master and Fellows were not slow in offering their congratulations, in a formal Latin letter, on his promotion to the Privy Council ; they did not hesitate to pronounce that it was a tardy recognition.[60] After his death, in sending down the library, the Countess wrote to the college : 'the great love and affection that my dearest lord, now with God, did ever bear unto the honour and good of that worthy society of yours, and that respect and honour which hath reflected from you all again, both towards himself and his house, do oblige me also, by what means I may, to endeavour that his name and memory may forever live and be fresh amongst you. And to that purpose, having found that in his lifetime and of his own noble inclination he had designed certain books unto the new library of your house, which have been all this time carefully by me preserved entire, I hope, in number — for the catalogue is with you and not with me — and safe from harm. Now, so soon as notice could be taken that the place grew to a readiness to receive them, I have herewithal sent them unto you as a testimony of the good will and affection borne unto the house from hence. For I must needs take notice of the great honour and respect done to my son at his late being with you, who, as I hope, he will therein also imitate his noble father in his love to learning and to you.'

This refers, of course, to the second son, who survived his father and elder brother to become the fourth Earl. On his going up to St. John's his tutor wrote, 'to no place can he come with more affection, either of her ladyship's or his own, desiring to succeed his noble father and brother as in other things so in that kind respect they did both bear unto, and find again ever from, that worthy society'.

Three months after Southampton had buried his little girl at Titchfield, in the chapel dominated by the great monument of marble, an earlier friend and follower was buried in the church at Stratford. We know nothing of any continuing connection between the poet and his patron, though something of the stress of the latter's career, at the time of the Essex conspiracy, is reflected in *Troilus and Cressida*, and something of his situation and youthful personality may appear in *All's Well That Ends Well*. That title might indeed be taken for epigraph of the way the young patron's life had turned out. Amid so many pressures that his later life had accumulated upon him, of office, interests political, military, territorial, commercial, of family and society, Court and country, there can have been little time to devote much thought to the actor-dramatist who had gone his own way and fulfilled himself in his independent, so busy, so dedicated and reserved, life. And yet, in 1609, the Sonnets had been given to the public, in which one might read :

> Not marble, nor the gilded monuments
> Of princes, shall outlive this powerful rhyme ;
> But you shall shine more bright in these contents
> Than unswept stone, besmeared with sluttish time.

When wasteful war shall statues overturn,
And broils root out the work of masonry,
Nor Mars's sword nor war's quick fire shall burn
The living record of your memory.

That, of course, was only the commonplace of poets. It would probably have surprised the noble Earl, as well as the society of the time, that he should be remembered by posterity only as the patron of that poet.

CHAPTER XII

The Virginia Company

THE responsible headship of the Virginia Company became a prime concern and leading activity of Southampton's last and busiest years. But his interest in the plantation of America, in maritime and commercial affairs, in a forward, activist policy, went back a long way. It was this that aligned this former Catholic more and more with an aggressive, Protestant line of policy, and brought him very much to Ralegh's standpoint, even to become a continuator of his colonial work — though there is no evidence of contact between the two men, and Southampton had belonged to Essex's circle, Ralegh's enemy. The pressures of life effect such transformations.

Perhaps, like Ralegh, his spell in the Tower gave him the time to devote his mind to more fruitful projects ; for it was during his imprisonment there, in 1602, that he became a chief backer of Captain Gosnold's voyage to prospect the American coast and thus to open up again the colonising activity that had been quenched by the developing maritime war a decade or more before. Gosnold had served Ralegh on one or two earlier expeditions, and here was Southampton carrying on the work in which Ralegh had grown discouraged. In his *History of Travel into Virginia Britannia* William Strachey, Secretary to the colony, makes the specific link and pays an eloquent tribute to the newcomer now coming to the fore.

Thus Sir Walter Ralegh, wearied with so great an expense and abused with the unfaithfulness of those he employed, after he had sent by these five several times colonies and supplies at his own charges . . . he was even now content to commit the fortune of the poor men's lives and life of the holy action itself into the favour and protection of the God of all mercy. . . . By which means for seventeen or eighteen years together it lay neglected, until it pleased God at length to move again the heart of a great and right noble earl amongst us —

'Candidus, et talos a vertice pulcher ad imos —'

Henry, Earl of Southampton, to take it in consideration and seriously to advise how to recreate and dip it anew into spirit and life. Who therefore . . . began to make new enquiries and much scrutiny after the country, to examine the former proceedings, together with the lawfulness and pious end thereof. And then, having well weighed the greatness and goodness of the cause, he largely contributed to the furnishing out of a ship to be commanded by Captain Bartholomew Gosnold and Captain Bartholomew Gilbert and accompanied with divers other gentlemen, to discover a convenient place for a new colony to be sent thither : who accordingly, in March anno 1602 from Falmouth, in a bark of Dartmouth called the *Concord*, set forward holding a course for the north part of Virginia.[1]

Virginia, to the Elizabethans, meant the whole of North America between Spanish Florida and the French St. Lawrence, which they regarded as the sphere of the New World 'providentially reserved', in Hakluyt's phrase, for English settlement. It was not until James I's reign that the northern parts of Virginia came to be designated New England — appropriately, for they are very like. It is amusing to find Strachey still referring, in the decency of Latin, to Southampton's physical beauty — 'bright and shining, beautiful from top to toe'.

Gosnold and Gilbert made for the Azores and then for a direct course to the American coast — where the Elizabethan voyages had made for the West Indies and then come up out of the Florida channel. Thus the captains coasted along New England, naming Martha's Vineyard, and reached the spacious Main — in time to become the state of Maine. They waxed eloquent over the country : 'this Main is the goodliest continent that ever we saw, promising more by far than we any way did expect. For it is replenished with fair fields, and in them fragrant flowers, also meadows, and hedged in with stately groves, being furnished also with pleasant brooks, and beautified with two main rivers that (as we judge) may haply become good harbours and conduct us to the hopes men so greedily do thirst after.' ² That means the North West Passage to the riches of the East.

Strachey continues the story : 'This voyage alone could not satisfy so intent a spirit and ambitious in so great and glorious an enterprise as his lordship's, the aforesaid earl of Southampton : who laboured to have it so begun as that it might be continued with all due and prepared circumstances and safety. And therefore would his lordship be concurrent the second time in a new survey and despatch to be made thither with his brother-in-law, Thomas Arundell, Baron of Wardour : who prepared a ship for Captain George Weymouth, which set sail from Ratcliffe in March 1605.' ³ His share in this little American voyage is much the best thing we know about Southampton's brother-in-law ; from Rosier's narrative we know that at least a couple of Arundell's servants were among the small ship's company of twenty-nine.

They made straight for the coast of Maine, where they arrived in May. The account of the country that Rosier gives is very much on the same lines as Gosnold's — the ways of the Indians, deerskins, furs, tobacco, salmon, and so on. But he adds a lyrical account of the grand river Kennebec : 'as we passed with a gentle wind up with our ship in this river any man may conceive with what admiration we all consented with joy. Many who had been travellers in sundry countries and in the most famous rivers yet affirmed them not comparable to this they now beheld. Some that were with Sir Walter Ralegh in his voyage to Guiana in the discovery of the river Orinoco, which echoed fame to the world's ears, gave reasons why it was not to be compared with this.' ⁴ Perhaps this was going a little far, but we observe how Ralegh set the standard for all these men and how effective was his sense of publicity.

They observed, 'here are made by nature most excellent places as docks to grave and careen ships of all burdens, secured from all winds . . . such that few places in England or in any other parts of Christendom art with great charges can make the like'. The subsequent maritime history of Maine, with the part it played in colonial times in the history of the British Navy, bears out the perspicacity of that observation. Of more immediate importance, they brought back with them five Indians, three of whom they handed over to Sir Ferdinando Gorges at Plymouth, who took them under his wing for the next three years and used them to learn everything he could from them about their country. It was this more than anything else that gave Gorges his fixation on planting New England : 'this accident must be acknowledged the means under God of putting on foot and giving life to all our plantations'.[5] For the rest of his life Gorges persevered with his efforts, and ultimately emerged as the founder of the province of Maine.

With the peace of 1604 came England's chance to go forward with the plantation of her sphere of the New World. After all, this was what she had fought Spain for twenty years for — the open door in America and the independence of the Netherlands. Immediately upon these voyages, the second of which aroused great interest, two companies were founded to plant colonies in America : the Plymouth Company, based mainly on South Western support and the fishing interest there ; the London Company, which naturally had greater resources and more staying power. The former, interested in the northern area, planted the first northern colony, at the mouth of the Kennebec — at Popham's Beach — in 1607 ; the second, interested in the southern area, planted Jamestown the same year. The northern colony did not last ; we shall see what heroic efforts were necessary to see the southern colony through.

Lord Chancellor Egerton said later, 'we always thought at first we would send people there little by little'.[6] The first colony at Jamestown consisted of the usual number, such as had been sent out to Roanoke by Ralegh, of about a hundred. At the end of seven months they had exhausted their provisions and cultivated no more : only thirty-eight were left alive. The first supply sent out another one hundred and twenty, the second another seventy. The tale of misfortune grew worse ; famine and fever stalked the colony hand in hand with idleness and indiscipline — this is where the Puritans had such an advantage in New England later ; only John Smith's energy saved the colony from perishing. Something more drastic was necessary ; a bigger effort at home, more effective command in the colony, if possible a military man with full powers to exert discipline.

In London there was an enlargement of the Council in 1607 by which the Company, and its colony, were governed — sixteen more members, among them Sir Edwin Sandys. But now the colonial idea caught on; the Privy Council whipped up support ; the country, but especially the City, responded like a prairie fire. The nation felt that its honour was involved — or perhaps instinctively its future, as it certainly was. The Spanish ambassador, Zuñiga, protested and obstructed, but in vain. The Virginia Company was granted a new charter in 1609, with full powers to govern and regulate the colony. It recruited among its subscribers no less than fifty-six City companies and six hundred and fifty members. The membership reads like a fascinating roll-call of Jacobean society, beginning with the Lord Treasurer, Salisbury ; Southampton's name stands third, immediately followed by Pembroke and, lower down, Montgomery. Here are all the people who were interested in the nation's future overseas, especially in the New World.[7] Of the amount of money they were ready to put into the venture we find later on, by 1618, that Lord De la Warr comes first with £500, Pembroke second with £400, Southampton third with £350.[8] Richard Hakluyt's holding was £21 — but he had invested his life's work in the cause. The Treasurer of the Company and the leading spirit in the whole enterprise, for the next ten years, was the greatest of English businessmen at the time, Sir Thomas Smythe, also Governor of the East India Company; from his house in Philpot lane, principally, Virginia's affairs were directed.

A great effort was made for 1609. Lord De la Warr himself was to go out as governor, but since he was unable to leave for the time, Sir Thomas Gates — a Netherlands soldier, an acquaintance of Southampton — went in his place. A fleet of nine vessels, with some six hundred colonists on board, made their rendezvous at Plymouth for the New World at the beginning of June. Setting a direct course for the Chesapeake, the flagship under Sir George Somers ran into a hurricane, which became famous as *The Tempest*. The rest of the fleet got to Virginia, but the *Sea Venture* was driven in on the coast of the uninhabited island of Bermuda and split up, though not a life was lost. There they spent the winter and spring, with food in plenty — the woods swarming with hogs and fowl, the sea with fish — and built themselves a couple of pinnaces in which they reached Virginia in May.

William Strachey, the new Secretary of the colony, sent home a letter recounting these events, addressed to a 'Noble Lady'. It is not known who this lady was, but the social usage of the time indicates that she was the wife of a nobleman. The likeliest candidate is the celebrated literary patroness, Lucy, Countess of Bedford, since she was a member of the Company in her own right, and later her name appears on the Council. Strachey's news-letter was read by Shakespeare, who may well have known the writer, for he was a resident of Blackfriars, with which the dramatist was closely connected in these years. It was this that suggested the theme of Shakespeare's penultimate play, with its undertone of farewell to the theatre, and even the details of the pamphlet are caught up into the piece.

There is, for example, the phenomenon of St. Elmo's fire, which the terrified colonists had experienced in the hurricane:

> Now in the waist, the deck, in every cabin,
> I flamed amazement: sometime I'd divide

And burn in many places ; on the topmast,
The yards and bowsprit would I flame distinctly,
Then meet and join.

When the *Sea Venture* ran in on the rocks no one was drowned.
When Prospero in the play asks, 'But are they, Ariel, safe ?'
Ariel replies, 'Not a hair perished'. The colonists were convinced that their island was haunted, full of spirits and noises.
Shakespeare's island was full of magic, and had moreover
Caliban and his witch-mother, Sycorax, imprisoned by Prospero in a tree. On coming upon Caliban, Stephano says,
'have we devils here ? Do you put tricks upon's with savages
and men of Ind ?' (i.e. Indians). The conspiracy against
Prospero comes straight out of events on Bermuda : two or
three attempts at mutiny were capped by a conspiracy against
the life of the governor. Strachey mentions the first description of the island by Gonzalo Ferdinando Oviedo — thus we
have the names of Gonzalo and Ferdinand in the play.

A major theme behind the play is that of the relations
between advanced and backward peoples, a suggestion of what
happens when the two come in contact — the colonial, the
human, the racial problem then opening up for the English,
as for the Spaniards before them, with the colonisation of
Virginia.

'Thus early were the fortunes of Virginia linked with those
of Bermuda.'⁹ The encouraging report of conditions on the
enchanted isle turned the stream of colonisation in that direction during the next few years, 1612–18 ; and in 1615 the
Somers Islands, or Bermuda, Company came into existence to
deal with its separate, if closely connected, interests. The two
companies ran in harness, since their membership was much
the same — Southampton, for example, was a member of
both ; their business was interconnected, and sometimes, later,
they met together.

In Virginia the fearful winter of 1609–10 became known as
the 'starving time' : of five hundred colonists only sixty were
left alive. (The ground round Jamestown must be strewn with

dead men's bones.) In 1610 Lord De la Warr arrived with three ships and a hundred and fifty men, and began to put things in order once more. In 1611 a new subscription was called for in London, some £18,000 for the relief of Virginia. Three ships went out under Southampton's follower, Sir Thomas Dale, as knight-marshal, who took steps to restore some discipline to the hopeless colonists. 'Unto such calamity', wrote Strachey, 'can sloth, riot and vanity bring the most plentiful estate.' [10] 'No man would acknowledge a superior nor could from this headless and unbridled multitude be anything expected but disorder and riot,' sadly commented the Virginia Council, contemplating the fruit of all their efforts.[11] In short, the usual foolery of mankind left to their own devices.

In 1612 a revision of the Charter transferred the powers of the nominated Council to the elected Court and assembly of the Company, and this opened the way eventually for a transfer of power to the opposition to Smythe's leadership growing up under all these set-backs and misfortunes, the endless discouragements. By 1616, for all the sacrifices made, only three hundred people were left in the colony ; the Company had no money left to cover even the costs of administration. 'Not even Dale's return home with Pocahontas and nine or ten other Indians and the concerted effort to play up her status as a royal convert could overcome the fact that thousands of pounds, hundreds of lives, the devoted efforts at home of Smythe, Johnson, and Sandys, and abroad of Smith, Newport, Argall, Gates and Dale had seemingly been expended for nought.' [12] A change of administration and policy at home was sought ; in Virginia there remained the resort to a land-grant policy — fifty acres for every person transported. That ultimately saw the colony through — that and the tobacco crop, with the spread of the habit of smoking, particularly, it was observed, among soldiers at home and abroad.

Meanwhile, what of Southampton's continuing part in the colonial and commercial expansion of the time ?

The East India Company was, along with the Virginia Company, under Sir Thomas Smythe's leadership. In May 1609 the Lord Treasurer, Lord Admiral Nottingham, and Southampton were admitted free members as favourers of the Company.[13] In July Southampton sent a brace of bucks, evidently for their feast, 'to make merry withal, in regard of their kindness in accepting him of their Company'. In October Lord Monteagle requested to be made free of the Company on the same terms as Southampton, he adventuring £500, with a brace of bucks yearly at election. In January 1610 Southampton requested that Mr. Haines might be admitted, whom he had appointed to manage his adventure. Southampton's interest in the Company continued, for in 1619 we find him recommending a couple of sea-captains to command their next fleets.

In 1616 Southampton's friend, Sir Thomas Roe, sent him an entertaining Journal of his residence at the decadent Court of the great Moghul, Jehangir, at Agra. Roe was a grandson of a Lord Mayor of London, who inherited a good deal of wealth, which he spent on voyages, among other things, so he went East hoping to recoup himself. In 1610–11 he had made a voyage to the Amazon and the Orinoco, and in subsequent years sent out two more expeditions to those hopeful parts. This left him poor, and in 1613 he went soldiering in the Netherlands. One sees the Protestant pattern. Fat and jolly, 'Honest Tom' was all his life a great crony of the Protestant Elizabeth, the Winter Queen. She was always friendly, too, to Southampton : they were of the same circle and opinions.

In February 1616 Roe wrote, sending part of his Journal to Southampton : 'my lord, since my arrival in this country I have had but one month of health, and that mingled with many relapses, and am now your poor servant, scarce a crow's dinner. The fame of this place hath done it great credit in England but lost as much with me, for though the king be as rich as the Turk and every way as great, yet for want of laws, learning and civil arts all things, even the Court, are mingled with such barbarism as makes all contemptible. The king sits out, like a player, in the gallery over a stage to be seen, but no man but eunuchs comes up to him, so that he spends all but hunting hours among his women.' [14] Roe excused himself from turning historiographer, for he had the unwearied Coryat with him, 'who now is in my house and hath not left a pillar nor tomb nor old character unobserved almost in all Asia. And is now going to Samarkand in Tartary, from thence to Prester John in Africa [i.e. Abyssinia], and hath written more volumes than leaves in his last Venetian travel, wherein he holds still the correspondence of going on foot.' Alas for Coryat's plans, this was his last journey : he died next year at Surat.

The purpose of Roe's embassy was to push the failing Portuguese out of their predominant position in India and instal the rising English in their place. An able diplomat, he succeeded in getting the concession of a factory at Surat, the kernel from which the Indian Empire grew ; but it was the increasing power behind the East India Company that achieved it. As Roe expressed it to Southampton : 'I stand in good terms with the king, who never gave that respect to any ambassador, of Turk or Persian ; but our residency here inconstant, for we stand or fall as the Portugal is in disgrace or credit. They fear both, cannot hold friendship with both, and watch occasion to adhere to the stronger.' That was it — as it is apt to be in all politics at all times and in all places.

Roe was anxious that the Spanish empire should not take the place of the Portuguese in India. 'First, it will advance the king of Spain's revenue a million of dollars yearly, enrich his subjects that shall engross the greatest commodity of the East into their hands ... It will restore him all his credit here, where he lay languishing for breath. O what happiness, how it had advanced the peace of Christendom, if he had lost these Indies, and it had been *malum omen* to have one branch fall off in the

height of an empire which hath his period! . . . I could enlarge
this, but if your lordship please to consider it farther, you shall
see my grounds if you will command the copy of my discourse
to the committees, though I know your own judgment will
pierce into the inwards of this negotiation.'

On the more personal side, 'I thought all India a China shop,
and that I should furnish all my friends with rarities. But this
is not that part : here are almost no civil arts but such as
straggling Christians have lately taught, only good carpets and
fine lawn, all commodities of bulk, whereby I can make no
profit but publicly. . . . Though I live . . . perhaps many ways
in more state and with many more servants than any ambassador in Europe, such is the custom here to be carried in a bed,
all richly furnished, on men's backs up and down — though it
needs not, for there are the finest horses that I ever saw of
jennet size and infinite store, besides guards and footmen, of
which only I keep twenty four.' Roe concluded, 'you expect
no ceremony and I have learned none here, but I am ever, and
will die so, your lordship's most affectionate servant'. He
added a postscript : 'give me leave to present my humble
service to my lady, my lady Penelope, my little lady mistress
for whom I will be provided with presents'. He had no idea,
at that distance, that the little girl was already dead.

Southampton's main overseas interest, however, was in
American plantation and exploration. In 1610 he put down
money to aid the eminent navigator, Henry Hudson, make his
last voyage in search of the North West Passage[15]. Hudson
penetrated into Hudson's Bay, explored all round its coasts,
but, refusing to give up, was set adrift by mutineers to die in
the bay that winter. Two years later Southampton became an
incorporator of the North West Passage Company. In 1614
he subscribed £100 to Edward Harlow's voyage to the New
England coast. In May of this year the Virginia Company
petitioned the new House of Commons for aid in its increasing
difficulties — after all, it was a national enterprise and the

honour of the nation was at stake. The Company engaged an eminent lawyer to put its case to the Commons, and South- ampton, with Lord De la Warr and Lord Sheffield, was per- mitted to attend — really to give their advocate countenance and prestige. The Commons stipulated that the peers should 'sit with uncovered heads until otherwise requested by the Speaker', and ordered that 'there should be a great silence while the lords were present'. There was evidently expected to be a great deal of interest in the occasion, for a fine was to be exacted of any M.P. standing in the entry.[16]

The lawyer engaged, Richard Martin — later Recorder of London — was supposed to be a celebrated wit, but he must have been a great ass, for, instead of putting the case of the Company, he made a pedantic speech reciting the whole history of the case, patronising the House 'as a schoolmaster teaching his scholars', and then proceeded to attack their record. Next day he was called to the bar of the House to make submission, 'but the lords that accompanied him are more angry with him than all the rest, and will not be satisfied'. Thus the chance of aid for Virginia, along with everything else, was lost in the Parliament of 1614.

Under the pressure of continuing discouragements and mounting dissatisfaction the demand within the Company for a change of administration and a more active policy became irresistible. By 1619 the minority that looked to Sir Edwin Sandys for leadership became a definite majority. At the Quarter Court and assembly held at Sir Thomas Smythe's house, 28 April 1619, at which Southampton, Warwick, Lord Cavendish and most of the grandees who took an active interest were present, Sandys was elected Treasurer, with John Ferrar as Deputy, and their party took over control.[17] South- ampton was an active supporter of Sandys, took a constant interest in the Company's proceedings, exerted himself on its behalf, and — in spite of all the other demands on him — gave up a good deal of time to its business. We find him appealed to as an honest broker, for example, in the difficulties caused by Captain Argall's privateering voyage from Virginia to the West Indies.[18]   The Riches were much incensed ; Southampton, as a Privy Councillor, was able and willing to bring both sides together and quieten the dispute.   Later on we find that he was able to retain Warwick's good will, when Sandys had lost it, and Sir Nathaniel had an express belief in his 'justice and nobleness'.   This made him the obvious candidate to take over the leadership of the Company when the time came.

At once the new spirit in the conduct of the Company was evident.   Sandys was an enthusiastic, pushing, devoted man, who gave himself to the affairs of Virginia with ardour, where the ageing Smythe had too many irons in the fire, what with the East India Company, and the Bermuda Company which he continued to control for the next two years.   Sandys pushed forward emigration to Virginia for all he was worth : in the next four years he sent out four thousand people.   It was setting too fast a pace, without the Puritan impulse and morale to keep them straight and at work.   When he took over only £1,000 remained in cash of all the money subscribed ; urgent appeals went out to backsliders to pay up their quota, to the bishops for money to found a college, resort was made to a lottery to raise funds for the ambitious programme proposed. From the colony Sir George Yardley, the governor, reported a great scarcity of corn and asked that the planting of tobacco might be diminished.   But tobacco was the only crop that brought in any money.   The Privy Council itself pressed for a diversification of crops and commodities in Virginia, especially for producing silk and wine.   Sandys was only too willing to do his best, spent money on sending out vines and silk-worms and experienced French and Italians to introduce the arts ; he put a lot of money into trying to establish iron-works in the colony — all to no avail : it was money wasted, with no return.

Southampton was attending not only Court meetings, but preparative Courts and committees.   In July Alderman Johnson, Smythe's supporter, was censured for unseemly words against the new administration, uttered at a committee meeting at Southampton House. The new administration was engaged in the hopeless task of trying to bring order out of Smythe's accounts, Southampton being on this committee. He was present again when a communion cup and platter, a crimson carpet and linen for the communion table were presented for Jamestown by an unknown person. Southampton was Sandys's foremost backer, and Sandys looked up to him as in a sense his leader. We find him while away at his country house at Northbourne in Kent, under a course of physic in September, assuring Southampton that in the meantime 'I am, have been and will be careful that there should be no defect in our Virginia business. The chief whereof is now the paying of mariners' wages and freight of ships returned.' Sir George Yardley, who had taken extraordinary pains in putting matters in order and laying the foundation of a regular state has 'suddenly fallen into a violent resolution of quitting his place', under the error that Smythe, with whom he had a quarrel, was still Treasurer. Sandys asked Southampton to take no notice of Yardley's rash offer but to pass it over in silence. It is clear that Southampton must have arranged matters, for we find Yardley writing, 'now since it hath pleased God to dispose of the business into the hands of my most honoured lord of Southampton, wherein every good man hath cause to rejoice. . . . No man shall more desire to win the favour of so noble a person as my lord of Southampton.'

One sees that he was a man to whom people resorted with their troubles in entire confidence in his uprightness and justice, and also that his concern in the Company's affairs was close and practical. Sometimes the Council sat at Southampton House. In November they voted that they were 'exceedingly beholden to my lord of Southampton for his many honourable favours and nobly countenancing them in all their businesses, and especially such as is of greatest importance'. They now asked him, with regard to matters causing dissension — evidently with regard to the Magazine Account, accounting for the stocks sent to the colony — 'to vouchsafe his presence at that meeting of the Council, that by his lordship's and their authority those differences might be concluded'. Again later in November his presence was 'humbly desired' to conclude the cause of dissension. There was not a dissentient from the proposition. One observes again and again throughout the Company's proceedings the tone of deference with which he is regarded — mainly, of course, due to his rank, but there is also a tone of personal respect. At this meeting of the General Court, 17 November, there was a large attendance to hear a full report on the state of Virginia: besides the usual peers there were Sir Ferdinando Gorges, Sir Thomas Roe, Sir Thomas Gates, Shakespeare's acquaintance, Sir Dudley Digges, and Drayton's, Sir Henry Rainsford — so many of the familiar names so much interested in Virginia.

In December there came up the dispute as to fishing latitudes between the Virginia Company and the Northern Company, of which Gorges was the leading spirit and was present at the meeting. Southampton was called in as honest broker once more, and undertook to reach an agreement with Gorges on the matter.[19] Towards building the church at Jamestown £200 had been collected, along with some plate. In January 1620 we find Sandys writing to the Earl of Huntingdon, as one of the principal Virginia Adventurers, inviting him, for planting his own private land, to join a particular group of some thirty persons of whom Southampton was chief.[20] In February at the Quarter Court held in Sandys's house near Aldersgate — at which Pembroke was present (almost the only occasion) with the other peers — an unknown person signing himself 'Dust and Ashes' gave £500 for converting infidel children. It brings home to one the strange, fanatic world of the Jacobean age, John Donne's cult of the shroud and keeping his coffin in his bedroom. A few months later Nicholas Ferrar, senior, parent of the holy Mr. Ferrar of Little Gidding, also interested in the Virginia Company, as all the family were — left £300 for converting infidel children.

In May the Quarter Court, with a large attendance, heard a discouraging report from Virginia : the colony was weak, the treasury exhausted. 'Divers lords, knights, gentlemen and citizens, grieved to see this great action fall to nothing,' decided 'to take the matter in hand anew and at their private charges set up divers particular plantations, whereof the first of any moment now called Southampton hundred hath had three hundred and ten persons sent unto it'. This hundred lay along the Chickahominy river, which for a time was also known as the Southampton river ; the Hampton river too, was originally named after him. In June Southampton sent out to his plantation, with Lord De la Warr, ten men who were allotted fifty acres a piece according to custom. At the next Court it fell to Southampton to end the dispute between Alderman Johnson and the Bermuda Company. He struck off some £80 profit due to the Company 'as wishing peace and quietness'. Johnson denied that it had been due, but Southampton produced the evidences vouched for by the auditors.

Sandys was now under attack, having to defend himself against aspersions of having incensed the Spanish ambassador against the Virginia captains Argall and North, who had gone cruising in the West Indies for what they could catch. Once more he looks to Southampton for protection; writing from Northbourne he asks Ferrar to inform the Earl of 'the necessity of my stay here, to stop such suggestions as my unfriends may make'.

Now the King took a hand. Before the next annual election he sent a peremptory message excluding Sandys, whom he never forgave for his opposition in the Parliament of 1614, and recommending the Company to choose Smythe or Alderman Johnson, or one of two others.[21] A meeting was held at Southampton House, which decided to send a strong delegation to the King asking that they might put off their election for the time being. Southampton headed the party of a dozen — peers, knights, lawyers, businessmen — that waited on James, who was much displeased at first but then calmed down to indicate that he would prefer them to choose a Treasurer with regular access to his person, i.e. a peer or Privy Councillor. He absolutely excepted against Sandys. Southampton was the obvious person, and at the next General Court was nominated 'with much joy and applause'. He accepted 'for the redeeming of this noble plantation and Company from the ruins that seemed to hang over it'. His election was acclaimed without any ballot, while he was dispensed from routine business 'other than his own more weighty businesses did permit'. Ferrar continued as Deputy, while Sandys remained the driving spirit. This did not mean that Southampton was 'merely a screen' for Sandys ; [22] we have seen how actively involved he was in the Company's business. It meant that he now came forward to take full responsibility for the Company in the public eye, and this position he retained for the remainder of its existence.

His election gave renewed confidence. Chamberlain reported it : 'there is hope matters will go forward there better than heretofore'.[23] At once Sandys brought forward a new project for managing affairs, to remove dissensions and achieve unity. He proposed that they should send out 800 people to Virginia, with 100 young maids to make wives ; that they should procure silk-worms and vines, and skilled men to manage these things. The whole project to cost £17,800. It was an impossible sum in the circumstances of the Company — though not a tithe of what James spent on his favourites. At a General Court in July, Southampton could not be present until three in the afternoon — they regularly met in the mornings : he was detained with the Privy Council, discussing the question of a restraint on the import of tobacco, against which the Company was protesting. A proposal was made to concentrate the sale of Virginia tobacco on the Netherlands, leaving the English market to the Bermuda Company.

Southampton was prevented by his own affairs from keeping Court again until November, when the dispute with the

Northern company over fishing in northern waters came up again. The King had assured Southampton that no prejudice was intended to the southern colony in the matter. Two days later a stranger stepped in and presented Ralegh's Map and Description of Guiana, with four great books for the use of the college (three of them the Works of the indispensable, the prolix, the tedious Perkins). In December Southampton was detained for many hours away on the Company's business, and on going out of town asked that Sandys might sign for receipt of money for the Company in his place. At the end of January 1621 he reported that Yardley was anxious to return, after three years' service as governor, and recommended Sir Francis Wyatt as 'well reputed of, both in respect of his parentage, good education, integrity of life and fair fortunes . . . as also for his sufficiency otherwise'. Wyatt was chosen governor. At the Quarter Court, 31 January 1622, South-ampton reported that he had been all that morning with Doncaster (formerly James Hay) and that the King was willing to renew their patent. The Court expressed their thankfulness to him for his great pains and care taken in their business. He was granted a patent for 300 shares, 'being one of the greatest and most ancient adventurers . . . having now a desire, with the help and assistance of some of his friends, to undertake and advance a particular plantation in Virginia'. The Court expressed itself grateful for what 'by example might draw on others with like resolution to advance more particular plantations in Virginia and thereby in short time replenish that country with great multitudes of people'. Such was Sandys's hasty, perhaps over-hasty, intent. Sir Francis Wyatt was chosen to go out as governor.

On 22 February an extraordinary Court was held, from which Southampton was absent on account of the new Parlia-ment which had been summoned and in which he was taking a busier, more leading part than he had ever done before. At this time the Northern Adventurers settled on the name of New England for their territories, while the Southern adhered to Virginia. On 12 April he was present when Mr. Smith proposed 'a fair and perspicuous history of Virginia from her first discovery to this day ; and to have the memory and fame of many of her worthies, though they be dead, to live and be transmitted to all posterities'. The proposal was exceedingly commended and elicited very great applause. (Was this a characteristic piece of self-advertising on the part of Captain John Smith, with his own *General History of Virginia* in mind ?) Southampton proposed Sandys's brother George for treasurer in Virginia, 'for his approved fidelity, sufficiency and integrity'. George Sandys, who distinguished himself as a poet, was already widely travelled in the Middle East, and had published a Relation of his journeys. At the next Quarter Court South-ampton could not be present at the beginning because of special business in Parliament. George Sandys was balloted for and elected, with only three balls against. He went out with Sir Francis Wyatt, carrying forward his translation of Ovid's *Metamorphoses* 'amongst the roaring of the seas, the rustling of the shrouds and clamour of sailors'.

The day was far spent and Southampton not yet come, when his re-election as Treasurer took place, with not one ball against, but 'with the greatest thanks that possibly they could for his honourable care, pains and endeavours to uphold and advance the plantation ever since his happy entrance into this place of government'. At the end Captain John Smith put forward a petition for the reward of his services in that he had twice built Jamestown and four other particular plantations 'as he allegeth', that he explored the country and relieved the colony for three years with what he got from the savages with the peril and hazard of his life. His request was referred to the auditors.

From the preparative Court on 11 June prior to the General Quarter Court Southampton was absent ; but the previous Saturday he had had conference for hours together at South-ampton House, on the business of establishing a council of state in the colony. It was reported that Mr. Pory had not carried

himself well as secretary of the colony ; we happen to know
that the interesting Mr. Pory, full of scientific observations
which he should have written down, an acquaintance of
Chamberlain's, was a drunkard. Sir Edwin Sandys reported
that it was displeasing to the King that for 'so much effort over
so many years yet hath it not produced any other effect than that
smoky weed of tobacco'. One of James's sensible points was
that he hated smoking. Sandys pointed out that maintaining
a high price for tobacco — the growth of which in England
was prohibited to benefit Virginia — was responsible for the
neglect of other commodities. Two days later Southampton
was present at the General Court, when he was asked to join
with the Archbishop of Canterbury to chivvy the bishops to
bring in the remains of the money they had collected for the
college. Southampton was not present on 24 July, but he had
subscribed £200 to further shipwrights and workmen for
building vessels in Virginia, and Sandys another £200, 'to
witness their zeal and constant resolution to advance the
plantation, notwithstanding the many discouragements they
had received'.

Southampton was absent not without good reason. In the
Parliament which had been summoned early that year to face
the European crisis — James's son-in-law had lost his kingdom,
was about to lose his own Palatinate, the great war was at last
under way — Southampton had come out in open opposition
to James's government, had indeed taken the lead and fallen
foul of the favourite, Buckingham, in an angry scuffle in the
Lords. Southampton had thereupon been taken into custody
and held in honourable confinement from mid-June to the end
of July.

At this moment the *Mayflower* was at Southampton ready
to sail with her Pilgrims, though they did not leave from
Plymouth until September. They had obtained their patent
from the Company, authorising them to settle, in the previous
year. Since this particular boat-load of colonists made such a
mark in history and literature, in the American folk-memory

and the myth of the English-speaking peoples everywhere —
not without desert — it would be fair to recall the efforts the
Company itself was making at this very time. In the seven
months from August 1620 to February 1621 6 ships had been
sent out. In August 3 ships had sailed : the *Bona Nova* of 200
tons, carrying 120 persons ; the *Elizabeth* of 40 tons with 20
people ; the *Mayflower* (was this another ship of the same
name ?) of 140 tons, with 100 colonists. In September the
Supply of Bristol, 80 tons, took 45 people, in December the
Margaret and John, 150 tons, took 85 ; in February the *Abigail*,
350 tons, carried 230. In all 600 colonists — most of whom
perished, one way or another. In a full year of the Southamp-
ton-Sandys administration we find the exertions of the Company stepped up to 21 ships with a total of 1,300 persons, while
250 went to Bermuda. 'So there is twenty-four sail of ships
with five hundred mariners in them employed to these plantations in this year.'

Meanwhile, from way down under the equator, the East
Indiamen were collecting so that Virginia might have a school.
While at anchor at the Cape this year, before the long haul
across the Indian Ocean, the *Royal James* collected £70 8s. 6d.
for the good purpose : 10 marks from the excellent captain,
Martin Pring of Bristol, down to the shillings of the mariners.
An unknown person contributed £30 ; two other ships collected 100 marks. Altogether £192 1s. 10d. This simple
sum, contributed mostly by hard-fisted mariners and younger
sons going to find a fortune — though far more frequently, a
grave — in India, speaks more eloquently than verse what
Virginia meant for the nation.

Once more this summer the royal James attempted to intervene in the Company's election, and once more in vain. The
King sent a note of names from which he wished them to
choose. The Venetian envoy reports that they made a dia-
metrically opposite election : Southampton, 'the only one
whom the generality of the people resolutely designated, but
whom the king regards with suspicion as a poppy higher than

the rest, which must be abased'.[24]   Perhaps James's intervention, ineffectual as usual, contributed to the highest vote recorded in the assembly — 117 : tribute to the general confidence felt in Southampton, rather than a muster of undiluted Sandys's support.[25]   On Southampton's acceptance of office once more, the Court acknowledged 'their bounden thankfulness for his noble favour and affection unto the plantation, under whom it had pleased God to prosper it so well in the two precedent years of his government as there was now greater hopes than ever of a flourishing state and commonwealth in Virginia'.

Alas, for their hopes!   At this sanguine moment — so like life — there had already befallen, unknown to the Company, the greatest disaster ever to happen to the colony : the great Massacre of March 1622. The Virginia colonists — unlike the more wary, the more aggressive and harsher Puritans of New England — had been lulled into a sense of false security after years of peace. Suddenly, at the beginning of the sowing time in March, the Indians struck back with savage brutality, cutting off isolated settlements and individual farms, obliterating everything in their path. Altogether 347 persons were massacred : it is affecting to read the names of them all in the Virginia Company's records. But that is not the full tale of the tragedy : worse was to come. The colony was so much disorganised and thrown out of gear, stores and equipment lost, sowing neglected, that that winter 'starving-time' came again : another 500 perished. Of 4,000 people sent to Virginia in the previous four years, together with the colonists who had managed to survive, a census of 1624 showed a population of only 1,275. During that period a proportion of three out of four had perished.

Such was the price, in English lives, of the foundation of Virginia.

In the sanguine, hopeful time of 1621 the friends of Southampton and Sandys had gained control of the Bermuda

Company, too ; so that for the remaining years of the Virginia Company the two could work together, or at least their affairs be considered together. We find Lord Cavendish, as head of the Bermuda Company, proceeding hand in hand with Southampton ; sometimes there were joint meetings, when Southampton, enjoying the precedence of his rank, took the chair.

The question that dominated the last two years of the Company was that of the Tobacco Contract. Whatever the Company did, for all the efforts that it made to diversify its products, the colony came to depend on 'this weed that so readily took root in soil where more desirable commodities perversely withered and died'.[26] (It was a merciful blessing for Virginia that the noxious habit spread.) It became urgent, in the circumstances of the Company, to assure an advantageous market for its importation into England, if possible a monopoly ; a joint policy with the Bermuda Company to this end (Bermuda tobacco was inferior to Virginia) and to keep out Spanish tobacco. On the other hand, the government, which was doing what it could to keep up the price of tobacco, prohibiting its cultivation in England, wanted to raise a revenue upon the import in return. Could a bargain be struck ?

Negotiations to this end, in which Southampton took the lead, occupied a great deal of his time for the remainder of the year. The two Companies joined together to consider Lord Treasurer Middlesex's (formerly Cranfield) proposal for a monopoly in return for a revenue. Sandys thought that a proportion of the revenue from the tobacco would be safer than a fixed revenue in money : 'considering the uncertainty of this deceivable weed tobacco, which served neither for necessity nor for ornament to the life of man, but was founded only upon an humour which might soon vanish into smoke and come to nothing'. In June and July there were long discussions of the terms of the Contract which Southampton was negotiating with the Lord Treasurer. In July a discussion of the incorrigible Captain Argall's conduct, acting more like a privateer than an explorer off the American coast, took up time. After a long pause it was agreed that the propositions regarding the Contract should go forward. Southampton and Sandys had both been with Middlesex trying to get better terms.

The Companies wanted the complete monopoly of import, or the exclusion of all Spanish tobacco. This was unobtainable, but they finally accepted a limitation to 40,000 lb. though they considered this 'the hardest part and article in the whole contract'.[27] The Lord Treasurer, a hard bargainer, insisted on one-third share of the profits for the Crown ; the Companies wanted to reduce this to one-fourth, but had to give way. On 22 November 1622 Southampton presided at a joint Court of the two Companies. He reported that the bargain was the best they had been able to obtain ; it seemed a necessity for the continuance of the plantation — as they were advised by a noble person, 'not as good meat well sauced, but of a portion necessary for their health, being willing, as his lordship said, *devorare molestiam* of this bitter pill'. There was no enthusiasm for the Contract. We have a rare pen-portrait of Southampton at this moment by an opponent of it. The Earl 'set him down in his chair, pulling his hat over his eyes and folding his arms across and leaning backward in his chair, as if all were lost'. Everyone must have known that this was all that could be got out of the government, and the bargain was approved.

As a consequence of the Contract it was necessary to set up a scheme for its administration : a Tobacco House, with salaried officials. And here arose the final, fatal trouble. The Company made the mistake of fixing the salaries too high, Sandys and Ferrar, who were to be the officers, of opening their mouths too wide. At a joint Court, 27 November, Southampton made a long speech setting forth the proposals and arrangements, the schedules and rates, with a discussion of each item. There was an ominous long silence. He desired the assembly to speak their minds freely — he and his colleagues had acted only as their servants to prepare measures for their conclusion. There was then some discussion. After another pause he put the proposals and they were carried — Sandys to be Director, Ferrar as Deputy and Treasurer. Upon dissolving the Court Southampton and Cavendish, as leaders, 'stood up and both of them praying God that this business might be to the advancement of the plantations . . . desired the whole Company now to make their best of that which themselves had concluded and, like honest and worthy-minded men, to give their best helps for the good execution thereof'.

For the Virginia Company this was the beginning of the end. The salaries question gave a handle to Sandys's opponents which not all Southampton's prestige or the general respect for him could overpower. The lead was taken by John Wroth, a member of the Council who was disappointed at not getting one of the salaried offices and was, moreover, a cousin of the Lord Treasurer, to whom he reported the Company's proceedings unfavourably. He kept up a constant campaign of objections and aspersions within and without the Company ; Southampton had to descend from his eminence and come into the open to deal with him.

At the December meeting the Earl was not present ; the Court was much scandalised at the calling in question of matters that had been already settled at the General Court. On 29 January 1623 Wroth acknowledged Southampton's proceedings 'to be always like himself, most noble, direct, just and plain', but complained that things had been done in the Earl's absence out of town. Several times Southampton recalled Wroth to the matter in hand and whether the Court record was correct or no. For his complaints against Lord Cavendish, Southampton rebuked Wroth : though they were all councillors 'yet there was very great difference between the persons of divers of them, and in particular between Mr. Wroth and the Lord Cavendish, to whom he owed more respectful behaviour and language'. At length Southampton was moved to anger and to say that 'he should be sorry to have lived so that it should be in the power of Mr. Wroth to wrong him in his honour or reputation'. And Mr. Wroth was censured.

This did not quench him. Two days later, at an extraordinary Court, he claimed that he could not speak freely, for Southampton, as a Privy Councillor, could commit him to prison. The Earl answered that 'he need not fear any such thing from him, for, whatsoever respects and additions he had, he left them all when he came to this place and came here only as the Treasurer'. After further obstruction the Earl flamed up : in any other place than this he would not have endured it and 'sharply willed him to behave himself after a better manner'. Standing on dignity was no use with such a persistent type : Southampton called it 'no other but a persistent swaggering'.

At the next meeting he put it whether the record were correct or no — passed in the affirmative without one dissentient. Nevertheless Wroth was allowed to bring forward his own project for offices and salaries. It was by general consent disallowed. There was a large attendance — including Dr. Donne, Dean of St. Paul's — at the Quarter Court on 5 February, at which Southampton reported the whole proceeding relative to salaries and offices, and how the report of Mr. Wroth's abusive and improper behaviour had caused him to come up immediately from the country. One man's unruliness had put them to extreme trouble, forcing them to keep so many Courts day after day and neglect their proper business — for eight weeks all other proceedings had been hindered. It was proposed that Wroth should be suspended from the Council. Southampton suggested a middle way — temporary suspension till he submitted. Sandys reported that Sir Thomas Smythe's accounts for the twelve years of his administration were so defective, disorderly and intricate that they could not be cleared up. Smythe desired that 'he might go with peace into his grave, being already far stricken in years'.

In February the Lord Treasurer demanded that the proclamation of the Contract might be put off for three or four

months. Southampton took the lead in the prolonged discussions regarding it in the Companies and their committees,
on one February day lasting for six hours. It had been reported
to the Lord Treasurer that the Company were overawed and
durst not speak. The Court condemned the report as false and
scandalous, and recorded, without dissent, that the Court had
never been overawed over passing the Contract. In April
Sandys presented his report on the colony. In December 1618,
after twelve years of Smythe's administration, after spending
over £80,000 of public stock, besides private and voluntary
planters, there were 600 colonists and 300 cattle in the colony.
And the Company was £5,000 in debt, which had since been
paid off. In 1623 — in spite of the Massacre and the great
mortality that followed it — for an expenditure of £30,000 of
public stock, plus private planters, there were 2,500 persons,
1,000 beasts, besides infinite goats and swine. This was, like
Sandys himself, over-optimistic, as we have seen. Undoubtedly, if it had not been for the malign disaster of the Massacre
— no fault of his — he would have had a much better report
to make. But nothing could explain away the death-roll in
Virginia, or what little there was to show for such pertinacious
and heroic efforts.

Now Sandys in turn was on the defensive, and his old
opponents gaining the upper hand. News of the faction-
fighting within the Company got abroad : on one side,
Southampton, Cavendish, Sandys, and Sir Edward Sackville ;
on the other, the Earl of Warwick and Sir Nathaniel Rich —
who together represented the largest interest in Bermuda —
Alderman Johnson and Smythe. The King called the parties
before him in the hope of establishing concord, but Sir Edward
Sackville was so insolent towards him that James 'was fain to
take him down soundly and roundly'.[28] The government
appointed a commission under Sir William Jones to investigate
the whole affairs of the two Companies ; all records and papers
had to be turned over to the commissioners at the Quest house
next St. Andrew's, Holborn. Personal feelings were so exacer-

bated, especially between the Earl of Warwick and Lord Cavendish, who held the leading interests in Bermuda, that that summer they were trying to leave the country to fight it out on foreign soil. The King stayed Cavendish from going abroad in order to prevent the fight.[29] One observes the contrast with Southampton's behaviour : impulsive as he had been in youth he had achieved greater self-control than most, and behaved with the dignity and decorum proper to a grandee. Everyone refers to his conduct as 'noble' and 'just' : these seem to have been the keynotes of his character in full maturity. It is what earned him people's confidence and general respect — and a measure of jealousy at his unfailing popularity from King James, who could not command it.

Southampton remained as Treasurer until the end, though in its last year the Company operated under the orders of the Privy Council. It is difficult to see what else could have been done if the colony were to be sustained ; the Company's resources were exhausted, itself divided into two factions. Necessary wages were paid out of the Exchequer, and somehow or other supplies and provisions continued to be sent out : from May to November 1623 14 sail with 340 persons. In that November he and Sandys were voted twenty shares each, 'in a thankful acknowledgment of his noble deserts and merits both from themselves and the plantation, they having no other means to express their love'. The expiring Company put it on record that Southampton had 'performed his place with singular wisdom, prudence and care, and much noble pains and industry, and with unquestionable integrity, to the advancement of the plantation and full satisfaction of us the Company'.

The Company had already been called upon to surrender its patent the previous month. This it refused to do ; it determined to go down with flying colours. On receiving the Privy Council's demand it called an extraordinary Court, which voted down the surrender by all but nine votes present — the leading opponents, the Riches, Smythe and Johnson being conspicuous by their absence, perhaps for very shame at such a conclusion to the story.[30] The Company had to be taken to the law-courts, where its charter was declared vacated and so, after a life of eighteen years, it came to an end. In that same month of April 1624 there arrived a petition from the planters in Virginia against the Company, which it considered unfair, as we may consider it, in view of all the efforts made. The colony was taken into the hands of the Crown — Virginia became the first of the Crown colonies; this was agreeable to the planters — it left them freer to go their own way.

Meanwhile, the leading spirits in the Company transferred their fight to the floor of the House of Commons. Sandys and Cavendish attacked the Lord Treasurer and charged with partiality the commissioners appointed by him to investigate the Company's affairs. The King forbade the House to proceed any further in the matter. But Sandys now broadened his attack on Middlesex, demanding a complete investigation of his conduct of the Treasury. His revenge was complete : he carried the Commons with him in demanding the impeachment of Middlesex before the Lords, where Southampton took a leading part in his condemnation. The Lord Treasurer was driven from office, sent to the Tower (briefly), and condemned to pay an enormous fine.

When Southampton had been asked to deliver up the records of his administration to the commissioners, he replied that 'he would as soon part with the evidences of his land as with the said copies, being the evidence of his honour in that service'. These must have been the Records that Colonel William Byrd of Westover purchased from the executors of Southampton's son, which now repose in the Library of Congress and upon which our story is based.

In spite of everything, Virginia had been launched on her way.

CHAPTER XIII

Parliament Man

THE last years of James's reign, like those of Elizabeth, were a time of crisis. The early 1620's saw the convergence of the opening moves of the Thirty Years War in Europe with an internal crisis at home, in which the frustrations, demands, conflicts of the reign as a whole, open or latent, came to a point. The two reacted on one another, inevitably, but also dramatically. Frederick's loss of Bohemia and imminent loss of the Palatinate to the Catholic cause, Spanish and Imperialist in alliance, aroused the fear, hostility and anger of a country becoming ever more aggressively Protestant. The political crisis was accompanied by economic depression — also interconnected, for European war meant a large loss of textile exports, the 'decay of trade' which appears frequently on the lips of House of Commons men, in speeches, petitions, the literature of the time.

The atmosphere was one of continuing crisis, with tempers not steeled as in the heroic age of Elizabeth but on edge with frustration. For there was a deep division as to how to deal with it. The responsibility for executive action rested with James's government — government was the king's in those days ; and there was more to be said than has been allowed for James's policy of keeping in touch, if not in line, with Spain, in the hope of eventually coming to terms over the Palatinate, among other things. The diminished resources of the Crown, an impoverishment real enough even without James's extravagant kindness to favourites, meant a weak hand in foreign policy, without the support of Parliament — and Parliament, undeviatingly, distressingly, boringly Protestant, did not like the policy. The Crown's financial needs, which Parliament would not attend to — having no confidence in James's policy abroad or at home — made the King all the more anxious for a gilt-edged Spanish Infanta for his son and heir, with the fantasy-dowry of American treasure of which Gondómar gave him constant hopes. And not James only, sufficiently convinced Protestant as he was ; even such a good patriot as Cranfield, James's finance minister in these years, favoured the Spanish marriage with the best intentions. But the policy — like James himself and his son, involving the Crown increasingly with their unpopular, unrepresentative courses — was out of sympathy with the nation. In the end the Commons, more representative of the English people, were justified by the complete collapse of James's foreign policy and the whole edifice of his diplomacy in his last year.

Anyone who experienced in the 1930's the comparable confusion, the cross-purposes and frustrations flowing from a real enough dilemma, ending in the utter bankruptcy of policy and consequent war, should be able the better to understand the situation in the 1620's.

These years offer not only a background to Southampton's life : his activity reached its height, his career attained its full significance, in them — really once more, but more soberly and effectually — as an Opposition leader. He took the leading part in the Lords in bringing Lord Chancellor Bacon to book, was prominent in the impeachments of Mompesson and Lord Treasurer Middlesex, he defended Yelverton in trouble for his aspersions upon the sacred person of the favourite, he had an open quarrel with Buckingham in the Lords ; he collogued with, and probably concerted measures with, leaders of the Commons in opposition to the Court. He was looked upon as the champion of the cause of the Palatinate, expected to head the English forces in its defence, kept in touch with the States General and died in the Netherlands as a commander of

the forces sent over to fight there. His career was achieving co-
gency and power, the various disparate strands coming together
in a pattern of significance, when it was cut short by death.

From the point of view of the student of constitutional
history his career has a further interest to observe. The
seventeenth century was the most critical, as it was the most
dramatic and exciting, period in the evolution of the English
constitution. Constitutional development in James's reign was
as yet immature, imprecise, lagging and backward. The situation was ambiguous. Constitutional and political forms and
techniques were increasingly unrepresentative of the realities
and facts of the nation's life, in particular the economic realities
and the facts of social and class power. In the end it took a
revolution to bring them into closer correlation. From this
point of view Southampton, an entire Englishman and a
patriot, was on the side of the future, a Parliament man. All
his associates were with the Opposition to the Court. But he
himself was a courtier, a Privy Councillor, an official member
of the government, though recognised by all to be on the
popular side. So there is a certain dilemma in his political
situation too : a member of the government who is really, and
recognised to be, a leader of the Opposition! One must not
think of these things in modern terms : Jacobeans did not
enjoy the constitutional refinements of our beautifully ordered
and so mature society.

One catches a better glimpse of how things were in those
years from a contemporary, Arthur Wilson.

There were some gallant spirits that aimed at the public liberty
more than their own interest . . . among which the principal were
Henry, earl of Oxford, Henry, earl of Southampton, Robert, earl
of Essex, Robert, earl of Warwick, the Lord Saye, the Lord
Spencer, and divers others, that supported the old English
honour and would not let it fall to the ground. . . . Southampton,
though he were one of the king's Privy Council, yet was he no
great courtier. Salisbury kept him at a bay and pinched him so
by reason of his relation to old Essex, that he never flourished

much in his time ; nor was his spirit, after him, so smooth-shod as to go always the Court pace, but that now and then he would make a carrier that was not very acceptable to them ; for he carried his business closely and slyly, and was rather an adviser than an actor.[1]

This gives us the clue to the picture not always apparent superficially to the sight, a key to the understanding of his part in the following events : a certain political ambivalence enjoined by his position, though his sympathies were obvious ; the expression of those sympathies in general prudent and restrained, though occasionally the clash of events causes them to break out into the open.[2] He has come a long way from the intemperate partisanship of his youth ; he is now an old and practised hand at the game, experienced in the ways of politics and Courts. Nevertheless, as he had been looked up to in his youth for the candour and generosity of his nature, the ardour of his loyalty, so now he is looked up to for his incorruptibility, his absence of self-seeking, his honesty and patriotism. As in his youth, so in his last years, there is an aesthetic propriety in that an apparent ambivalence does not conceal an essential integrity.

In 1619 Lord Admiral Nottingham — the ancient hero, as Lord Howard of Effingham, of 1588 — at length resigned. Southampton, as the only high official who had held command at sea, might well expect the succession. But he was not the man for James, who in any case had a candidate ready in the spirited Buckingham, of the exquisite manners, who had hardly seen the inside of a ship. At New Year 1620 Prince Rupert was born, at Prague, to James's daughter, the Winter Queen ; with the spring her husband would have to fight for his kingdom.[3] In London there were rumours of levies to go out to the remote little country, of which people knew little, to aid him against the German onrush, led by Catholic Austrians. It was rumoured that Southampton would take command and had offered a large subvention out of his own pocket. In April the City was wanting a Parliament to deal with the situation. In June the Venetian envoy was reporting that if Southampton got leave, 'a leading nobleman, rich and experienced, with considerable influence . . . he would have a larger following than anybody else, and no one but he would achieve much'.[4] But the King disliked entrusting great powers to such a man and regarded it as not fitting that 'a member of his own Privy Council should engage in a matter in which he does not wish to declare himself openly'. This seems fair enough in the circumstances, and though Frederick's ambassador, Dohna, had asked for Southampton to command the troops to be sent, he was excluded and their second choice, Sir Horace Vere, appointed instead. That summer Southampton was at work as usual in his area taking the musters, with the additional duty of impressing 100 men, Hampshire's quota, towards manning six royal ships for suppressing pirates.[5] There was not money for any more, and Southampton had already been cheated of the hope of a larger command. He must have been used to it : it had been a familiar experience all the way along.

The crisis abroad necessitated the calling of a Parliament, if the government were to face the possibility of a war. The Council of War advised the King that this would need £900,000 a year — an unprecedented sum ; after a direct appeal from James Parliament voted two subsidies, about £160,000, hardly enough for current needs, nothing like enough for war. But then they had no guarantee that James would follow their activist policy, while on the other hand their lack of confidence made it impossible for him to follow it. (The comparison with the 1930's becomes still closer.) Having voted this inadequate sum the Commons proceeded with more gusto to take up their grievances where they had been left by James's hasty dissolution in 1614, and added to them more recent vexations and complaints, in particular regarding monopolies, licences and patents being increasingly used to raise money. The Commons demanded the stricter execution of the laws against Catholics, a Protestant marriage for the heir to the Crown, no appeasement with Spain.

In the Lords Southampton at last plays a foremost rôle.[6] We find him very regular in attendance, missing only one sitting in February, for example. He is elected to all the important committees of the House, one of the triers of petitions of England, Scotland and Ireland, along with the Archbishop, Buckingham and the Lord Treasurer ; on the committee of privileges for the House, on that of the bill for restraining the export of ordnance — important in view of the danger of war, for England now enjoyed a leading place in the manufacture of cannon. The Commons asked for a conference with the Lords for the better executing of the laws against recusants and seminary priests ; a strong committee was named, Southampton being one of them, with his special knowledge of the subject. He was also placed on a number of committees dealing with private matters — for freeing some of the Earl of Bedford's lands from fee farms to the Crown (another loss to future revenue), for conveying the splendid manor of Temple Newsam to the King's French cousin, Esmé Stuart, Lord Aubigny.

In March he was on the committee of the bill confirming the charter for Charterhouse. As the King's special pupil in politics and other things, Buckingham proposed the founding of an Academy for the education of youth, especially of quality and worth (such as himself). 'This motion was generally liked and much commended, and thereupon many grave and judicious speeches used by sundry lords.' That cost no money, nor did the polite formation of a large committee, of whom Southampton was one: it was, of course, all talk. In the subsidy bill Oxford was named before Cambridge ; thereupon 'it was much debated among the Lords what course may be taken for an equality between the said two universities that the one might not have precedency of the other ; but nothing was concluded therein, neither in the forenoon (when this was principally urged) nor now'. Just the kind of thing to engage the attention, and waste the time, of such assemblies — nor would it be any more conclusive today.

All this was small beer ; far more important matters were coming up from the Commons. They were bringing their grievances for the attention of the Lords : the monopolies, such as that for making gold and silver thread — which had led to a good deal of fleecing the public, the patents for licensing inns (still more so in the hands of the monopolist Mompesson), abuses of the grants of concealments of Crown and Church lands, the penal statutes against Catholics. Southampton was on the committee for considering the grievances of the Commons, along with the Prince and Buckingham. He moved that since three patents were complained of three committees be appointed, each to examine the complaints regarding one patent. Since the commissioners could not take examinations on oath, he moved that witnesses might be sworn to the examinations they had yielded. Both motions were agreed. He then moved that for greater freedom of debate the whole House might go into committee. It is the first time the business of the House is given in such detail in the Journals — for those who like that sort of thing. It seems that in these matters Southampton was operating in liaison with the Opposition leaders, or opponents of the Court, in the Commons.

As such he took the lead against the notorious over-reacher Mompesson, who had thought up various schemes for recovering moneys to the Crown, which brought in, however, far more to himself and his unpleasing agents. The Earl reported the proceedings of his own committee on Concealments of Crown lands, which found that Mompesson had called up the king's officers and filled his own book with some £200 a year in concealed lands. Mompesson was a very pertinacious projector : over three thousand innkeepers had been vexed with prosecutions for the breach of obsolete statutes. Southampton must have heard the complaints of his own county that, of sixty inns licensed by this tolerant patentee, sixteen had been previously closed by the J.P.s as disorderly houses.[7] Enough of him! Treated to a very severe sentence, the patentee gave another mark of his ingenuity by jumping out of a window and escaping to France. Sir Giles Mompesson was on his way to immortality in English literature as Sir Giles Overreach.

A much larger and more glittering prize was to fall to the Opposition — the Lord Chancellor Bacon himself. Before this dramatic and famous event there occurred the open quarrel between Southampton and Buckingham that may have had a part in it, that helped to frighten the favourite into currying favour with the Commons, and resulted in Southampton's imprisonment at the end of the session. It seems that Buckingham, who was no fool, having plenty of address and many of the gifts of the politician (though none of the statesman), saw the danger-signals and decided to sacrifice the offending monopolists, including some of his own kinsmen, to stave off an attack on himself. For maximum effect he chose to make his declaration at a conference between Lords and Commons, a committee of which he was not a member. He was at once silenced by Southampton. Nothing daunted, Buckingham got leave from the King to say what he pleased and returned to the Lords to complain of Southampton's interruption. Southampton said that they had heard it all before and that Buckingham went on repeating the same thing. There was an angry scuffle between the two, and it was said that but for the intervention of the Prince swords would have been drawn. This incident was not forgotten among graver matters.

The fall of Bacon made a great sensation — when before, or since, has such a Lord Chancellor been driven from office for bribery, with such ignominy? Southampton took a leading part in bringing down this brilliant-plumaged bird. Bacon realised that the persistent attack of the Commons on the 'referees' — those to whom the patents had been referred and who had allowed them — was aimed at himself and warned James that 'those who will strike at your Chancellor it is much to be feared will strike at your Crown'. Lulled by a sense of his own greatness and a (perhaps justified) contempt for ordinary mortals, he did not realise the danger he was in. When the attack on him opened, he wrote to the King, 'when I look into myself, I find not the materials of such a tempest as is come upon me'.[8] In his lofty philosophic isolation he was careless of forms — unlike a true professional, his cousin Salisbury, for example — and much hurried under the press of business. And he was too grand to notice what his servants and officials were doing in his name. The most venal of them was John Churchill, his Registrar — founder of the family fortunes — who, to save his own skin, turned into chief witness against the Chancellor.[9] A train of bribes and dubious dealings was uncovered, of most of which Bacon was ignorant, and for a time he retained his confidence.

It turned out to be a sense of false security, as his enemies got to work on the evidence he was himself largely unaware of. Southampton took the lead on the committee of the Lords investigating the charges, examining numerous witnesses in April. There is no reason to think that Southampton's conduct was personally motivated; he said in the Lords, 'I will deal with the Lord Chancellor as with my best friend, I will not seek to circumvent him. The truth is, our only aim is that the truth may appear. The Lord Chancellor is accused to be a corrupt judge. I'll deny the delinquent nothing without which he may pretend he cannot clear himself.' Nevertheless, Southampton was not contented with the general submission the Chancellor made and which was read to the House : he wanted an answer to the particular charges direct from his own mouth. There followed a debate whether it was proper to bring the Great Seal to the bar of the House. The Prince pleaded that they should be merciful; Buckingham followed with an argument that had particular point coming from his lips, that they might 'attribute this thing to the corruption of the time, in respect of the quality of the person'.[10] They were all conscious of the corruption of the time — but Southampton was above it.

He demanded that Bacon should make a full confession, and the long schedule of twenty-eight charges was sent to him. Four days at the end of April were occupied in hearing and debating his answers. When the sensitive Chancellor realised the extent of the charges that had piled up against him, the impossibility of accounting for them all — if 'he had given way to great exactions by his servants', he was responsible for them — and the inevitability of his disgrace and fall from office, he fell ill and took to his bed. A deputation was sent to him to exact his confession, particular and general — three earls, Southampton, Pembroke, Arundel, three bishops — this must have been particularly chastening — and six barons attended upon the fallen great man in bed, and returned with a full submission to everything : 'my lords, it is my act, my hand, my heart. I beseech your lordships to be merciful unto a broken reed.' The author of the essay 'Of Adversity' had not lost his sense of style when he came to it in person.

Their lordships were more merciful to the great offender than Southampton was willing to be. His group of friends pressed for Bacon's degradation from the peerage ; but this was voted down by a majority — their sense of their order was against this, it might turn out a precedent to be used against themselves. (It was all right to degrade knights from their knighthood, as with Sir Giles Mompesson and Sir Francis Michell, but not a peer from his peerage.) 'Is it well that he whom this House thinks unfit to be a constable shall come to the Parliament ?' asked Southampton, and he took credit to himself for not having proposed banishment, of which he declared the late Chancellor worthy.[11] He pressed for Bacon's relegation to the Tower — the inside of which he well knew himself ; but the King respited Bacon from this on the ground of his sickness.

I fear that, after all, we cannot altogether acquit Southampton of all personal animus against Bacon ; but the line-up was essentially a political one, the Opposition against the Court. The Commons — with whose leaders Southampton was in touch — were out to get those members of the Court camarilla who were vulnerable. One person, the tallest and most brilliant poppy of them all, was untouchable. In the middle of these excitements, on 26 March, the King had paid the Lords a visit, making a gracious speech accepting the reforms of the patents and monopolies and ending up with a tender tribute to Buckingham as his own cherished pupil in statecraft. This in itself was a rebuke to Southampton, who had come almost to blows with him. Now the person of the favourite was in question once more in the case of Yelverton, the unpopular Attorney-General, who had dared to reflect on him — this was regarded as a scandal to his Majesty's person, as perhaps it was. Southampton and his friends did what they could to defend Yelverton in the Lords, but this did not save him from imprisonment. Over this there were heated exchanges in the Lords between the two parties, Arundel — Northampton's heir — leading for the Court, Southampton for the Opposition, with a large party following him. In one of these occurred the celebrated exchange between Arundel and Southampton's son-in-law, Spencer. Everyone knew that the Spencer fortune, a fairly recent one, rested on its sheep pastures. The insufferably stuck-up Arundel, with his longer Howard ancestry, said that his ancestors were serving the Crown while Spencer's were still keeping sheep. Spencer replied that while his ancestors were keeping sheep Arundel's were plotting treason — a fair riposte in view of the record of the Howards.

All that May Southampton was hard at work on the committees of the House dealing with various kinds of business — contentious suits brought against J.P.s, mayors and local officers, bills to protect subjects against concealments, for avoiding lawsuits, dealing with monopolies and dispensation from the penal laws. There were further cases to be dealt with and examinations taken — that of Sir John Bennett, Judge of the Prerogative Court of Canterbury, for bribery and corruption. (The common lawyers of the Commons were on the warpath.) Then there was the case of the absurd Floyd, a

Catholic, upon whom the Commons inflicted a savage sentence
for insulting their Protestant heroes, Frederick and Elizabeth.
They had ordered him to be whipped, among other things.
Only Sandys showed some moderation and charity, and he
submitted that it was improper to whip a gentleman. The
Lords understandably followed this lead : they increased
Floyd's fine, to show that they were good Protestants, but
introduced a bill to exempt gentlemen from the servile punishment of whipping.

At the beginning of June the Lords lined up with the
Commons to press three petitions upon the King, two of
which were significant : to prevent bullion leaving the realm
and ordnance from being exported. These were measures
with the possibility of war in view, and Southampton was on an
influential small committee to press them on the King. It was
rumoured that there were meetings with the Commons
leaders at Southampton House — likely enough, had not
Southampton plenty of Virginia business to transact with
Sandys and their friends ? James was being pressed on every
side — Buckingham, in some alarm for himself, joining with
Gondómar to urge a dissolution of Parliament. James, as
usual, compromised. He did not dissolve Parliament, but
suddenly sent a message warning that it would be prorogued
and recommending business to be wound up in a week. The
Commons were indignant, and full of foreboding. Sandys
spoke what was in all their minds : 'the country is in a dangerous state. Our religion is rooted out of Bohemia and Germany.
It will soon be rooted out of France . . . Their hearts were full
of grief and fear.' [12]

Now that the dangerous assembly was dispersed, and the
country gentlemen sent home to their counties, measures
could be taken to visit the offences of the Opposition leaders
upon their heads. On 15 June, shortly after leaving the Council
table, Southampton was arrested and taken into custody ; the
same day Sandys and the brilliant lawyer Selden — most con-

genial of Caroline intellectuals — were confined. Some time
later the Earl of Oxford followed. Southampton was put
into honourable confinement with the Dean of Westminster,
Williams, shortly to become Lord Keeper, in charge of Sir
William Parkhurst, and to be allowed no intercourse with any
other person. Southampton asked that 'his lady being much
subject to sudden grief and passion, his letter might be the first
messenger of his detention . . . and that his son being ready to
go to travel he might first speak with him and give him some
directions'.[13] These requests were granted, on condition that
his keeper were present. His request to answer charges against
him in the King's presence was refused. Chamberlain tells us
that on his part Southampton 'refuseth to answer, alleging
that he will give no advantage to be drawn *ore tenus* into Star
Chamber, but requires to know what he can be charged withal
and to see his accusers. It is like this refusal will do him no
good, but give further cause of suspicion and so of stricter
restraint.' [14]

We are now dealing with an old experienced hand, and it is
from the questions put to him, not from his replies, that we
learn what he had been up to. The first query asked 'whether
his own conscience did not accuse him of unfaithfulness
towards the king in the latter part of Parliament, which his
Majesty had cause to doubt both in his own carriage, in the
Upper House and by the carriage of those near to him in the
Lower House?'[15] Southampton's reply was that his conscience was free, and his Majesty too just to charge him with
the carriage of anyone in the Lower House, howsoever near
to him. This is a reference to Sandys, and reminds us how
closely associated the two were : not only in the Virginia
Company, but now by marriage, Sandys's and Southampton's
daughters having married the two Spencer brothers. In the
week before his arrest the two had had conference for hours
together one day at Southampton house on Virginia business
— it is unlikely that all other matters were excluded from their
discussions. The next question suggests 'whether he was not

a party to a practice about Easter to hinder the king's ends at that meeting, and were there not meetings and consultations held to that intent ?' Southampton denied this — after all, he did not have to accuse himself. The third question suggested that some of the Commons came up to the committee chamber of the Lords to receive their directions from him as to their conduct in the Lower House that day. Other queries asked whether he had not practised with some of the Lower House to hold up the King's bills upon the adjournment being announced, and to work for some of the subsidies granted to be sent direct to the King and Queen of Bohemia without coming into the Exchequer.

Southampton's parrying replies gave no satisfaction, for he was subjected to another examination : 'whether upon more consideration he found no cause to answer otherwise than he had done ?' The second examination came closer home to the cause of dissension — Buckingham. What discontents had he lately received, and how had he expressed them, towards the King and his government, or any other person near them ? He replied that he had expressed none towards the King or his government ; and, short and sharp, 'if there had been any unkindness between him and anyone near the King, that concerned not his Majesty'. (But that was precisely whom any aspersions on the favourite did most concern.) Had he not said that things were amiss in the state and that there would never be a good reformation of them while one did so wholly govern the King ? Had he said that he liked not to come to the Council table, there were so many boys and base fellows there ? With regard to the controversy with Buckingham in the Lords and his putting on his sword there, he admitted that if the Prince had not been there they had like to come to blows. A more significant matter than this — the government tried to get out of him once more whether he had not encouraged the Commons to put pressure on the King to prolong Parliament by holding up bills ?

Constitutionally, as James assured Gondómar, the really

effective power that remained to the Crown in relation to Parliament was that of dissolution. When James's son, Charles I, was forced to yield this up to the Long Parliament in 1641, the revolution was on the way. The parting of the ways was hardly so clear twenty years before, but it was clear enough on which side Southampton really was : he was a Parliament man.

A month later he was still in custody in the comfortable deanery at Westminster — and the new Dean, Williams, was a friend. Chamberlain writes, 14 July 1621 : 'the Earl of Southampton and the rest continue in the same case and place as they were, saving that Sir Edwin Sandys is kept more close'.[16] Now Williams — on his way to the bishopric of Lincoln, the archbishopric of York — was suddenly and surprisingly made Lord Keeper, in Bacon's place. The poor King had had enough of lawyers, and always found bishops more congenial company. The new Lord Keeper, who was a client of Buckingham's, at once exerted himself, in a Christian spirit to obtain Southampton's release. After all, were they not both Johnians ? — and this would be a most popular inauguration for himself. It was : it reaped good will. His efforts were aided by another famous ecclesiastic, Southampton's own diocesan — what more appropriate ? — Lancelot Andrewes, Bishop of Winchester.

Together they produced, if not a miracle, a transformation of the scene. Chamberlain's next letter to Carleton, 21 July, tells us : 'on Monday the Marquis Buckingham came to town and made many visits. He was with the earl of Northumberland [a prisoner since Gunpowder Plot] and Sir Henry Yelverton in the Tower ; with the earl of Southampton two hours together at Westminster ; with the earl of Oxford at Sir William Cockaigne's, with Sir Thomas Lake at his house. In all which places his coming was taken for a good presage, like the appearing of St. Elmo after a tempest.'[17] (I think we may infer from this comment that Chamberlain, a shareholder in the Virginia Company, had read William Strachey's letter, even if, no theatre-goer, he had not seen the play based upon it.) But was it not polite of the new Marquis to pay all these visits ? — courtesy was always a part of his irresistibility. Accordingly it was arranged that very early on Wednesday morning Lord Keeper Williams should take his friend Southampton to Theobalds for an interview with the King himself — which is what Southampton had asked in the first place. There all four had a long conference together — James and Buckingham, Southampton and Williams — with no one else present. It all ended satisfactorily, James dismissing his malcontent Councillor kindly ; the Lord Keeper brought him back to his own Southampton House, dined with him and left him at liberty — or so he thought.

He was disappointed to find that he was not yet out of restraint and surveyance, that he might go down to Titchfield but still in charge of his keeper. The rumour among the foreign envoys in London was that Southampton was too closely in sympathy with the Queen of Bohemia and her children to please James and the Prince, as yet unmarried. If anything untoward happened to Charles — and what a good thing that would have been for the country, for he made a hopeless king — Elizabeth would have succeeded to the throne. Ultimately her line did succeed with the Hanoverians, as against the descendants of Charles I, irretrievably Catholic and out of touch with the sentiments of the country.

Bishop Williams's task as honest broker was incomplete. He addressed himself anew to Buckingham : 'I do not doubt but his Majesty and your lordship do now enjoy the general applause of your goodness to the earl of Southampton. Saturday last he came and dined with me, and I find him more cordially affected to the service of the king and your lordship's love and friendship than ever he was when he lay a prisoner in my house. Yet the sunshine of his Majesty's favour, though most bright upon others — more open offenders — is noted to be somewhat eclipsed towards him. What direction soever his Majesty gave, the order is somewhat tart upon the earl. The word of "Confinement" spread about the City — though

I observed not one syllable so quick to fall from his Majesty — his keeper much wondered at. The act of the Council published in our names, who were neither present thereat, nor heard one word of the same. Yet, upon my credit, the earl takes all things patiently and thankfully, though others wonder at the same.'[18]

Evidently Southampton's restraint was unpopular, particularly in the City ; it was Buckingham, not the King, who was behind it and acting arbitrarily in the matter. The politics of the business we can descry from Southampton's letter to the good bishop : 'you may see what is expected from me : that I may not only magnify his Majesty's gracious dealing with me but cause all my friends to do the like, and restrain them from making any extenuation of my errors — which, if they be disposed to do or not to do, is impossible for me to alter, that am not likely for a good time to see any other than mine own family. . . . I can hardly persuade myself that any error by me committed deserved more punishment than I have had, and hope that his Majesty will not expect that I should not confess myself to have been subject to a Star Chamber sentence.' Underneath the rather lordly manner of the expression, and a certain disingenuousness implicit in the situation, we can see Southampton's resentment and his determination not to alter his line. He ended up tartly that he intended to keep one part of Buckingham's advice, 'to speak of it as little as I can . . . I purpose, God willing, to go tomorrow to Titchfield — the place of my confinement — there to stay as long as the king shall please'.[19]

The game is obvious enough : young Buckingham was trying to drive a wedge between this old hand and his associates, to get him to discountenance them, to isolate him. And there was a weapon the favourite could bring into play : Southampton was not only a Privy Councillor, a member of the government, but a pensioner of the Crown — whose pensions could be withdrawn. In August the kind Lord Keeper applied himself to bring both sides, if possible, together. To Southampton's resentment at having been subjected to a Star Chamber investigation he applied the episcopal balm of reminding him of other noble persons who had had the same experience without any derogation of their honour. On the King's side, his mercy 'had a great cloud of jealousies and suspicions to break through before it came to shine upon you'. The bishop warned him 'to avoid that *complacentia*, as the divines call it, that itching and inviting of any interpretation which shall so add to your innocency as it shall derogate from the king's mercy'. He ended up with a paean in praise of Buckingham and adjuring Southampton to 'make good his professions to this noble lord, of whose extraordinary goodness your lordship and myself are remarkable reflections : the one of his sweetness in forgetting of wrongs and the other of his forwardness in conferring of courtesies'.[20]

To the paragon himself Williams wrote enjoining upon him that 'somewhat is to be finished in that excellent piece of mercy which his Majesty — your hand guiding the pencil [appropriate image !]—is about to express in the earl of Southampton. It is full time his attendant were revoked, in my poor opinion, and himself left to the custody of his own good angel. There is no readier way to stop the mouths of idle men, nor to draw their eyes from this remainder of an object of justice, to behold nothing but goodness and mercy. And the more breathing time you shall carve out between this total enlargement and the next access of the Parliament, the better it will be for his Majesty's service. . . . Remember your noble self, and forget the aggravations of malice and envy ; and then forget, if you can, the earl of Southampton.' [21]

This was very politic advice — really Williams would have made a so much wiser Archbishop of Canterbury than his rival Laud. It was like the bad judgment of Charles to appoint the wrong one — James would not have made that mistake. Buckingham listened to the good bishop's advice, and at the end of August Southampton's keeper was revoked and himself restored to complete liberty.[22]

Nevertheless James and Buckingham were taking no risks
from Southampton in the decisive session of Parliament
to meet that November, and they had their weapon at hand in
the pensions he drew from the Crown. On 13 November
Williams wrote to Buckingham that Southampton was in
town 'in hope to kiss his Majesty's hand' and was 'very
willing to follow his Majesty's directions in that business your
lordship understands of. He only . . . desires his Majesty's
leave of absence, which is usual and reasonable. . . . My lord of
Southampton is touched with some fear of his two pensions,
but relies altogether upon his Majesty's mercy and your lordship's good mediation ; and I cannot but wish him all good
success in that particular.' [23]

James and Buckingham had received no assurance from him
as to what his line in Parliament would be ; they could not
recruit him to their side, nor get him to desert his friends. On
the other hand, he was a Privy Councillor, officially a member
of the government. The ambiguity of his position is reflected
in the comments in London : people did not know what to
think — and he was not telling them. On 21 November the
Venetian envoy reported that James was trying to conciliate
Southampton every way.[24] Three days later Chamberlain
wrote : 'the earl of Southampton went home from hence
about a fortnight since, being rather wished and advised to do
so — for aught I can learn — than enjoined or commanded'.[25]
In December the Venetian envoy reported that there was some
dissatisfaction, in Parliament, that the Earl and some others
'abstained from appearing from fear that they could not
express their opinions safely, according to the liberty they
claim. This has aroused a noisy discussion in the Lower
Chamber with the Secretary of State about the prerogatives of
the Crown'.[26]

When Parliament met on 21 November Southampton
was granted leave of absence on the polite ground of sickness.
He stayed down in the country : we have already noticed
his absence from meetings of the Virginia Company that

autumn and the dissensions that broke out while he was away.

The urgent question before Parliament was that of a supply for the Palatinate before it was too late : Frederick and his Queen had already lost Bohemia, the attack was now closing in upon them on the Rhine. There is no doubt that if James acted in concert with the nation he could have exerted some influence in Europe : Spain's policy was not in itself unreasonable, and the full deployment of English power would have met with concessions. But the crisis was now an internal one, a crisis of confidence in James and his conduct of the government : 'he had asked for a supply, but he had not disclosed his policy'.[27] (More and more like the incoherence of policy in the 1930's — the demand for armaments, but with no guarantees as to policy.) And, at heart, James did not mean to follow the policy so passionately desired by the Protestant English Commons : the son of Mary Stuart, he meant to be a king in his own right, assert his prerogative and not take his orders from English commoners. And it was undoubtedly his right and prerogative to resolve on peace and war, and to choose a wife for his son.

It is true that the Commons had no conception of James's larger-minded objectives, religious toleration, an end to religious war, some measure of religious liberty, a truce on the Continent. The Commons were Protestant partisans, and they now had no confidence in the government conducting the nation's business. They were willing, indeed anxious, to grant a supply for the Protestant Palatinate, but — a Spanish marriage, a Catholic dynasty on the English throne ? The debate was wide open at once, and in Sandys's absence the lead was taken by Sir Dudley Digges, his colleague in the Virginia Company, an active figure in overseas expansion — and an acquaintance of Shakespeare. And why was Sandys absent, Digges inquired : the debate got off on the wrong foot at once. It is noticeable that several of the leaders in the debate were leading figures in the Virginia Company — Sir Edward Sackville and Sir Robert Phillips, for example. They were joined by two young speakers now to make their names in Parliament, names of ill-omen to the House of Stuart, Wentworth and Pym. Pym made a speech that gave a foretaste of his immense political ability. Over the penal laws against Catholics he made a significant and politic distinction : 'the aim of the laws in the penalties and restraint of Papists was not to punish them for believing and thinking, but that they might be disabled to do that which they think and believe they ought to do'.[28] In contemporary circumstances, and as the situation stood in Europe, this was fair enough.

The King remained at Newmarket, out of touch with Parliament as he was out of sympathy with it. But he had the unwisdom to intervene in their proceedings with a letter calling in question their right to discuss the matters the Commons had debated. This united the whole House against him, which now proceeded to enter a solemn Protestation of their liberties in their Journals. When he came up to Whitehall he sent for the offending Journals and, in the presence of the Council, himself tore out the Protestation. Rather than put up with it he would do without a subsidy, do without Parliament, fend for himself.

The dissolution that followed was Gondómar's triumph : 'it is the best thing that has happened in the interests of Spain and the Catholic religion since Luther began to preach heresy a hundred years ago. The king will no longer be able to succour his son-in-law or to hinder the advance of the Catholics.' [29] That is what putting his trust in Gondómar had brought James to. 'The dissolution of Parliament marked the eclipse of James as a potent and respected ruler.' [30] There was nothing now for him to do but cast himself on the mercy of Spain and hope for the best. James understood the indignity of his position well enough : Gondómar wrote, a few days later, 'the king seems at times deeply distressed at the resolution he has taken to leave all and attach himself to Spain'. Henceforth, he was to get the worst of both worlds — and to console himself more and more with the bottle.

These events can have brought Southampton, in his rustication, nothing but grief, though he maintained an absolute silence.

The consequences were what were to be expected. In 1622 Frederick's cause in the Palatinate was ruined ; his capital, Heidelberg, fell, the country was ravaged by the invading Spanish-Imperialists, through the folly and obstinacy of its ruler. In England, after the dissolution, the finances of the Crown were in chaos, the debt mounted to £900,000 again, and Cranfield was called in as Lord Treasurer to make an heroic effort, single-handed, to bring some order out of the mess. He uncovered the corruption general throughout the administration, 'the continued increase of an expensive and unpopular largesse against which, since his first entry into public life, Cranfield had repeatedly protested', and with which he was now called upon, too late, to deal.[31]

For special purposes the government was reduced to send out privy seals, or demands for a benevolence, as for the Princess Elizabeth now an exile. In May the Privy Council were trying to raise £5,000 for her. Southampton, as Lord Lieutenant, had to raise the contribution from Hampshire. The Privy Council 'could have wished' that the first meeting of the J.P.s about this had been assisted by his presence.[32] He reported that he had taken much pains about the contribution, but the sum was likely to fall short of expectations. The J.P.s of Hampshire reported to him that they had taxed themselves at 5d. in the £ upon their subsidy assessments towards the contribution.[33] In August came his annual report on the state of the musters : there had been a decrease owing to the decay of some parties, which must be supplied by others of increasing ability ; some pleaded privilege and sought to be let off their obligations, others refused to show arms — he subjoined their names, with a report on the supplies of arms and powder.

In June and July we know that Southampton had been busy

in London negotiating the terms of the Tobacco Contract for the Virginia Company with the Lord Treasurer. From Chamberlain we learn that he had awkward business of his own to negotiate, too : 'the earl of Southampton is here about the stopping of his pension out of the sweet wines and other payments granted him out of the Exchequer for the damage done him and his tenants by the increase of deer in the New Forest. He hath taken the best way and addressed himself to the lord of Buckingham, from whom he hath fair promises.' [34] One day in August, at Aldershot, he had a meeting with the King and Buckingham, 'being brought up the back stairs one night after supper by the Lord Admiral, who only was locked into the chamber with them. What their discourse was I know not, but their meeting and parting seemed very fair.' [35] Thus Sir Francis Fane, whose other news — not very reliable — was that the match with Spain was absolutely concluded and the Elector Palatine to be restored.

The year 1623 resounded with the reverberations of the fantastic episode of Baby Charles and Buckingham's journey to Madrid to bring home the Infanta — and her dowry. James knew what nonsense it was, but was over-ruled by them and had to put the best face he could on it. Anyone with any sense could have seen that England's hand in the negotiations would be weakened, the Spaniards bound to put up their terms. In addition to the folly, there were the danger and expense of it all, adding greatly to Cranfield's labours to raise cash and make ends meet. He himself was anxious that the Prince should bring back his bride, if only to give a bottom to the bottomless debt. Impossible to tell the story here, for Southampton had nothing to do with it : he was clearly opposed to it, one of those whose hopes rested on the Princess Elizabeth in exile. Which is perhaps why James — a better politician than Baby Charles or Buckingham — assured Southampton in June, when hopes ran high, that he should have the honour of receiving the Prince and the Infanta. The Venetian envoy commented that this courtesy was all the more noted because the Earl was not always in favour.[36] The intention, however, was obvious : politics rather than courtesy.

At this moment James almost embroiled himself with the Dutch, whom no Stuart liked. The Dutch were making rapid strides in the East Indies, pushing the Portuguese out and showing themselves aggressive to the English. It was in this year, 1623, that they perpetrated their horrid massacre upon the English at Amboyna. News of this friendly exploit cannot as yet have reached home, but that of other depredations had. In April a couple of Dutch ships ran into Cowes water, under Southampton's jurisdiction. Captain Lambert of the Dutch warship broke his word to Southampton and departed incontinently to Holland, leaving a number of Dutch prisoners on his hands.[37] Lambert pleaded that he was acting by order of the States General, and that the prisoners were from a pirate ship. In May, Southampton reported, the Captain of Cowes castle was agitating for their release, as they were now at his charge ; if liberated, they would be at their own expense. But James was unwilling to free Dutchmen who were held as pirates and guilty of outrages in Scotland ; he sought redress of the Dutch ambassador.

In August the Court was at Salisbury on the King's summer peregrination : he requested the favour of a brace of bucks out of Beaulieu woods, since more venison would be required than the low condition of the game in the New Forest could spare.[38] On 14 August Southampton was at Beaulieu, requesting a pass for his son, Lord Wriothesley, to go to the Low Countries with Sir Horace Vere, with four servants and four horses, and that he might take leave of the King. It seems that James paid his last visit to Beaulieu this month, with Pembroke and Montgomery in his train as usual.[39] Then they all went on board the *Prince* at Portsmouth, to pay Southampton's island-province a visit at Calshot. In September the gossip was that Southampton had suggested a match between his son and the Lord Treasurer Middlesex's daughter, adding that now was the time when the Treasurer would stand in need of friends.[40]

Though this came true, the match did not. Meanwhile, his son accompanied Sir Horace Vere on a visit to the exiled Winter Queen at the Hague.

The return of Charles and Buckingham from Madrid in October, in defeat, bitterness and resentment, brought about another transformation in the political scene. They had found every obstacle put in their way, terms heightened, difficulties increased, in the end a humiliating treaty imposed, which Charles had to accept to get away from the country, but which there was no hope, and perhaps now no intention, of his implementing. To cap all, Buckingham had quarrelled with Olivares, who ruled all, and the Princess herself took a hand — she would rather become a nun than marry a heretic. The safe return of the heir to the throne without a Spanish bride caused transports of delight in London, and Charles and Buckingham savoured the unwonted, and delusive, delights of popularity. James's reception of his returned boys, who had been abroad like knights-errant in a *romanso*, he declared, was in character : meeting on the stairs at Royston, they all embraced and cried together before going in to tell their shame-making, indignant story. Buckingham and Charles now went over to the popular side and became as irresponsibly opposed to carrying out the match as they had earlier been irresponsibly rash in embarking for it. Meanwhile, since there was no dowry and their journey had cost a great deal of money, they urged the calling of a Parliament upon the reluctant James. They all knew that it would be vehemently anti-Spanish, and the young men, unlike the old King, did not mind if it led to war. Affairs were on the brink of a decisive change : Charles was pushing his father aside, and beginning to reign before James was out of the way.

Evidences of the new turn were not slow to affect South-ampton. In December the Venetian envoy reported that the Prince was very gracious to the Earl, who had been out of favour with the King, though even he was now regarding him with a more friendly eye.[41] And we learn that Charles favoured Southampton for the command in the Netherlands. Clearly war — as distasteful as ever to the King, though little notice was taken of him, now breaking up — was envisaged. On his last Christmas eve by the family hearth at Titchfield Southampton wrote his reflections to his friend, Sir Thomas Roe :

> You must not impute it to neglect that I have not written unto you since I saw you. I have been wholly a countryman, and seldom seen either the Court or London, and you know that between Titchfield and Constantinople there is no ordinary correspondence. In this life I have found so much quiet and content that I think I should hardly brook any other ; sure I am I envy none, and shall unwillingly leave this, if any occasion shall draw me from it. This last term going to London about some business [Virginia affairs] I met with a letter from you, which I was glad of, because it brought me the news of your well-being. I stayed there till the week before Christmas, when I came home to keep that time with my wife and children.

Then, with a turn to public affairs :

> I will write no news, because of things past you cannot want notice, and of any future, which we can know only by con-jecture, there is no certainty. Yet, this I will say, I think the time is near wherein we shall see the crisis of our affairs. When I came from London the opinion was we should have a Parliament very shortly. I have not yet heard that the day is appointed, but I believe it will soon be. God send the Lower House may be composed of discreet and honest men, else all may be naught ; but I hope the best and persuade myself I have reason to do so. I have no more to say but that you may be out of doubt that I wish you as well as any of your friends and am and will be your very assured friend.[42]

This letter brings him fully before us at the end of his career — as the Sonnets of Shakespeare at the beginning. It does not seem that he had taken his place at the Council-table, probably not since he left it for confinement in 1621. He was not one of the inner ring of the government, and it does not appear that he was closely informed of what was going on.

His convictions were with the popular, patriotic party, as they always had been ; he wished to see them strong in the new House of Commons — if so, all might yet be well. On the other hand, the years and harsh experience had taught him prudence, particularly of expression. Though it is perfectly clear where he stands, he does not state it in any partisan, let alone crude or vulgar, manner. So far from that, there is a clear nobility of style, a certain lordliness even — very appropriate in one who in his golden youth had been the pupil of a great lord of language.

CHAPTER XIV

Fate

WHEN the new Parliament met on 19 February 1624 Southampton was in his place once more, ready to take a leading part
in the deliberations of the Lords. Things had come his way:
he was not now swimming against the tide but with it. Not
for him the feebleness of a Pembroke, whose instincts were
sound enough, with plenty of commonsense, but without
strength of character. Pembroke was not in sympathy with
the turn things had taken: he was a sensible middle-of-the-
road man. But, to quote Gardiner, 'Pembroke was not a man
to persist long in opposition. His character was wanting in
that robustness which is needed for such a task. Again and
again in the course of his career we find him clashing with
Buckingham; but a few words from the King or the Prince
were always enough to soothe his easy temper, and he would
be again on the old footing, giving the support of his respected
name to a policy which he distrusted.' [1] What a contrast with
Southampton! — who, from the time of the Sonnets, had a
mind of his own and, beneath his mother's charm, had something of his father's temper, self-willed and obstinate.

The political transformation was reflected in the King's
speech, which pathetically expressed the collapse of his hopes,
the bankruptcy of his policy. Where he had been accustomed
to lecture Parliament on the wisdom of his statecraft and the
absoluteness of his prerogative, he now took a defensive line,
saying that he was ready to follow *their* advice, capitulating on
the main point over which he had dissolved the last Parliament

in anger. Nevertheless the old King was wiser than they, and by far his ablest ministers, Middlesex and Bristol, were with him — they were made to pay for their superior wisdom. What James had hoped was that, if Spain and England would work together, they would give the law to Europe and stop the war. And at the summit of high politics it is often rational, rather than personal, considerations that count. The consideration that had defeated James was a political one: he had found that not all his appeasement of Spain could procure the return of the Palatinate. It was this that disarmed him, left him and his best ministers, who went on hoping against hope, defenceless against the combination of the Prince and Buckingham with the whole weight of Parliament.

Southampton was now both with the great majority and in favour. No one had a more sensitive nose for power than the late Lord Chancellor Bacon, and on the approach of the Parliament we find him applying to Southampton. Apparently there had been a *rapprochement* between them on his fall and Southampton was far from vindictive.

It pleased your lordship when we last met and did not think, I dare say, that a Parliament would have been so soon, to assure me of your love and favour. And it is true that, out of that which I have heard and observed of your noble nature, I have a great affiance in your lordship. I would be glad to receive my writ this Parliament, that since the root of my dignity is saved to me [i.e. his peerage], it might also bear fruit, and that I may not die in dishonour. But it is far from me to desire this except it may be with the love and consent of the Lords. If their lordships shall vouchsafe to think me worthy of their company or fit to do them service, or to have suffered sufficiently, whereby I may now be, after three years, a subject of their grace as I was before a subject of their justice. In this matter I hold your lordship's favour so essential as, if God shall put it into your heart to give me your favour and furtherance, I will apply my industry and other friends to co-operate with your lordship. Otherwise I shall give over to think of it.[2]

Evidently Southampton was recognised as a leader of the

Lords, at least one who enjoyed the respect of the whole House and had much sway with it. From exile at The Hague there piped up the Queen of Hearts to her crony, Roe, on 'the day of good St. Davie' (1 March) : 'since my dear brother's return into England all is changed from being Spanish, in which I assure you that Buckingham doth most nobly and faithfully for me. Worthy Southampton is much in favour, and all those that are not Spanish.' [3]

We find Southampton as usual on all the leading committees of the House, the regular customary committee of privileges, for example.[4] The first important business was the Spanish treaties that had been in such prolonged negotiation. Buckingham and Bristol's reports, with their differing implications, were considered, and Southampton placed on the select committee to examine the precedents of former treaties. Buckingham moved for a committee to consider war-measures, to report on the country's stores of munition, make further provision, transport ordnance, survey forts, report defects : Buckingham himself, Southampton, Essex, and the men of war manned this. The Spanish envoys protested to the King against Buckingham's slights upon the King of Spain. He was formally exonerated by the House ; the House of Commons went further, where the frightful Coke orated, 'And shall he lose his head ?' [5] (As if there were any danger of it !) 'Never any man deserved better of his king and country.' (What a reversal in the course of a year !) The impassioned West-countryman, Eliot, demanded 'War only will secure and repair us . . . Are we poor ? Spain is rich. There are our Indies. Break with them ; we shall break our necessities together !' Such was the atmosphere that spring.

The fatuity of Spanish orthodoxy had produced its own reaction. So far from its obtaining a relaxation of the penal laws against Catholics, the delighted Commons were now free to give themselves up to increasing the penalties against recusancy. On hearing Bristol's report of the marriage negotiations, the Lords concluded that the King could not proceed any further with them nor rely on any treaty for the recovery of the Palatinate. Southampton was on a powerful committee to confer with the Commons and offer advice, which meant putting pressure on the unhappy King — and Southampton took a leading part it in. We have the heads of his speech, very urgent and uncompromising. 'What to do now ? What at the conference ? . . . To let them know that we are of opinion that the whole proceeding hath been to delude. We find no ground to think that hereafter they will proceed with more integrity. Therefore of opinion not to rely upon any further treaties. If the Lower House agree with us in their opinion, then a conclusion.' [6]

Of course, the Lower House agreed — Southampton, as we have seen, was always in touch with the leaders of the Commons. There follow in his notes the steps by which to bring pressure on the King. 'Delay dangerous. Tonight if possible ; that impossible, tomorrow ; or as soon as it is possible.' The conference of the committees of both Houses was held in the Painted Chamber on 3 March. Next day Southampton was able to report : 'what was moved is now grown to a resolution of both Houses. . . . His Majesty will receive it graciously but consider of it, and it maybe, will say you know what depends on it. Hope of the Palatinate gone, the care of the rest to be recovered by war, your assistance in it.' War was envisaged : if James enlarged on this, he was to be assured 'we will be ready with our persons and our estates to be assistant and with the utmost'. Next day, 5 March, Southampton went with a small committee headed powerfully by the Archbishop of Canterbury to present the resolution of both Houses to the King. James was in no condition to resist : himself bullied now by Buckingham as he had been formerly by Carr, sabotaged by his son and heir, it was Parliament's policy that was to rule.

James came to the House with a pathetic plea (so like Chamberlain, in a worse cause, in 1939) that he was a man of peace, proud of being styled *Rex Pacificus*. Then, 'show me the means how I may do what you would have me!' War needs money : 'yourselves, by your own deputies, shall have the disposing of the money'.[7] It was a capitulation, in this last year of his reign, of all that he had stood for throughout it. What both Houses advised was a breach with Spain — at the news of which bonfires were lit in the streets of London — and the Commons voted £300,000 for war. Still James hesitated. All throughout March and April the committee-wheels turned, with their war-measures, Southampton propelling them. (It is interesting that he was fated never to see eye to eye with James.) Committees to stay the export of money, committees on munitions, to make the kingdom's arms more serviceable in future, for enforcing the laws against recusants more severely ; conferences with the Commons over recusants, concerning his Majesty's affairs — which meant bringing further pressure on his reluctant Majesty.

For where was the snag ? Who could be holding things up ? Who was persuading him from taking the last irrevocable step ? Buckingham and Charles were managing to isolate the King. They had prevented the wise Bristol from seeing him on his return from his last mission to Spain — by having him confined to his house (Ralegh's old house), at Sherborne. There remained the staunch Lord Treasurer, Middlesex, who was not afraid to announce his opposition to war, and, an old Parliament man himself, no aristocrat, had no fear of Parliament either. It was for this, really, that he was brought down, rather than for malversation in his office.

The ablest finance-minister James ever had to serve him, Middlesex had raised a host of enemies against himself. There was no one who liked him — indeed he was a very unlikeable man — no one to stand by him, except the King, who was now in no condition to stand up for anyone. He did make a plea on behalf of his Treasurer to the Lords, not without reason : 'all Treasurers, if they do good service to their masters, must be generally hated'.[8] Middlesex was more hated than any, for he was brutally frank, of a damaging candour, without

address, or any of the aristocratic arts of reserve, disingenuousness, and deception. A contemporary described him as 'as
open-hearted a man as ever I knew, who did not desire to
cover the nakedness of his thoughts'. Evidently he was no
politician, just an able business man and an expert finance-
minister. Of course he did well for himself and was a very
rich man ; but he had done superbly well for the state in
bringing order out of financial chaos and even achieving a
modest surplus out of an impossible morass. In the course of
his efforts he had offended Buckingham and his exorbitantly
demanding relations along with everybody else ; in Buckingham's absence he had groomed a presentable young kinsman,
Arthur Brett, to take the favourite's place with the King.
This was unforgivable, and Buckingham gave the word that
unleashed all his enemies at him.

We have seen the ill will that had grown up on the part of
the leaders of the Virginia Company against the Treasurer
over the Tobacco Contract, and his hand in their affairs
through his kinsman, the pertinacious Wroth. Now Sir
Edwin Sandys was in a position to get his own back and bring
the great man to book. The account was a long and tangled
one, and the minister had the hardihood to defend himself with
spirit and conviction. He was made to pay for that : when the
investigations of the Commons' committees were complete he
was impeached before the Lords. Here again, as in the case of
Lord Chancellor Bacon, it fell to Southampton to take the
lead on the committee dealing with the case, examining witnesses, auditing accounts. Southampton seems to have been
convinced that Middlesex was a greater offender than Bacon.
In fact, the charges against both were greatly exaggerated,
though it was difficult for either, in the circumstances of the
time, the corruptions of office, to come through with clean
hands. Even Professor Tawney, Middlesex's sympathetic bio-
grapher, admits that the consensus of opinion against him was
impressive and that he was not an easy client to defend.

The Treasurer defended himself with skill, though, after

being kept for eight hours standing at the bar doing so, he retired to bed pleading sickness like Bacon before him. A deputation was sent to wait on him — two earls, Southampton and Essex, two bishops, and two barons with a physician — and demand his attendance upon the House. Southampton reported that indeed the Lord Treasurer was in bed, but he was not sick 'for aught their lordships or the physician could perceive'. He was brought to the House to receive a severe sentence and the largest fine, £50,000, yet imposed. James had not been able to help his minister, but he was able to give Buckingham and Charles a piece of his mind. To the one, 'By God, Steenie, you are a fool and will shortly repent of this folly : you are making a rod with which you will be scourged yourself'.9 And he told the Prince who was already usurping his place that 'he would live to have his belly-ful of Parliaments'. Middlesex himself lived on to see this come true — and to be called into consultation when Charles I's affairs reached an inextricable impasse.

In May Parliament was prorogued, having taken all the steps to prepare for war. The subsidies were voted, the Spanish envoys dismissed, the Dutch commissioners in London to renew the alliance for a defensive war for the recovery of the Palatinate. The war in Europe, which James had hoped to arbitrate, or at least to compromise, was to go on and on for another twenty-four years — until 1648, when the Treaty of Westphalia confirmed things much as they had been before.

Southampton continued to be painted, as he had been at intervals all his life ; in his later portraits we watch the imprint of time upon the familiar features. A portrait of him in his middle years, now at Beaulieu, gives the slightly foreign impression, if with all the refinement and delicacy of feeling, of a de Critz. There is refinement, along with an aristocratic reserve, in the subject. Nothing has essentially changed : there is the elegant oval of the head, rather sharpened now; the hair that was once so beautiful has slightly receded, though

not much, upon the noble forehead. There is a fine distinction
in the poise, somewhat aloof, reticence in every lineament. The
eyes are as alive as ever, but with the fatigues of the years
beginning to show in the lines underneath them.

This impression is much enforced by the last portraits we
have of him, that painted by Mytens and its derivatives, like
the copy at St. John's, Cambridge, which would have been
presented to go along with his gift of books. The basic
portrait in this group was painted not long before he left the
country for his last service in the Netherlands. He is in full
armour, with a resplendent gold-lace scarf across his breast-
plate, full ruff of white lace, hands in leather gloves, deep lace
at the wrists. But there is lassitude in the pose, the stance —
right hand on thigh — of a man who has been vigorous, with
whom the sands are running out. For the face is that of an
ageing and weary man, fatigue showing most clearly in the
eyes that have at length become 'deep-sunken', as the poet
foresaw so many years before :

> When forty winters shall besiege thy brow
> And dig deep trenches in thy beauty's field . . .

'Winter's ragged hand' had at length defaced the beauty of
that golden spring :

> Sap checked with frost and lusty leaves quite gone,
> Beauty o'ersnowed and bareness everywhere.

In pursuance of the treaty with the States General 6,000
volunteers were to be raised for service in the Netherlands. In
June Chamberlain reported, 'here is much canvassing about the
making of captains and colonels for these new forces. . . . Sunday last was appointed and then put off till Tuesday, when they
flocking to Theobalds with great expectation, the king would
not vouchsafe to see any of them, nor once look out of his
chamber till they were all gone. . . . The prime competitors
are the earls of Oxford, Essex and Southampton. . . . It hath
seldom been seen that men of their rank and privy councillors
should hunt after so mean places, in respect of the countenance

our ancient nobility was wont to carry. But it is answered that they do it to raise the companies of voluntaries by their credit — which I doubt will hardly stretch to furnish 6,000 men without pressing, for our people apprehend too much the misery and hard usage of soldiers in these times.' [10]

On the contrary, Chamberlain seems to have been wrong for once. There was no difficulty in raising these regiments or equipping them, but it must have meant a great deal of hard work. Southampton, for example, in addition to his own county, was responsible for Huntingdon, Sussex, Somerset, Wiltshire, Bristol, Norfolk, Wales, Devon, and Exeter. [11] His colleagues in command were also peers, the Earls of Oxford and Essex, and Lord Willoughby. This led to a dispute as to precedency, which had to be settled, for both Oxford and Southampton were members of the Council of War, and, though Southampton was naturally the leader, Oxford was by far the senior earldom. This was just the kind of thing that could give untold trouble, though there seems to have been no ill will between Southampton and Oxford : they were both imbued with conviction and fighting for a cause for which they had long fought politically. It was now a question of carrying their convictions into action, sacrificing their lives, if need be. This was the answer to Chamberlain's surprise at these lords being content to serve as colonels.

The issue of precedency caused much discussion, many letters and some public comment — since this was the Jacobean age, interested in such things. Buckingham astutely passed the buck, saying that he was too ill to settle the matter ; and the Council of War arranged a sensible compromise : Oxford to have precedence in Court and all civil matters, Southampton in all military matters 'in respect of his former commands in the wars'. The King was glad to assent to this — in effect leaving the command to Southampton.

Meanwhile, there was the main business to attend to — raising the levies. We have a last letter of his to his friend, Lord Spencer :

After many stops and delays we are now ready to begin to levy our men for the Low Countries and our drums shall beat, I think, within two days. We now stay only for that which in matters of this nature is the principal verb — money, without which we can entertain no men. You know no part of the subsidies is yet come in, and our Council of War are troubled to advance so much as will serve for the levy. Which, though it be no great sum, being not above £5000 that will do it, yet are our treasurers so wary that they will not engage themselves for so much. But I think Burlamachi will furnish it, and, that once had, we shall go on.[12]

For a chaplain to attend him Southampton naturally turned to his old Cambridge college, and wrote to the Master of St. John's, with some confidence, for him and the Fellows to give leave to one of the society to accompany him while still enjoying his Fellowship.[13] By the end of July the regiments, well-equipped and in good order, were on the way. But the colonels, with their personal following and baggage, were held up in the Thames, since 'the skippers dare not go forth for fear of the Dunkirkers, who are, they say, very busy in the mouth of the river and have of late rifled many passengers coming from the Low Countries'.[14] However, by 7 August, Southampton was ready to depart, going direct to Holland by a Dutch ship : 'I hear my lord of Oxford and his lady are gone in the *Seven Stars*. I will not now trouble the king's ship, whose pilots I think are not so well acquainted with the Maas as the Dutchmen, who will, God willing, carry me to Rotterdam.'[15]

By the end of August all was in order : the regiments had been divided among the garrisons of the Dutch towns : the troops were reported as being very fine and well ordered.[16] Ambassador Carleton — Southampton's acquaintance, Chamberlain's friend — introduced the four commanders to the assembly of the States General, when they took the oath prescribed by the treaty. There at The Hague would be many old friends and acquaintance, to whom to introduce his son and heir — principally the Princess Elizabeth, titular Queen of

Bohemia, keeping her impoverished little Court as a pensioner of the States.

The next we hear is the death of both son and father. Plague was reigning in their winter quarters at Rosendaal; both sickened and the son died on 5 November. Arthur Wilson, who was present, tells us, 'the drooping father, having overcome the fever, departed from Rosendaal with an intention to bring his son's body into England; but at Bergen-op-Zoom he died of a lethargy, in the view and presence of the relator, and were both in one small bark brought to Southampton'.[17] This means that he was worn out by fever and strain, and certainly should not have moved so soon after his son's death — he died only five days after, 10 November.[18]

We may conclude that he had given his life for the cause he believed in as much as if he had died on the field of battle. Certainly this was the feeling in England, as the Venetian envoy reports : the loss was acutely felt at the English Court 'as a good Englishman and one interested in the common cause'.[19] And to the Doge a few days later, 'thus England has lost one of the bravest and noblest of her cavaliers'. The loss came more closely home to the fugitive Queen for whom he had left home to fight. To the young Essex she wrote : 'you may well conceive that the death of the worthy earl of Southampton did trouble me, which I cannot think [of] but with grief. I have lost in him a most true and faithful friend, both in him and his son. I have written to my brother to the same effect as you desire . . . and to the Duke of Buckingham, to whom, if I had not written, he might have crossed all. I have entreated my brother to get the wardship of this young lord for his mother, and, if it be possible he might enjoy his father's pensions.'[20] And to their good-hearted friend, Sir Thomas Roe : 'I am sure you have already heard the infinite loss we have all had of the brave worthy earl of Southampton and his son the Lord Wriothesley; you know how true a friend I have lost in them both, and may imagine easily how much my grief is for them'.[21] That other Elizabeth, whom we know better as Elizabeth Vernon, was inconsolable under the double blow of the loss of husband and son. She had always been in love with Southampton, and their married life, as everything shows, was singularly happy — never a shadow upon it. Now she asked to be prayed for in the churches. Kind Bishop Williams exerted himself to obtain for her the guardianship of her delicate younger son in his minority.[22] The father and his elder son were buried together in the great tomb at Titchfield on 28 December. We know that the bells of Basingstoke were rung on his funeral day, so it is likely that all the bells of Hampshire were rung that day for their Lord Lieutenant.[23]

Tributes to Southampton in death poured out as they had done all through his life. Of varying quality they at least serve to give us a picture of how he was thought of by contemporaries. For the departure of the four eminent Colonels into the Netherlands, Gervase Markham — prolific literary journeyman — was bringing out a little volume with tributes to their families, descents, and themselves.[24] Underneath the rhetoric of Jacobean literary journalism we see that Markham had known Southampton, ever welcoming to literary men, rather well. He emphasises the combination in Southampton of the man of action, brave and anxious to shine in battle, with the well-educated and well-read man, loyal to Cambridge, his nursing mother, with his care for good letters. Markham proceeds to give us the fullest account we have of the young Earl's exploit on the Islands Voyage of 1597 in sinking a Spanish prize. Now, at his death, Markham inserted a sonnet which gives a balanced and informative little miniature of the Earl's life, character, and career.

> When thy good stars met in thy natal hour
> An evil planet slipped into their field
> To thwart their purpose and frustrate thy power
> To make thy labours their full harvest yield.

301

This was true : all his life, in spite of the propitious prospects of his birth and his brilliant promise, circumstances had contrived to cheat him of the full fruition of his powers, and he had never enjoyed the command he pined for. At the end of his life, though he does not precisely express himself as such, I suspect that he was a dissatisfied man, cheated of the fame the fates (and poets) had promised him. For all the favouring portents he had not achieved the first rank, as some others had done — an enemy like Ralegh, for instance, for all his broken life, or a questionable acquaintance like Bacon with his dubious record. But, then, they were men of genius : Southampton did not have that in him. On the other hand, there were consolations : he had grown, in maturity, into a universally respected man, a man of probity and rectitude, of high standards and public spirit, incorruptible in that corrupt age, in which he stood out as such. In all tributes to him changes are rung on the word 'noble' : he did exemplify true nobility, no mean achievement in that glittering, false world of the Jacobean Court.

Markham makes the point of these consolations :

> Yet, from benign aspect, they moved thy soul,
> Made it a treasure-house of virtues rare,
> Courage and wisdom, truth and self-control,
> Clean-handed rectitude beyond compare.

There follows a just tribute to both public and private life :

> Loved by the nobler spirits of thy time,
> Blessed by thy constant, most devoted wife,
> Praised by thy grateful poet in his rhyme,
> Thy country all the better for thy life.

Here is the point, in verse, that honest Tom Roe made in his letter of consolation to the Princess Elizabeth : 'I know not what private loss I have had in the death of the most worthy earl of Southampton, but I am sure it is an honour to him to have it truly said, England and the public have the greatest loss'. And he, too, took to verse to console himself and her for their loss.[25]

Sir John Beaumont, son of the dramatist, drew together the two ends of Southampton's life, that stood in some contrast, the golden youth unspoiled by fortune, the grave and politic senior much respected in counsel :

> When he was young no ornament of youth
> Was wanting in him, acting that in truth
> Which Cyrus did in shadow, and to men
> Appeared like Peleus' son from Chiron's den ;
> While through this island Fame his praise reports
> As best in martial deeds and courtly sports.
> When riper age with wingèd feet repairs
> Grave care adorns his head with silver hairs ;
> His valiant fervour was not then decayed
> But joined with counsel as a further aid.[26]

'Valiant fervour' : it is a good phrase, and it is just. Beaumont expresses the keynote of Southampton's character in a couplet :

> No power, no strong persuasion could him draw
> From that which he conceived as right and law.

He goes on to the virtues of Southampton's private life, which, once he attained maturity, remained unspotted in that singularly tarnished age :

> When shall we in this realm a father find
> So truly sweet, or husband half so kind ?
> Thus he enjoyed the best contents of life,
> Obedient children, and a loving wife.

Lastly, there was his delight in learning and the arts :

> I keep that glory last, which is the best :
> The love of learning, which he oft expressed
> By conversation and respect to those
> Who had a name in arts, in verse or prose.

The poem closes with a picture of Southampton scanning his friends' amateur verses :

> Shall ever I forget with what delight
> He on my simple lines would cast his sight ?

Simpler verses still were contributed by the Earl's rustic acquaintance in the Isle of Wight, where he was much beloved. One of these, a Mr. Jones, on coming to London 'found in public and private many monuments of honour, love and grief' to their late Governor, most of which are now lost. However, Mr. Jones bethought of him of producing a volume, in which all classes of the Earl's subjects in his little kingdom might join : *The Tears of the Isle of Wight.* 'We of the lower sort' gave their absurd expression to their grief :

> But thou accursèd Netherland, the stage
> And common theatre of blood and rage,
> On thee I'll vent my uncontrollèd spleen
> And stab thee to the heart with my sharp teen . . .
> Cursed be thy cheese and butter — all the good
> That e'er the world received from so much blood —
> May maggots breed in them until they fly
> Away in swarms. May all thy kine go dry
> Or cast their calves, and when to bull they gad
> May they grow wild and all thy bulls run mad.

Several of these country contributors thought up anagrams and acrostics — though without any crackpot suggestions as to the identity of Mr. W. H.

In the end, we come to the tribute of Shakespeare, written when Southampton was young, and now both were dead — at the same age, 52 :

> Or I shall live your epitaph to make,
> Or you survive when I in earth am rotten ;
> From hence your memory death cannot take,
> Although in me each part will be forgotten.
> Your name from hence immortal life shall have,
> Though I, once gone, to all the world must die :
> The earth can yield me but a common grave,
> When you entombèd in men's eyes shall lie.

This is the commonplace of the poet, written with a genuine, if considered, modesty. We are then electrified, as so often with Shakespeare, by the sudden psychic intuition of genius —

when we think of Southampton hundred and Southampton
River and Hampton Roads, if all unrealised by those who know
those places and those waters, when we think of Virginia and
Bermuda, the *Sonnets* at the beginning, *The Tempest* at the end,
the tombs at Stratford and at Titchfield and what secrets they
contain :

> Your monument shall be my gentle verse,
> Which eyes not yet created shall o'er-read ;
> And tongues-to-be your being shall rehearse,
> When all the breathers of this world are dead.

And, at the last, with magnificent affirmation :

> You still shall live — such virtue hath my pen —
> Where breath most breathes, even in the mouths of men.

Notes

Chapter I : THE KING'S SERVANT

1 The pedigree of the family in B. J. Greenfield, 'The Wriothesley Tomb in Titchfield Church', *Hampshire Field Club* (1889), 65 ff., gives five generations before Sir John Writh : a very respectable ancestry.

2 J. Anstis, *Register of the Order of the Garter*, ii. 355 ff.

3 J. Stow, *A Survey of London*, ed. C. L. Kingsford, i. 299–300.

4 Ibid. i. 302–3.

5 *Dict. Nat. Biog.*, *sub* Sir Thomas Wriothesley.

6 J. Leland, *Collectanea*, ed. T. Hearne (edn. 1774), v. 159–61, where the name of Wriothesley is hardly recognisable under its latinised form, 'Ad Thomam Uriteslegum . . .'.

7 *Letters and Papers of Henry VIII*, ed. J. Gairdner, v. 527.

8 *L.P.* ix. 73.

9 *L.P.* xi. 280, 296, 329, 334.

10 *L.P.* xii, pt. i. 593.

11 *L.P.* xi. 1455.

12 Cf. R. W. Goulding, 'Wriothesley Portraits', *Walpole Society*, viii. 17–94.

13 I owe this reference to the kindness of Professor Madeleine Doran.

14 *L.P.* xii, pt. i. 557.

15 *L.P.* xiii, pt. 2. 168–9.

16 *V.C.H. Hampshire and the Isle of Wight*, ii. 139.

17 *L.P.* xii. pt. 2. 204.

18 *V.C.H. Hampshire*, ii. 185.

19 Ibid. 140.

20 *L.P.* xiii, pt. 2. 155.

21 Ibid., pt. 1. 51.

22 Ibid. 6.

23 Ibid. 220.

24 *q.* W. H. St. J. Hope, 'The Making of Place House at Titchfield, near Southampton, in 1538', *Archaeological Journal*, lxiii. 231 ff.

25 *L.P.* xiii, pt. 1. 281.

26 J. K. Fowler, *A History of Beaulieu Abbey*, 206.

27 *L.P.* xiii, pt. i. 296, 314.

28 W. H. St. J. Hope and H. Brakespear, 'The Cistercian Abbey of Beaulieu in the County of Southampton', *Arch. J.* lxiii. 129 ff.

29 *L.P.* xiii, pt. i. 7, 282.

30 *The Itinerary of John Leland*, ed. L. Toulmin Smith, i. 281.

31 *L.P.* xiii, pt. 2. 214.

32 *L.P.* xiv. 78.

33 *L.P.* xv. 423.

34 Ibid. 390.

35 Ibid. 437, 457.

36 *Cal. S.P. Foreign, 1547–53,* 196.

37 Cf., Goulding, loc. cit.

38 *L.P.* xxi, pt. 2. 13.

39 *Acts of the Privy Council, 1547–50,* 3–4, 15–16.

40 Ibid. 48, 59, 103.

41 *Cal. S.P. Spanish, 1547–9,* 91, 100.

42 Ibid. 345.

43 Ibid. 477.

44 Ibid. 8, 44.

45 Ibid. 47.

46 *Wriothesley's Chronicle*, ed. W. D. Hamilton, Camden Soc. ii. 41.

47 *Diary of Henry Machyn*, ed. J. G. Nichols, Camden Soc. i.

48 *Trevelyan Papers*, ed. J. P. Collier, Camden Soc. i. 206 ff.

49 *Wriothesley's Chronicle*, i. 154.

CHAPTER II : THE HEIR

1 H.M.C., *Salisbury MSS.* xiii. Addenda, 27.

2 *A.P.C., 1550–52,* 184.

3 *A.P.C., 1558–70,* 174.

4 q. C. C. Stopes, *The Life of Henry, Third Earl of Southampton, Shakespeare's Patron,* 501.

5 Cf. Goulding, loc. cit., plate xvi.

6 *Cal. S.P. Spanish, 1568–79,* 214, 218.

7 *Cal. S.P. Foreign, 1569–71,* 31. This is dated 11 February 1569, which I think should be 1570.

8 *The Loseley Manuscripts*, ed. A. J. Kempe, 231.

9 *Cal. S.P. Spanish, 1568–79,* 274.

10 Kempe, op. cit. 233–4.

11 W. Murdin, *A Collection of State Papers,* i. 30, 39.

12 Cf. Southampton's examination, 31 October 1571, when he denied everything, *Salisbury MSS.* i. 558.

[13] S.P. 12. lxxxvi, 2.

[14] Little-Ease was a notorious, narrowly confined dungeon within the Tower.

[15] *Salisbury MSS.* ii. 21.

[16] Murdin, op. cit. ii. 222–4.

[17] Cotton MSS. Titus, B. ii. 161, 308.

[18] *A.P.C., 1571–5*, 92.

[19] Kempe, op. cit. 238.

[20] *A.P.C., 1571–5*, 109, 111.

[21] Kempe, op. cit. 238–9.

[22] Ibid. 240.

[23] *A.P.C., 1571–5*, 267 ; *Cal. S.P. Dom., 1547–80*, 483, 632.

[24] P.C.C., Martyn 43.

[25] *A.P.C., 1578–80*, 398.

[26] Cotton MSS. Titus, B. ii. 174.

[27] *A.P.C., 1581–2*, 153.

[28] P.C.C., Rowe, 45.

CHAPTER III : LORD BURGHLEY AND HIS WARD

[1] Cottrell-Dormer MSS., *q.* in full, with some mistakes in transcription, Stopes, 9 ff.

[2] *A.P.C., 1581–2*, 298.

[3] *Cal. S.P. Dom., 1581–90*, 448.

[4] *A.P.C., 1581–2*, 296, 376.

[5] T. Baker, *History of St. John's College, Cambridge*, ed. J. E. B. Mayor, 187.

[6] Cf. J. B. Mullinger, *The University of Cambridge, From the Royal Injunctions of 1535 to the Accession of Charles I*, 196 ff.

[7] J. B. Mullinger, *St. John's College*, 72.

[8] H. C. Porter, *Reformation and Reaction in Tudor Cambridge*, 186. It is a pity that in his account Mr. Porter omits all mention of Digby's intellectual distinction.

[9] *q.* Mullinger, *St. John's College*, 79 ff.

[10] Lansdowne MSS. vol. 50, 23 ; vol. 53, 51.

[11] *A.P.C., 1586–7*, 340.

[12] *Register of Admissions to Gray's Inn, 1521–1889*, ed. J. Foster, 66.

[13] *Cal. S.P. Dom., 1581–90*, 500.

[14] *Salisbury MSS.* iii. 365.

[15] *Cal. S.P. Dom., 1581–90*, 680.

[16] *Rutland MSS. H.M.C.*, i. 293.

[17] H. P. Stokes, *Corpus Christi College, Cambridge*, 80.

[18] *Cal. S.P. Dom., 1581–90*, 693.

Notes

19 Ibid., 680.

20 Ibid. 688.

21 *Salisbury MSS.* iv. 96.

CHAPTER IV : THE PATRON AND THE POET

1 Hyder Rollins, ed. *A New Variorum Edition of Shakespeare. The Poems,* 586.

2 *q.* E. K. Chambers, *William Shakespeare,* ii. 188.

3 *q.* ibid., 189.

4 It would be like him to coin the word 'o'er-green' (i.e. o'er-Greene), not otherwise known.

5 *q.* ibid. 210.

6 Aubrey's *Brief Lives,* ed. A. Clark, ii. 226.

7 *q. D.N.B. sub* Robert Greene.

8 *q.* Stopes, 49.

9 C. Plummer, *Elizabethan Oxford,* 294.

10 *A.P.C., 1592,* 176 ; *A.P.C., 1592-3,* 109.

CHAPTER V : THE POET AND THE PATRON

1 In reviewing my *William Shakespeare,* Professor L. C. Knights said oracularly that my interpretation of this sonnet 'has no value at all' ; while Professor Terence Spencer, of Birmingham, said that it 'is a mistaken interpretation of the syntax of the poem . . . because Shakespeare uses the past tense of the verb at the beginning of Sonnet 86'. Now, as a matter of plain fact, there are *nine* verbs in the past tense in that sonnet, and two past participles ; two verbs are rightly in the present tense, for they refer to the current situation. The whole sense of the Sonnet is a summing up of a rivalry now over, in the past.

2 *q.* J. Bakeless, *The Tragical History of Christopher Marlowe,* i. 99.

3 *D.N.B. sub* Sir Thomas Heneage.

4 *Cal. S.P. Dom., 1591-4,* 357, 359, 503, 510.

CHAPTER VI : THE FOLLOWER OF ESSEX

1 *Salisbury MSS.* xiii. Addenda, 508.

2 *Rutland MSS.* i. 321.

3 *Aubrey's Brief Lives,* ed. A. Clark, i. 193-5.

4 *Salisbury MSS.* vi. 267-8.

5 Ibid. v. 55 ff.

6 *q.* F. A. Yates, *John Florio*, 125.

7 *q. D.N.B. sub* Sir Charles Danvers.

8 Foley, *Records of the English Jesuits*, iv. 49.

9 *Sidney Papers*, ed. A. Collins, i. 348–9.

10 R. W. Goulding, loc. cit. 32.

11 *Salisbury MSS.* v. 294.

12 Ibid. 299–300.

13 Ibid. 309–10.

14 Ibid. 359–60.

15 P.C.C., Huddleston, 86.

16 P.C.C., Scott 70.

17 *De l'Isle and Dudley MSS.* ii. 175–6.

18 *Cal. S.P. Dom., 1595–1597*, 204–5.

19 *Salisbury MSS.* vi. 102.

20 *Cal. S.P. Dom., 1595–1597*, 203.

21 E. P. Cheyney, *A History of England from the Defeat of the Armada to the Death of Elizabeth*, ii. 58.

22 *Salisbury MSS.* vi. 158.

23 *q. D.N.B. sub* Essex.

24 T. Birch, *Memoirs of the Reign of Elizabeth*, ii. 274.

25 *Sidney Papers*, A. Collins, ed. ii. 18.

26 *Cal. S.P. Dom., 1595–7*, 448.

27 Ibid. 456.

28 Ibid. 480.

29 *Salisbury MSS.* vii. 369, 372.

30 Collins, ii. 72.

31 *Salisbury MSS.* vii. 499, 537.

32 Ibid. vi. 43.

33 Ibid. 297.

34 M. St. Clare Byrne, 'The Social Background', in H. Granville-Barker and G. B. Harrison, ed., *A Companion to Shakespeare Studies*, 192.

CHAPTER VII : MARRIAGE AND DISCONTENTMENTS

1 *Salisbury MSS.* viii. 31–32.

2 Collins, ii. 81.

3 Ibid. 82.

4 Ibid. 87.

5 Ibid. 90.

6 *Salisbury MSS.* viii. 91–92.

7 Ibid. 241.

8 Ibid. 313.

9 *The Letters of John Chamberlain*, ed. N. E. McClure, i. 41.
10 *Cal. S.P. Dom., 1598–1601*, 90.
11 Stowe MSS. 167, f. 38.
12 *Cal. S.P. Dom., 1598–1601*, 92.
13 *Salisbury MSS.* viii. 353.
14 *Cal. S.P. Dom., 1598–1601*, 97.
15 *Salisbury MSS.* viii. 355.
16 Ibid. 358–9.
17 Ibid. 557.
18 Ibid. 392–3.
19 Chamberlain, I. 52.
20 *Cal. S.P. Dom., 1598–1601*, 121.
21 *Salisbury MSS.* viii. 379.
22 Ibid. xiv. 79–81.
23 Ibid. viii. 371–3.
24 Chamberlain, i. 52.
25 *Salisbury MSS.* viii. 508–9.
26 Ibid. 518.
27 Ibid. 528.
28 The Huntington Library copy was once Edmund Malone's — greatest of Shakespearean scholars — and has his notes. But its first owner, whose name is inscribed on the decorative title-page, was Sir Thomas Chaloner, the naturalist. He was the son of the diplomatist, upon whose early death Lord Burghley took the son's education under his care. Chaloner was well acquainted with Italy, which he visited on his continental tour 1580–3 and again in 1596–7, whence he corresponded with Essex. He made use of his knowledge of the Papal alum-works, a chief source of Papal revenue, to open up the alum deposits on his estate at Guisborough in Yorkshire. Florio's Italian Dictionary would be very much to the purpose for such a person.

CHAPTER VIII : SOLDIERING IN IRELAND

1 Chamberlain, i. 64–65.
2 Ibid. 71–72.
3 W. B. Devereux, *Lives and Letters of the Devereux, Earls of Essex*, ii. 16.
4 *Salisbury MSS.* ix. 438.
5 Ibid. 173.
6 q. Stopes, 157, 158.
7 *Salisbury MSS.* ix. 166.
8 *Salisbury MSS.*, 91.
9 Devereux, ii. 44–45.

[10] *Salisbury MSS.* xiv. 107.

[11] *Cal. S. P. Ireland, 1599–1600,* 100–101.

[12] *Salisbury MSS.* ix. 236.

[13] Ibid. 245.

[14] Ibid. 340–2.

[15] *Salisbury MSS.,* 16.

[16] Devereux, ii. 61–64.

[17] Collins, ii. 132.

[18] Cf. *Thomas Platter's Travels in England,* trans. C. Williams, 166. I have adapted the translation.

[19] *Cal. S.P. Dom., Addenda, 1580–1625,* 397–8.

[20] *Salisbury MSS.* xiv. 147.

[21] Ibid., x. 34.

[22] Collins, ii. 189.

[23] *Cal. S.P. Ireland, 1600,* 224.

[24] Ibid. 231.

[25] *Letters from Sir Robert Cecil to Sir George Carew,* ed. J. Maclean, *Camden Soc.,* 14–15.

[26] *Salisbury MSS.* xiv. 138.

[27] Ibid. x. 262.

Chapter IX : THE ESSEX CATASTROPHE

[1] *De L'Isle and Dudley MSS.* ii. 398.

[2] *Salisbury MSS.* xi. 63.

[3] Ibid. 20.

[4] *Cal. S.P. Dom., 1598–1601,* 575, 578.

[5] Sir E. Brydges, *Life of Sir Thomas Egerton,* 29.

[6] T. B. Howell, *State Trials,* i. 1334 ff.

[7] Chamberlain, i. 119–20.

[8] q. J. E. Neale, *Queen Elizabeth I,* 375.

[9] *Cal. S.P. Dom., 1601–3,* 15.

[10] *Salisbury MSS.* xi. 72–73.

[11] Ibid. 94.

[12] Ibid. 35.

[13] Ibid. 71–72.

[14] *Cal. S.P. Dom., 1598–1601,* 598.

[15] *Cal. S.P. Dom., 1601–3,* 16, 19.

[16] *Letters of Sir Robert Cecil to Sir George Carew,* ed. J. Maclean, *Camden Soc.,* 74.

[17] *Salisbury MSS.* xii. 610.

[18] *A.P.C., 1600–1,* 237–8. For Dr. Paddy, prescribing for Sir Arthur Throckmorton, *v.* my *Ralegh and the Throckmortons,* 194.

Notes

19 *A.P.C.*, *1601–4*, 175.
20 Ibid. 256.

CHAPTER X : A NEW REIGN : THE REWARDS OF FAVOUR

1 *Salisbury MSS.* xii. 562.
2 *The Diary of John Manningham*, ed. J. Bruce. Camden Soc., 148, 168, 171.
3 Chamberlain, i. 192.
4 J. Nichols, *The Progresses of James I*, i. 197–8.
5 *The Letters and the Life of Francis Bacon*, ed. J. Spedding, iii. 75–76.
6 *q.* D. H. Willson, *King James VI and I*, 165.
7 *q.* ibid. 178.
8 Sir Anthony Weldon, *The Court and Character of King James*, ed. 1817, 16, 56.
9 Ibid. 55.
10 Manningham, 170.
11 *Cal. S.P. Venetian, 1603–1607*, 42.
12 *Cal. S.P. Dom., 1603–1610*, 8, 19, 23, 34.
13 Chamberlain, i. 204 ; *Cal. S.P. Dom., 1603–1610*, 126.
14 *Salisbury MSS.* xv. 190–1.
15 Ibid. 244 ; *Cal. S.P. Venetian, 1603–1607*, 178.
16 *Cal. S.P. Dom., 1603–1610*, 89, 106.
17 *Cal. S.P. Venetian, 1603–1607*, 165, 168 ; *Gawdy MSS.* 92.
18 Weldon, 13.
19 *q. Dict. Nat. Biog. sub* Hay.
20 *Cal. S.P. Dom., 1603–1610*, 137, 162, 184.
21 *Salisbury MSS.* xvi. 415.
22 Cf. my *William Shakespeare*, 213 ff.
23 S. R. Gardiner, *History of England, 1603–1642*, i. 168.
24 For the following account *v. Journals of the House of Lords*, ii. 264 ff. *passim*, from which quotations are taken.
25 E. Lodge, *Illustrations of British History*, iii. 269.
26 *Salisbury MSS.* xvii. 100.
27 Chamberlain, i, 226 ; *Cal. S.P. Dom., 1603–1610*, 344.
28 *Salisbury MSS.* xvii. 276, 286.
29 Ibid. 333.
30 Nichols, i. 548.
31 *Salisbury MSS.* xvii. 423.
32 *Buccleuch MSS.* i. 55–56.
33 Cf. my edition of Shakespeare's *Sonnets*, 254–7.
34 *Salisbury MSS.* xviii. 378.
35 Ibid. 304.

36 Nichols, i. 593.
37 *Salisbury MSS.* xviii. 36.
38 Sir John Harington, *Nugae Antiquae*, i. 348 ff.
39 *Salisbury MSS.* xviii. 270, 446.
40 *Cal. S.P. Dom., 1603–1610*, 354.
41 P.C.C., Huddlestone, 86.
42 *The Complete Peerage*, G.E.C., new ed. by G. H. White, xii, pt. i. 131.
43 Willson, 261.
44 q. Stopes, 309, 310.
45 *Cal. S.P. Dom., 1603–1610*, 405, 453, 458.
46 *Cal. S.P. Venetian, 1607–1610*, 135, 206.
47 *The Oglander Memoirs*, ed. W. H. Long, 23.
48 *Cal. S.P. Dom., 1603–1610*, 524, 527, 528, 551.
49 *Cal. S.P. Colonial, 1574–1660*, 8.
50 *Salisbury MSS.* xv. 266.

Chapter XI : COURT AND COUNTRY

1 S. R. Gardiner, *History of England, 1603–1642* (ed. 1899), ii. 83.
2 *Journals of the House of Lords*, ii. 687 ff.
3 Nichols, ii. 332, 360.
4 Chamberlain, i. 297.
5 Clarendon, *History of the Rebellion* (ed. 1888), i. 72.
6 Ibid. 71–72.
7 q. *D.N.B. sub* William Herbert.
8 Clarendon, i. 74–75.
9 Ibid. ii. 539–41.
10 q. D. H. Willson, *King James VI and I*, 267.
11 *Downshire MSS.* iii. 2.
12 *Cal. S.P. Col., 1574–1660*, 8.
13 Chamberlain, i. 313.
14 *Cal. S.P. Venetian, 1610–1613*, 259.
15 *Cal. S.P. Dom., 1611–1618*, 96.
16 q. Willson, 269.
17 q. *Downshire MSS.* iii, p. xviii.
18 Chamberlain, i. 351.
19 q. Willson, 269.
20 *Cal. S.P. Dom., 1611–1618*, 144.
21 *Downshire MSS.* iii. 315.
22 *Cal. S.P. Dom., 1611–1618*, 145.
23 *Downshire MSS.* iii. 391.
24 Ibid. xviii.

25 Nichols, ii. 499.

26 *Cal. S.P. Dom., 1611–1618*, 154.

27 *Ancaster MSS.* 354.

28 Ibid. 361 ff.

29 Sir Ralph Winwood, *Memorials of Affairs of State*, iii. 478.

30 Nichols, ii. 702.

31 Gardiner, ii. 240 ff.

32 *q.* ibid. 251.

33 *Coke MSS.* 84, 86.

34 *De L'Isle MSS.* v., 221, 233.

35 *Portland MSS.* ix. 145.

36 *q.* Gardiner, ii. 328.

37 *Cal. S.P. Dom., 1611–1618*, 381.

38 Nichols, iii. 213, 219.

39 *Cal. S.P. Venetian, 1615–1617*, 496.

40 *Cal. S.P. Dom., 1611–1618*, 450.

41 *Cal. S.P. Venetian, 1615–1617*, 476.

42 Chamberlain, ii. 55.

43 *Kenyon MSS.* 19 ff.

44 Chamberlain, ii. 85.

45 *Cal. S.P. Dom., 1611–1618*, 507.

46 Chamberlain, ii. 67.

47 Ibid. 107.

48 *Cal. S.P. Dom., 1611–1618*, 544.

49 Chamberlain, ii. 187.

50 *Cal. S.P. Dom., 1619–1623*, 16.

51 Ibid. 16.

52 Ibid. 25.

53 Chamberlain, ii. 234.

54 *Cal. S.P. Dom., 1619–1623*, 41.

55 *The Complete Peerage*, by G.E.C., ed. G. H. White, xii, pt. i. 130 ff.

56 *De L'Isle MSS.* v. 412.

57 *A.P.C., 1615–1616*, 168.

58 Stopes, 415.

59 T. Baker, *History of St. John's College*, ed. J. E. B. Mayor, 201.

60 Ibid. 481, 493, 510.

CHAPTER XII : THE VIRGINIA COMPANY

1 William Strachey, *The Historie of Travell into Virginia Britania*, ed. L. B. Wright and Virginia Freund (Hakluyt Soc.), 150–1. I have modernised the text.

[2] *Purchas His Pilgrimes* (MacLehose edition), xviii. 309.

[3] Strachey, 155.

[4] Purchas, xviii. 350–1.

[5] q. J. P. Baxter, *Sir Ferdinando Gorges and his Province of Maine*, ii. 8.

[6] q. W. F. Craven, *The Southern Colonies in the Seventeenth Century*, 82.

[7] Alexander Brown, *The Genesis of the United States*, i. 209 ff.

[8] S. M. Kingsbury, ed. *The Records of the Virginia Company of London*, iii. 87.

[9] Craven, 97.

[10] Purchas, xix. 46.

[11] q. Brown, i. 347.

[12] Craven, 117.

[13] *Cal. S.P. Col., East Indies, 1513–1616*, 185, 188, 196, 203, 310, 317.

[14] Add. MSS. 6115.

[15] Brown, ii. 1062.

[16] Ibid. i. 692 ff.

[17] My account of the Company's proceedings, unless otherwise stated, is based on its *Records*, ed. Kingsbury, *passim*.

[18] W. F. Craven, *Dissolution of the Virginia Company*, 129–30, 144–5.

[19] Ibid. 293.

[20] *Hastings MSS.* ii. 57.

[21] Chamberlain, ii. 305.

[22] Craven's phrase, 145.

[23] Op. cit. 311.

[24] *Cal. S.P. Ven., 1621–3*, 372.

[25] Craven, 240–1.

[26] Craven, 147.

[27] q. Andrews, 161.

[28] *Cal. S.P. Col., 1504–1660*, 44.

[29] *Cal. S.P. Dom., 1623–1625*, 28.

[30] Andrews, 177.

CHAPTER XIII : PARLIAMENT MAN

[1] Arthur Wilson, *The History of Great Britain* (edn. 1653), 161–2.

[2] As against D. H. Willson's too summary judgment of Southampton, in his later years, as 'hot-headed and contentious'. *King James VI and I*, 335.

[3] *Cal. S.P. Ven., 1619–1621*, 137, 229.

[4] Ibid. 275, 283, 291.

[5] *A.P.C., July 1619–June 1621*, 248.

[6] This account is based on the *Journals of the House of Lords*, iii. *passim*, from which references come, unless otherwise stated.

[7] Gardiner, iv. 43.

8 Ibid. 82.

9 In writing *The Early Churchills* I unaccountably omitted to notice these amenities.

10 Gardiner, iv. 93.

11 Ibid. 102.

12 Ibid. 127.

13 *The Autobiography and Correspondence of Sir Simonds D'Ewes*, ed. J. O. Halliwell, 199.

14 Chamberlain, ii. 384–5.

15 *Cal. S.P. Dom., 1619–1623*, 269.

16 Ibid. 388.

17 Ibid. 389–90.

18 *Cabala* (edn. 1691), 261.

19 Ibid. 331.

20 Ibid 332.

21 Add. MSS. 34727.

22 *A.P.C., July 1621–May 1623*, 37.

23 *The Fortescue Papers*, ed. S. R. Gardiner (Camden Soc.), 166.

24 *Cal. S.P. Ven., 1621–1623*, 172.

25 Chamberlain, ii. 411.

26 *Cal. S.P. Ven., 1621–1623*, 174.

27 Gardiner, iv. 240.

28 Ibid. 243.

29 Ibid. 266.

30 Willson, 423.

31 R. H. Tawney, *Business and Politics under James I*, 216.

32 *A.P.C., July 1621–May 1623*, 220.

33 *Cal. S.P. Dom., 1619–1623*, 385, 441.

34 Chamberlain, ii. 438.

35 *Rutland MSS.* i. 467.

36 *Cal. S.P. Ven., 1623–1625*, 41.

37 *Cal. S.P. Dom., 1619–1623*, 556, 588, 599, 606.

38 *Cal. S.P. Dom., 1623–1625*, 38, 55.

39 Nichols, iv. 903.

40 *Cabala*, 230.

41 *Cal. S.P. Ven., 1623–1625*, 169.

42 S.P., 13, clv. 77.

CHAPTER XIV : FATE

1 Gardiner, v. 179.

2 Spedding, vii. 454.

[3] *The Negotiations of Sir Thomas Roe* (edn. 1740), 222.

[4] *Journals of the House of Lords*, iii. 208 ff.

[5] Gardiner, v. 188, 191, 199.

[6] *q.* Stopes 451.

[7] *Journals of the House of Lords*, iii. 250.

[8] *q.* Tawney, 231, 234.

[9] *q.* Willson, 443.

[10] Chamberlain, ii. 562.

[11] *A.P.C., June 1623–March 1625*, 249.

[12] MS. in the Hyde Collection, Somerville, New Jersey.

[13] Stopes, 456.

[14] *Cal. S.P. Dom., 1623–5*, 315.

[15] *Coke MSS.* 167.

[16] *Cal. S.P. Ven., 1624–1625*, 422, 429.

[17] Arthur Wilson, *History of Britain*, 284.

[18] In *State Papers Foreign, Holland*, the dates are given in modern style as 15 and 19 November.

[19] *Cal. S.P. Ven., 1623–1625*, 498.

[20] *Bath MSS.* ii. 73.

[21] Roe, 325.

[22] *Cabala*, 299.

[23] F. J. Baigent and J. E. Millard, *History of the Ancient Town and Manor of Basingstoke*, 513. The ringers were paid 1s.

[24] Gervase Markham, *Honour in his Perfection*.

[25] Roe, 353–4.

[26] These tributes are printed in Malone's edition of Shakespeare (edn. 1821), xx. 448 ff.

INDEX

319

Index